PREFACE

The **National Eligibility Test (NET)** is a test to determine eligibility for college and university level lectureship and for award of Junior Research Fellowship (JRF) for Indian nationals. It aims to ensure minimum standards for the entrants in teaching professions and research. On behalf of the University Grants Commission (UGC), the Central Board of Secondary Education (CBSE) holds the test for determining the eligibility of Indian nationals for the Eligibility for Assistant Professor only or Junior Research Fellowship & Eligibility for Assistant Professor both in Indian universities and colleges.

The present work is a small step to prepare for NET exam. The primary objective of this work is to provide information regarding the pattern of NET exam to the students. Indian students are facing various types of problems like unavailability of reach library, a good and high speed internet and good books. So I decided to collect the question papers (II & III), especially in the subject of Commerce and providing to the students in the form of this work. I express deep sense of gratitude to University Grant Commission, New Delhi. I thank my father Prakash Bholane, mother Sunanda Bholane, brother Vaibhav Bholane and father-in-law Gangadhar Sohani for their love, guidance and for always believing.

And, finally I am grateful to my loving and understanding wife Manjushree and my sweet son Atharva for their patience, love, encouragement and sacrifices.

Dr. Kishor P. Bholane

CONTENT

JUNE-2015

COMMERCE

PAPAR-II

Note: This paper contains fifty (50) objective type questions of two (2) marks each. All questions are compulsory.

1. The world's first electronic stock market is:

   (1) KOSPI   (2) Nikkie   (3) NASDAQ   (4) Dow Jones

2. The Human Development Index (HDI) is introduced by:

   (1) UNDP   (2) UNICEF   (3) IMF   (4) World Bank

3. Examine the following statements and choose the correct code:

   Assertion (A): American style option, compared to European style, provides more freedom to option holders in exercising the option.

   Reason (R): American style option can be exercised only at a specified date which is generally the expiration date.

   Codes:

   (1) Both (A) and (R) are correct.   (2) Both (A) and (R) are wrong.

   (3) (A) is correct, but (R) is wrong.   (4) (A) is not correct, but (R) is correct.

4. From the statements given below, identify the correct code:

   Statement (I):   The key strategy behind acquiring a company is to create shareholder's value.

   Statement (II):   Conglomeration is a merger between two companies that have common business areas.

   Statement (III): MRTP Act got replaced by the Competition Act, 2002 in India.

   Codes:

   (1) All the three statements are correct.

   (2) Statements (I) and (II) only are correct.

   (3) Statements (I) and (III) only are correct.

   (4) Statement (II) only is correct.

5. From the following, identify the tools of fiscal policy:

   (i) Public expenditure

   (ii) Open market operations

   (iii) Deficit financing

   (iv) Taxation

   (v) Reserve requirements

   Codes:

   (1) (i), (iii), (iv) and (v)   (2) (i), (ii), (iv) and (v)

   (3) (ii) and (v)   (4) (i), (iii) and (iv)

6. The basic difference between a static budget and flexible budget is that:

   (1) A flexible budget considers only variable costs but a static budget considers all costs.

   (2) Flexible budgets allow management latitude in meeting goals, whereas static budget is based on fixed standards.

   (3) A flexible budget is applicable for a single department only but a static budget for entire production facility.

   (4) A flexible budget can be prepared for any production level within a relevant range but a static budget is based on one specific level of production.

7. A retiring partner continues to be liable for obligations incurred after his retirement:

   (1) If unpaid amount is transferred to his loan account.

   (2) If he does not give public notice.

   (3) If he starts a similar business elsewhere.

   (4) In all the situations till he survives.

8. In what order, the following assets are shown in the balance sheet of a company?

   (i) Trade receivables

   (ii) Cash

   (iii) Furniture and fittings

   (iv) Investment in shares and debentures

   Codes:

   (1) (ii), (i), (iv), (iii)   (2) (i), (ii), (iii), (iv)

   (3) (iii), (iv), (i), (ii)   (4) (iv), (iii), (ii), (i)

9. When opening stock is Rs. 50,000, closing stock is Rs. 60,000 and the cost of goods sold is Rs. 2,20,000, the stock turnover ratio is :

    (1) 2 times   (2) 3 times   (3) 4 times   (4) 5 times

10. If : Stock turnover ratio is $=$ 6 times

            Average stock $=$ Rs. 8,000

            Selling price $=$ 25% above cost

    What is the amount of gross profit?

    (1) Rs. 2,000   (2) Rs. 4,000   (3) Rs. 10,000   (4) Rs. 12,000

11. A rectangular hyperbola shaped demand curve on all its points

    has : (1) Equal slopes of the price demand curve

    (2) Price elasticity equal to unity

    (3) Varying price elasticity

    (4) Both slope and price elasticity equal

12. In case of short-run equilibrium, a perfectly competitive firm while earning abnormal profits operates at an output level where :

    (1) Marginal cost is the minimum

    (2) Average cost is the minimum

    (3) Both marginal cost and average cost are equal

    (4) Marginal cost is higher than average cost

13. Which one of the following statements is false ?

    (1) Normally, a price demand curve slopes downward from left to right.

    (2) Economies of scale and economies of scope are the same.

    (3) For optimization, equality between marginal cost and marginal revenue is a necessary condition but it is not a sufficient one.

    (4) Law of variable proportions denotes input-output relationship during short-run.

14. Match the items of List-I with the items of List-II :

	List-I		List-II
(a)	Law of diminishing marginal utility	(i)	Cross demand
(b)	Relationship between price of one commodity and demand for other commodity	(ii)	Oligopoly
(c)	Skimming the cream policy	(iii)	Cardinal approach
(d)	Price rigidity	(iv)	Pioneer pricing

Codes:

	(a)	(b)	(c)	(d)
(1)	(i)	(ii)	(iii)	(iv)
(2)	(iii)	(i)	(ii)	(iv)
(3)	(ii)	(iv)	(i)	(iii)
(4)	(iv)	(iii)	(ii)	(i)

15. The following are the demand and supply equations in a perfectly competitive market:

$$P = 12 + 0.3 Q_s$$

$$P = 40 - 0.4 Q_d$$

The equilibrium market price would be:

(1) 24   (2) 10   (3) 40   (4) 20

16. Which of the following is not an accounting software package ?

(1) Quick Books   (2) Sage one   (3) Sage M   (4) Sage 50

17. Which one of the following formula is used to calculate probable error of correlation-coefficient between two variables of 'n' pairs of observations ?

(1) $0.6745 \left(\dfrac{1 - r^2}{\sqrt{n}} \right)$ (2) $0.5758 \left(\dfrac{1 - r^2}{\sqrt{n}} \right)$

(3) $0.675 \left(\dfrac{1 - r^2}{n} \right)$ (4) $0.5758 \left(\dfrac{1 - r^2}{n} \right)$

18. If the population is heterogeneous, which one of the following probability sampling methods is more appropriate ?

(1) Sequential sampling   (2) Quota sampling

(3) Double sampling   (4) Stratified sampling

19. Which of the following relating to normal distribution are not correct ? (i) Co-efficient of skewness is three.

(ii) It is mesokurtic.

(iii) Mean deviation for it is $\frac{2}{3}\sigma$

(iv) $\mu \pm 2\sigma$ covers 95.45% area.

(v) Mean, median and mode are equal.

(vi) The standard normal variate z has mean one and SD zero.

Codes:

(1) (i), (iii) and (vi)   (2) (iii), (iv) and (v)   (3) (i), (iii) and (v)   (4) (i), (iii) and (iv)

20. Which one of the following statements is false?

(1) Both correlation and regression co-efficients have same sign.

(2) Arithmetic mean of the regression co-efficients is always more than the correlation co-efficient.

(3) Regression co-efficients are independent of both the origin and scale.

(4) Correlation co-efficient is the square root of two regression co-efficients.

21. Match the items of List-I with List-II:

	List-I		List-II
(a)	"He who can manage, can manage Fayol anything".	(i)	Henry
(b)	"Due to these experiments, a factory Cornell does not remain a factory, it is converted into a laboratory".	(ii)	William B.
(c)	"Management succeeds or fails as human relations in business are intelligently or unintelligently handled".	(iii)	F.W. Taylor
(d)	"A place for everything, and Apply everything in its place".	(iv)	Lawrance A.

Codes:

	(a)	(b)	(c)	(d)
(1)	(i)	(ii)	(iii)	(iv)
(2)	(i)	(ii)	(iv)	(iii)

(3) (iv) (iii) (ii) (i)

(4) (iii) (ii) (i) (iv)

22. Assertion (A): Management is mainly associated with economic affairs.

Reasoning (R): Big business houses are the result of effective financial management.

Codes:

(1) (A) is correct and (R) is the right explanation of (A).

(2) Both (A) and (R) are correct but (R) is not the right explanation of (A).

(3) (A) is incorrect but (R) is correct in isolation.

(4) Both (A) and (R) are incorrect.

23. Areas of establishing objectives under MBO are:

(i) Market Standing

(ii) Innovation

(iii) Industrial Relations

(iv) Public Accountability

(v) Productivity

(vi) Industrial Policy

Codes:

(1) (iii), (iv), (v) and (vi)   (2) (i), (ii), (iv) and (v)

(3) (i), (ii), (v) and (vi)   (4) (ii), (iii), (iv) and (v)

24. Match the items of List-I with List-II:

	List-I		List-II
(a)	Management of Tomorrow	(i)	Chris Argyris
(b)	Motivation and Personality	(ii)	Fredrick Hergberg
(c)	The Motivation of Work	(iii)	L.F. Urwick
(d)	Personality and Organisation	(iv)	A.H.

Maslow Codes:

	(a)	(b)	(c)	(d)
(1)	(i)	(iv)	(ii)	(iii)

(2)   (iii)   (iv)   (i)   (ii)

(3)   (iv)   (iii)   (ii)   (i)

(4)   (iii)   (iv)   (ii)   (i)

25.   Narayan Murthy Committee revised its recommendations on Corporate Governance as on 29th October 2004 which diluted the following areas:

(i)   Independence of Directors

(ii)   Whistle Blower Policy

(iii)   Performance evaluation of Non-Executive Directors

(iv)   Mandatory training of Non-Executive Directors

Codes:

(1)   (i), (ii) and (iii) only

(2)   (i) and (iii) only

(3)   (i), (ii) and (iv) only

(4)   All (i), (ii), (iii) and (iv)

26.   The service marketing mix is an extended marketing mix and includes:

(i)   People

(ii)   Process

(iii)   Service

(iv)   Physical evidence

Codes:

(1)   (ii), (iii) and (iv)   (2)   (i), (ii) and (iii)   (3)   (i), (ii) and (iv)   (4)   (i), (iii) and (iv)

27.   Black box model in marketing relates to:

(1)   Marketing planning

(2)   Marketing mix

(3)   Marketing control

(4)   Consumer behaviour

28.   Items, considered part of the augmented product, do not include:

(1)   Guarantee

(2)   Warranty

(3)   Complementary products

(4)   Channels of distribution

29.   Which of the following is not a type of direct marketing?

(1)   Direct mail marketing

(2)   Retail marketing

(3)   Telemarketing

(4)   Email direct marketing

30. 'Press release' is a part of:

   (1) Public relations   (2) Advertising

   (3) Sales promotion   (4) None of the above

31. In capital budgeting, the term capital rationing implies :

   (1) that no retained earnings are available.

   (2) that limited funds are available for investment.

   (3) that no external funds can be raised.

   (4) that no fresh investment is required in current year.

32. In certainty equivalent approach, adjusted cash flows are discounted at:

   (1) Accounting Rate of Return   (2) Internal Rate of Return

   (3) Hurdle Rate   (4) Risk Free Rate

33. Combined leverage is calculated as:

   (1) Operating Leverage + Financial Leverage

   (2) Operating Leverage − Financial Leverage

   (3) Operating Leverage X Financial Leverage

   (4) Operating Leverage + Financial Leverage

34. Which of the following is not true with reference to capital budgeting?

   (1) Capital budgeting is related to asset replacement decisions.

   (2) Cost of capital is equal to minimum required return.

   (3) Existing investment in a project is not treated as sunk cost.

   (4) Timing of cash flows is relevant.

35. What is Economic Order Quantity?

   (1) Cost of an order   (2) Cost of stock

   (3) Reorder level   (4) Optimum order size

36. Which of the following is not a basic objective of HRM?

   (1) To attract HR into the organisation

(2) To develop and motivate HR for better performance

(3) To have the reward and punishment system for HR

(4) To integrate and maintain HR in the organization

37. What is 'gate hiring' ?

(1) To select people who approach on their own for employment in the organisation.

(2) To select people who are recommended by the employees.

(3) To select people from public employment exchanges.

(4) To select people supplied by labour contractors.

38. Matching essential managers and essential positions is a step in the process of:

(1) Career Cycle   (2) Succession Planning

(3) Career Planning   (4) Career Stages

39. The barriers to effective performance appraisal are:

(i) Psychological blocks of managers

(ii) Faulty assumptions of the parties concerned

(iii) Technical pitfalls

(iv) Faulty written communications

Codes:

(1) All are correct.   (2) Only (ii) and (iii) are correct.

(3) Only (i) and (ii) are correct.   (4) Only (i), (ii) and (iii) are correct.

40. Who has developed the 'Systems Approach' of industrial relations?

(1) John Dunlop   (2) Garry S. Becker

(3) Michael J. Jucius   (4) Edwin B. Flippo

41. In 1992, the banking sector reforms were introduced as per :

(1) C. Rangarajan Committee Report

(2)   M. Narasimham Committee Report

(3)   Suresh Tandulkar Committee Report

(4)   Sukhamoy Chakrabarty Committee Report

42.   For the purpose of extending rural banking and agro finance, the NABARD :

(1)   Directly lends and monitors the rural borrowers

(2)   Refinances the banks extending rural finance

(3)   Refinances the rural borrowers obtaining credit from banks

(4)   Directly finances the rural borrowers and gets refinance from government

43.   When RBI grants loan to commercial banks and charges interest on it, it is called :

(1)   Rapo rate   (2)   Reverse Rapo rate

(3)   Sweep stack rate, basic rate   (4)   Bank rate

44.   E-banking business is essentially regulated by the Information Technology Act, 2000, under which personal signature is replaced by:

(1)   Encrypted signature   (2)   Image signature

(3)   Digital signature   (4)   Online signature

45.   In order to control inflation and ensure stability in money market:

(1)   The RBI works under the direction of ministry of finance, government of India.

(2)   The RBI acts independently and can refuse the government directive.

(3)   The RBI acts under the board of directors.

(4)   The RBI's board of governors shall abide by the government directive.

46.   In respect of international business, a project is called a turnkey project because :

(1)   The licensee agrees to construct an entire plant in his home county and hands over the key.

(2)   The licensor starts the operation and hands over the key of the operating plant to the licensee.

(3)   The licensor starts the operation and then invites the licensee and hands over the key to complete the remaining work.

(4) The licensor and the licensee jointly carry out the project and agree to share profit equally.

47. Match the items in List-I with the items in List-II :

	List-I		List-II
(a)	Bretton woods conference	(i)	WTO
(b)	Soft loan window	(ii)	World Bank
(c)	Geneva	(iii)	IFC
(d)	Loan to private sector	(iv)	IDA

Codes :

	(a)	(b)	(c)	(d)
(1)	(i)	(iii)	(ii)	(iv)
(2)	(iv)	(iii)	(ii)	(i)
(3)	(ii)	(iv)	(i)	(iii)
(4)	(iv)	(ii)	(iii)	(i)

48. Assertion (A): The member nations, consistently finding balance of payments crisis, may approach the World Bank seeking financial accommodation to mitigate the cirsis.

Reasoning (R): The member nations facing balance of payments crisis can approach the IMF seeking redressal of the BOP crisis.

Codes:
(1) (A) is correct and (R) is correct explanation of (A).
(2) (A) is correct but (R) is wrong.
(3) (R) is correct and (A) is wrong.
(4) Both (A) and (R) are wrong.

49. In computation of balance of payments, overall balance of payments =
(1) Balance of current account + Balance of capital account + Statistical discrepancy
(2) Export of goods and invisibles — Import of goods
(3) Foreign exchange inflow — Foreign exchange outflow
(4) Export of goods and invisibles + Import of goods and invisibles

50. The instrument chosen for enhancement of international liquidity is:
(1) Society for World Wide Inter Bank Financial Telecommunications (SWIFT)
(2) Special Drawing Rights (SDRs)
(3) Multilateral Netting
(4) Netting of Payments

- o 0 o -

UGC - NET JUNE 2015

ANSWER KEYS (PAPER II)

SUBJECT : 08 (Commerce)

Qus. No.	Ans.	Qus. No.	Ans.
1	3	26	3
2	1	27	4
3	3	28	4
4	3	29	2
5	4	30	1
6	4	31	2
7	2	32	4
8	3	33	3
9	3	34	3
10	4	35	4
11	2	36	3
12	4	37	1
13	2	38	2
14	3	39	4
15	1	40	1
16	3	41	2
17	1	42	2
18	4	43	4
19	1	44	3
20	3	45	2
21	3	46	2
22	3	47	3
23	2	48	3
24	4	49	1
25	4	50	2

JUNE-2015

COMMERCE

PAPER - III

Note : This paper contains **seventy five (75)** objective type questions of **two (2)** marks each. **All** questions are **compulsory**.

1. GNP at market prices – Indirect taxes + subsidies is referred to as :

    (1) GNP at factor cost   (2) GDP at factor cost

    (3) NNP at factor cost   (4) NDP at factor cost

2. EDI system got legal recognition under which one of the following Acts ?

    (1) Electronics Act, 1996   (2) Right to Data Act, 1998

    (3) DGFT Act, 1999   (4) Information Technology Act, 2000

3. Following statements are related to futures contracts. Choose the statements that are **not** true :

    (a) Purchase of a futures contract is called short position.

    (b) Currency futures are traded on an exchange in standardised form and in fixed quantity.

    (c) Default risk in futures contract is high compared to forward contract.

    Codes :

    (1) only (a) and (b)   (2) only (a) and (c)   (3) (a), (b) and (c)   (4) only (b)

4. From the following, identify the trading blocks in the world and choose the **correct** code :

    (a) European Union

    (b) North American Free Trade Agreements

    (c) South Asian Association of Regional Co-operation

    (d) Central American Common Market

    (e) Central African Customs Union

    Codes :

    (1) (a), (b) and (c)   (2) (a), (b), (c) and (d)

    (3) (a), (b), (c), (d) and (e)   (4) (a), (b) and (e)

5. Match the items of **List - I** with items of **List - II** and choose the **correct** code :

	List - I		List - II
(a)	Carroll Model	(i)	International trade
(b)	Corlett - Hague Rule	(ii)	Interest rate
(c)	Hecksher Ohlin Theorem	(iii)	Principles of taxation
(d)	Knut Wick sell's Theory	(iv)	Social responsibility of business

Codes :

	(a)	(b)	(c)	(d)
(1)	(iv)	(iii)	(i)	(ii)
(2)	(iii)	(ii)	(i)	(iv)
(3)	(iii)	(i)	(ii)	(iv)
(4)	(ii)	(iii)	(i)	(iv)

6. Labour Rate of Pay Variance can be calculated by which one of the following equations ?

(1) Budgeted Labour Costs − Actual Labour Costs

(2) (Standard Hours − Actual Hours) × Actual Wage Rate

(3) (Standard Wage Rate − Actual Wage Rate) × Actual Hours Worked

(4) (Standard Wage Rate − Actual Wage Rate) × Standard Hours Worked

7. Given :

Margin of Safety	₹ 80,000
Profit	₹ 20,000
Sales	₹ 3,00,000

What is the amount of Fixed Cost ?

(1) ₹ 1,00,000   (2) ₹ 75,000   (3) ₹ 55,000   (4) ₹ 20,000

8. Preparation of consolidated statement of accounts as per AS - 21 is :

(1) Optional

(2) Mandatory for Private Ltd. Companies

(3) Mandatory for Listed Companies

(4) Mandatory for all Companies

9. Which one of the following is **not** true of cash Budget ?

(1) The shortage or excess of cash would appear in a particular period.

(2) All inflows would arise before outflows for those periods.

(3) Only revenue nature cash flows are shown.

(4) Proceeds from issue of share capital is shown as an inflow.

10. Study the following transactions :

(a) Raising of short term loans

(b) Goods purchased for cash

(c) Payment of bonus in the form of shares

(d) Issue of shares in lieu of raw materials

Flow of funds is :

(1) (a), (b), (c), and (d)

(2) (b), (c), and (d)

(3) (c) and (d)

(4) Only (d)

11. When a consumer increases units of X - commodity by giving up some units of Y- commodity and even to attain the same level of satisfaction, the marginal rate of substitution, will be calculated by :

(1) Change in X - Commodity divided by change in Y - Commodity

(2) Change in X - Commodity divided by marginal utility of Y - Commodity

(3) Change in Y - Commodity divided by change in X - Commodity

(4) Change in Y - Commodity divided by marginal utility of X - Commodity

12. The following is the demand function in the small market :

$Q = 50 - 5P$

Where 'Q' denotes quantity in physical units and 'P' denotes price of the commodity. At price ₹ 5, the point price elasticity of demand would be :

(1) Zero   (2) Equal to unity

(3) Highly elastic   (4) Highly inelastic

13. Match the items of **List - I** with the items of **List - II** and find out the **correct** matching.

List - I	List - II
Production functions	**Name of the shapes of returns to scale**
(a) $Q = 10.2\ K^{0.19}\ L^{0.88}$	(i) Constant Returns to scale
(b) $Q = 1.01\ L^{0.75}\ K^{0.25}$	(ii) Diminishing Returns to scale
(c) $Q = 0.84\ L^{0.63}\ K^{0.3}$	(iii) Increasing Returns to scale

Codes :

	(a)	(b)	(c)
(1)	(i)	(ii)	(iii)
(2)	(ii)	(i)	(iii)
(3)	(ii)	(iii)	(i)
(4)	(i)	(iii)	(ii)

14. In the short-run, when a simple monopoly firm attains equilibrium and earns only normal profit, its level of output will correspond to :

    (1) Lowest average cost

    (2) Average cost above optimum level of output

    (3) Average cost equals marginal cost

    (4) Marginal cost much below average cost

15. Which one of the following is a **false** statement ?

    (1) Ramsey pricing rates to the methodology of pricing to situations where firms are regulated and the maximization of allocative efficiency is the objective of pricing together with the objective of profit - maximization.

    (2) Peak-load pricing is a pricing practice where price varies with time of the day.

    (3) Value-pricing is the practice of pricing where the price is set based on its value to the customer.

    (4) Two - part tariff refers to a price structure which has two parts - a lump sum charge and a variable charge.

16. All the properties of order, interval and zero origin are simultaneously possessed by :

    (1) Nominal Data   (2) Interval Data   (3) Ratio Data   (4) Ordinal Data

17. Under which of the following situations, chi - square test is applicable ?

    (a) testing homogenity

    (b) testing goodness of fit

    (c) testing equality of two sample means

    (d) testing equality of two sample proportions

    (e) testing independence of attributes

    Codes :

    (1) Only (a), (b) and (c)   (2) Only (a), (b) and (e)

    (3) Only (c), (d) and (e)   (4) Only (a), (c) and (e)

18. Which one of the following is **not** the **correct** statement regarding sampling distribution of mean ?

    (1) Sampling distribution of mean is normally distributed for large sized samples.

    (2) Sampling distribution of mean is normally distributed for small sized samples drawn from not normally distributed population.

    (3) 't' distribution is not normally distributed.

    (4) Mean of the sampling distribution of mean is equal to the parametric value of mean.

19. Consider the following statements and identify the **wrong** statements :

    Statement - I : Accepting null hypothesis, when it is false, is called a level of significance.

    Statement - II : $1 - \alpha$ is called power of a test.

    Statement - III : Critical value of Z - static for two - tailed test at 5% level of significance is 1.96.

    Codes :

    (1) Statements I, II and III

    (2) Statements I and III

    (3) Statements II and III

    (4) Statements I and II

20. The process of thoroughly checking the collected data to ensure optimal quality level is referred to as :

    (1) Validation   (2) Editing   (3) Classification   (4) Entry

21. **Statement - (I)** : Management is the art of knowing what you want to do and then seeing that it is done in the best and the cheapest way.

   Statement - (II) : Management is the process of planning and regulating the activities of an enterprise.

   (1) **Statement (I)** is correct, but **(II)** is incorrect
   (2) **Statement (II)** is correct, but **(I)** is incorrect
   (3) Both the **statements (I)** and **(II)** are incorrect
   (4) Both the **statements (I)** and **(II)** are correct

22. **Assertion - (A)** : No business runs itself, even on momentum . . . . . every business needs repeated stimulus.

   Reasoning - (R) : The management is the dynamic, life giving element in every business, without its leadership, the resources of production remain as resources and never become production.

   (1) **Assertion (A)** and **Reasoning (R)**, both are correct, and **(R)** is the correct explanation of **(A)**.
   (2) **Assertion (A)** and **Reasoning (R)**, both are correct, but **(R)** is not the correct explanation of **(A)**.
   (3) **Assertion (A)** is correct, but **Reasoning (R)** is incorrect.
   (4) **Reasoning (R)** is correct, but **Assertion (A)** is incorrect.

23. Match the items of **List - I** with **List - II** :

	List - I		List - II
(a)	Credit Mobilier	(i)	Charles Babbage
(b)	Charleton Twist Company	(ii)	Henry Fayol
(c)	Difference Engine	(iii)	Claud Henri Saint Simon
(d)	Commentry Four Chambault	(iv)	Robert Owen

   Codes :

	(a)	(b)	(c)	(d)
(1)	(iii)	(iv)	(i)	(ii)
(2)	(iii)	(i)	(iv)	(ii)
(3)	(i)	(iii)	(iv)	(ii)
(4)	(ii)	(i)	(iv)	(iii)

24. Find out the **correct** combination of statements with regards to business ethics :
   (a) Business ethics is the behaviour that a business adheres to in its daily dealings.
   (b) The ethics of a particular business can be diverse.
   (c) Business ethics has normative and descriptive dimensions.
   (1) Only (a) and (b)
   (2) Only (a) and (c)
   (3) Only (b) and (c)
   (4) All (a), (b) and (c)

25. Which one of the following is **not** correct about business ethics ?

(1) Business ethics reflects the philosophy of business.

(2) Business ethics is a form of applied ethics.

(3) Business ethics are governed by the Government Policies.

(4) Ethics are the standards which govern decisions on daily basis.

26. A marketing network consists of :

(1) The tasks to devise marketing activities.

(2) The tasks of hiring, training and motivating employees.

(3) The activities that help in designing and implementing the marketing programmes.

(4) The company and its supporting stakeholders with whom it has built mutually profitable business relationships.

27. Target marketing involves which of the following activities ?

(a) Market positioning

(b) Market targeting

(c) Market behaviour

(d) Market segmentation

Code :

(1) (a) and (b)

(2) (b) and (d)

(3) (a), (b) and (d)

(4) (b), (c) and (d)

28. The pricing strategy which adjusts the basic price to accommodate differences in customers, products and locations is called :

(1) Differentiated pricing

(2) Promotional pricing

(3) Geographical pricing

(4) Price discounts and allowances

29. Horizontal marketing system comprises of :

    (1) the producer, wholesaler and retailer acting in a unified system.

    (2) multichannel marketing.

    (3) two or more marketing channels to reach one or more customer segments.

    (4) two or more unrelated companies put together resources to exploit an emerging market.

30. Match the items of **List - I** with the items of **List - II** :

	List - I		List - II
(a)	Face-to-face interaction with one or more prospective purchasers	(i)	Sales promotion
(b)	Any paid form of nonpersonal promotion	(ii)	Public relations
(c)	Short-term incentives to encourage purchase	(iii)	Personal selling
(d)	Programmes to promote company's image	(iv)	Advertising

    Codes :

	(a)	(b)	(c)	(d)
(1)	(iii)	(iv)	(ii)	(i)
(2)	(iii)	(iv)	(i)	(ii)
(3)	(ii)	(i)	(iii)	(iv)
(4)	(ii)	(iii)	(i)	(iv)

31. Which of the following techniques for appraisal of investment proposals are based on time value of money ?

    (a) Accounting Rate of Return

    (b) Internal Rate of Return

    (c) Profitability Index Method

    (d) Earnings Per Share

    Codes :

    (1) (a) and (b)   (2) (b) and (c)   (3) (a) and (d)   (4) (a), (b) and (d)

32. On the basis of the following information, what will be the EBIT corresponding to financial indifference point ?

Total capital outlay ₹ 60,00,000

Financing Plans

(a) 100% Equity @ ₹ 10/- per share

(b) Debt – equity ratio 2 : 1

Rate of interest 18% p.a., corporate tax rate 40%

(1) ₹ 10,00,000　　(2) ₹ 12,00,000　　(3) ₹ 10,80,000　　(4) ₹ 12,80,000

33. Which one of the following assumptions is **not** included in the James E. Walter Valuation model ?

(1) All financing by retained earnings only

(2) No change in the key variables such as EPS and DPS

(3) The firm has finite life

(4) All earnings are either distributed as dividends or invested internally immediately

34. Match the items of **List - I** with the items of **List - II** and find out the correct matching.

List - I (Formulae)		List - II (Type of leverages)
(a) $\dfrac{\text{Contribution}}{\text{EBIT}}$	(i)	Financial leverage
(b) $\dfrac{\text{EBIT}}{\text{Earnings before Tax (EBT)}}$	(ii)	Super – leverage
(c) $\dfrac{\text{Contribution}}{\text{EBT}}$	(iii)	Operating leverage

Codes :

	(a)	(b)	(c)
(1)	(ii)	(iii)	(i)
(2)	(i)	(ii)	(iii)
(3)	(iii)	(ii)	(i)
(4)	(ii)	(i)	(iii)

35. **Statement - I :** Working capital leverage measures the responsiveness of Return on Equity for changes in current Assets.

Statement - II : When the annual demand for an item is 3200 units, unit cost ₹ 6, inventory carrying charges 25% p.a. and cost of one procurement ₹ 150, the economic ordering quantity would be 700 units.

Codes :

(1) Both **statements** are correct

(2) Both **statements** are incorrect

(3) **Statement - I** is correct and **Statement - II** is incorrect

(4) **Statement - I** is incorrect and **Statement - II** is correct

36. Match the items of **List - I** with the items of **List - II** :

List - I	List - II
Conventional HRM	**Strategic HRM**
(a) Staff specialists	(i) Fast and proactive
(b) Slow and reactive	(ii) People and knowledge
(c) Capital and products	(iii) Line managers
(d) Cost centre	(iv) Investment centre

Codes :

	(a)	(b)	(c)	(d)
(1)	(ii)	(i)	(iii)	(iv)
(2)	(ii)	(iii)	(i)	(iv)
(3)	(iii)	(ii)	(i)	(iv)
(4)	(i)	(ii)	(iii)	(iv)

37. Which one of the following is a traditional method for selection of personnel ?

(1) Interview (2) Selection Test (3) Phrenology (4) Aptitude Test

38. The method of training in crafts, trades and technical areas is known as :

(1) Vestibule training (2) Coaching

(3) Mentoring (4) Apprenticeship

39. Behaviourally Anchored Rating Scale is a technique used for :

(1)   Selection   (2)   Succession Planning

(3)   Performance appraisal   (4)   Recruitment

40. Which one of the following is **not** a mechanism of managing stress ?

(1)   Rust out   (2)   Cognitive therapy

(3)   Job enrichment   (4)   Networking

41. Interest earned by a depositor against a deposit with a commercial bank for custodial service :

(1)   is a fund based income

(2)   is a fee based income

(3)   is a combination of fund and fee based gain

(4)   is a commitment based gain

42. Match the items in **List - I** with the items in **List - II** :

	List - I		**List - II**
(a)	ATM card	(i)	NPA
(b)	Debts due for more than 30 days	(ii)	John Shephard Barron
(c)	Micro finance	(iii)	State Finance Corporations Act
(d)	State level finance corporations	(iv)	NABARD

Codes :

	(a)	**(b)**	**(c)**	**(d)**
(1)	(i)	(iii)	(ii)	(iv)
(2)	(ii)	(i)	(iv)	(iii)
(3)	(iv)	(iii)	(ii)	(i)
(4)	(ii)	(i)	(iii)	(iv)

43. **Assertion (A) :** A well developed money market is the basis for an effective monetary policy. It is in the money market that the Central Bank comes into contact with the financial sectors of the economy as a whole and it is through the liquidity in the market that influence the cost and availability of credit.

   Reasoning (R) : A well organised money market is an essential condition for the successful operation of the Central Banking policies, and for holding the conditions of liquidity within the bounds of what the monetary authorities consider desirable.

   (1) **(A)** is true but **(R)** is false

   (2) **(R)** is true but **(A)** is false

   (3) **(A)** is true and **(R)** offers correct explanation to **(A)**

   (4) Both **(A)** and **(R)** are false

44. The operations of banks and financial institutions are regulated by :

   (1) The RBI Act 1934 only

   (2) The Banking Regulation Act 1949 only

   (3) Information Technology Act 2000 only

   (4) All of the above

45. To operationalise online, internet, mobile banking, debit card and credit card tools, some of the essential ingredients are :

   (1) Compliance with the Information Technology Act 2000

   (2) Satellite connection

   (3) Selection of a portal and server

   (4) All of the above

46. Any country consistently facing balance of payment deficiency can approach :

   (1) The World Bank

   (2) The Smithsonian Institute

   (3) IMF

   (4) The IMF and the IBRD

47. Counter–trade means :

(1) A sort of bilateral trade where one set of goods is exchanged for another set of goods and a seller provides a buyer with deliveries.

(2) A company takes full responsibility for making its goods available in the target market by selling directly to the end-users.

(3) The companies in two separate sovereigns agree to exchange one set of goods for another set of goods.

(4) A set of multilateral trade where one of goods and services may be exchanged for another set of goods and services among the trading partners.

48. The floating rate system is characterised by :

(1) the market forces that determine the exchange rate between two currencies.

(2) the central banking authorities of the two countries mutually agree upon the rate.

(3) help realigning the par value of major currencies.

(4) the rate of exchange mutually agreed upon between IMF and its member nations.

49. A practice of selling a commodity in a foreign market at a price lower than the domestic price; and even at equal to the cost of production to capture foreign market is known as :

(1) Gouging   (2) Forging   (3) Dumping   (4) Forfeiting

50. The highest percentage of export from India went to which of the following regions in 2013-14 ?

(1) OECD countries   (2) USA

(3) SAARC   (4) Latin America

51. Match the items of **List - I** with the items of **List - II** and select a **correct** code :

	List - I		List - II
(a)	SEBI	(i)	Exchange for small companies
(b)	RBI	(ii)	Secondary market in treasury bills
(c)	STCI	(iii)	Regulation of secondary market
(d)	OTCEI	(iv)	Ad-hoc treasury bills

Codes :

	(a)	(b)	(c)	(d)
(1)	(iv)	(ii)	(iii)	(i)
(2)	(iii)	(iv)	(ii)	(i)
(3)	(iii)	(i)	(ii)	(iv)
(4)	(ii)	(iii)	(i)	(iv)

52. X Ltd. goes into liquidation and a new company Z Ltd. purchases the business of X Ltd. It is a case of :

(1) Amalgamation   (2) Absorption

(3) Internal reconstruction   (4) External reconstruction

53. When the cost incurred on recruiting, training and developing the employees is considered for determining the value of employees, it is called :

(1) The replacement cost approach   (2) The historical cost approach

(3) The opportunity cost approach   (4) None of the above

54. In India, NIFTY and SENSEX are calculated on the basis of :

(1) Market capitalisation   (2) Paid up capital

(3) Free-float market capitalisation   (4) Authorized share capital

55. Financial Instruments which are issued with detachable warrants and are redeemable after certain period is known as :

(1) Deep Discount Bonds   (2) Secured Premium Notes

(3) Bunny Bonds   (4) Junk Bonds

56. Which of the following can be used by a company as communication mix to reach the target customers ?

(a) Advertising

(b) Sales promotion

(c) Events and experiences

(d) Public relations

(e) Direct marketing

(f) Personal selling

Codes :

(1) (a), (b), (d) and (f)   (2) (a), (b), (e) and (f)

(3) (a), (b), (d), (e) and (f)   (4) (a), (b), (c), (d), (e) and (f)

57. In addition to motivation, learning and memory, which one of the following is included in the main psychological processes affecting consumer behaviour ?

(1) Perception   (2) Life cycle   (3) Life style   (4) Social class

58. Match the items of **List - I** with the items of **List - II** :

	List - I		List - II
(a)	Geographic Segmentation	(i)	Gender, income, religion
(b)	Demographic Segmentation	(ii)	Knowledge, attitude, response
(c)	Psychographic Segmentation	(iii)	Regions, cities, neighbourhoods
(d)	Behavioural Segmentation	(iv)	Lifestyle, personality traits, values

Codes :

	(a)	(b)	(c)	(d)
(1)	(ii)	(iv)	(iii)	(i)
(2)	(ii)	(iv)	(i)	(iii)
(3)	(iv)	(ii)	(i)	(iii)
(4)	(iv)	(i)	(ii)	(iii)

59. Which one of the following is **not** a stage in the product life cycle ?

(1) Introduction   (2) Growth   (3) Equilibrium   (4) Decline

60. Which one of the following is **correct** statement in respect of co-branding ?

(1) Co-branding is an umbrella branding of goods of a company.

(2) In co-branding, two or more well-known existing brands are combined into a joint product.

(3) Co-branding is the process of combining two brands for promoting brand equity.

(4) All of the above

61. Which one of the following is **not** a major punishment ?

(1) Withholding of increments   (2) Demotion

(3) Transfer   (4) Suspension

62. **Assertion (A) :** Job evaluation is essentially a job rating process, not unlike the rating of employees.

Reasoning (R): Job evaluation is a practice which seeks to provide a degree of objectivity in measuring the comparative value of jobs within an organisation and among similar organisations.

(1) Both **Assertion (A)** and **Reasoning (R)** are correct

(2) Both **Assertion (A)** and **Reasoning (R)** are incorrect

(3) **Assertion (A)** is correct, but **Reasoning (R)** is incorrect

(4) **Reasoning (R)** is correct, but **Assertion (A)** is incorrect

63. Identify the **correct** combinations from the following :

	Skills	Training and Development Methods	Target Trainees
(a)	Knowledge	Deliberation/Lecture	Managerial
(b)	Multi-skills	Vestibule training	Operative
(c)	Decision-making skills	Management game	Managerial
(d)	Behavioural skills	Sensitivity training	Supervisory

Codes :

(1) (a), (b) and (c)

(2) (a), (c) and (d)

(3) (b), (c) and (d)

(4) (a), (b) and (d)

64. Which among the following are **not** part of staffing process ?

(a) Human Resource Planning

(b) Recruitment

(c) Selection

(d) Induction and Orientation

(e) Training and Development

(f) Performance Appraisal

(g) Transfers

(h) Separations

Codes :

(1) (e), (f), (g) and (h)

(2) (g) and (h)

(3) (f) and (h)

(4) None of the above

65. Match the items of **List - I** with **List - II** :

	List - I		List - II
(a)	INTUC	(i)	1920
(b)	AITUC	(ii)	1947
(c)	CITU	(iii)	1955
(d)	BMS	(iv)	1970

Codes :

	(a)	(b)	(c)	(d)
(1)	(i)	(ii)	(iii)	(iv)
(2)	(ii)	(i)	(iv)	(iii)
(3)	(ii)	(i)	(iii)	(iv)
(4)	(iii)	(i)	(iv)	(ii)

66. **Assertion (A) :** Amended Patent Act, in compliance with WTO, provides for grant of product patent as well as a process patent for a period of 20 years from the date of application.

Reasoning (R) : Under the Act, patent may be granted to an invention which means a new product or process involving an inventive step and capable of industrial application, a technical advance over existing knowledge.

Codes :

(1)   Both **(A)** and **(R)** are true but **(R)**, is not correct explanation to **(A)**.

(2)   **(A)** is false but **(R)** is correct.

(3)   Both **(A)** and **(R)** are true and **(R)**, is correct explanation to **(A)**.

(4)   **(A)** is correct but **(R)** is false.

67. Which of the following have been recognised under the intellectual property eligible for creation of rights as per WTO mandate ?

(a)   Computer software, music disc, performing art

(b)   Geographical indicator

(c)   Global positioning system

(d)   Journals, books, seeds, design, brand

Codes :

(1)   (a), (b) and (c)   (2)   (d), (c) and (a)

(3)   (a), (b) and (d)   (4)   (c), (a) and (b)

68. NAFTA came into force from January, 1994 embracing :

    (1)   The USA, Canada, Cuba, Trinidad and Tobago

    (2)   The USA, Canada, Mexico

    (3)   Cuba, Mexico, USA, Havana

    (4)   Trinidad, The USA, Mexico

69. A common market is one where :

    (1)   all the trading nations agree commonly to levy a common and uniform tariff rate for all goods.

    (2)   all the trading nations agree commonly to rationalise tariff and non-tariff barriers mutually to promote intra-region trade.

    (3)   there is a customs union along with free intra - union movement of factors of production.

    (4)   there is an economic union along with free intra-union movement of residents.

70. The Maastricht Treaty of February, 1992 renamed the European Community (EC) as :

    (1)   the European Union (EU)

    (2)   the European Economic Union (EEU)

    (3)   the European Monetary Union (EMU)

    (4)   the European Economic Community (EEC)

71. In which of the following cases, Assessing officer has the discretion to assess the income of the previous year in the previous year or in the subsequent assessment year ?

    (1)   Shipping business of non-residents

    (2)   Association of Persons (AOP) or Body of Individuals (BOI) formed for a particular event or purpose

    (3)   Assessment of persons likely to transfer property to avoid tax

    (4)   Discontinued business

72. Rental income received by a foreign individual, from another foreign individual, in respect of the property situated in Delhi is taxable in the hands of :

    (1)   Resident and Ordinarily Resident (OR) only

    (2)   Ordinarily Resident (OR) and Not Ordinarily Resident (NOR) only

    (3)   Non Resident (NR) only

    (4)   Ordinarily Resident (OR), Not Ordinarily Resident (NOR) and Non Resident (NR)

73. Which of the following income is **not** chargeable under the head 'income from business and profession' ?

    (1) Profits and Gains carried on by an assessee during the previous year.

    (2) Income derived by a trade professional or similar association from specific services performed for its members.

    (3) Income from the activity of owning or owning and maintaining race horses.

    (4) Salary received by a partner of a firm from the same firm.

74. Mr. A earned a capital gain of ₹ 100 lakhs on 31-2-2014 from the sale of a long term capital asset (land) within the limits of Jaipur corporation. If he invests ₹ 60 lakhs, out of ₹ 100 lakhs, in Rural Electricity Corporation Bonds approved under Sec. 54 EC in 20-2-2014, what is the amount of exemption he can claim under Sec. 54 EC of Income Tax Act for the AY 2014-15 ?

    (1) ₹ 60 lakhs   (2) ₹ 50 lakhs   (3) ₹ 100 lakhs   (4) ₹ 30 lakhs

75. Under which of the following situations, the Appellate Tribunal can rectify the mistake in the order passed by it under Sec 254 (2) of Income Tax Act ?

    (a) If subsequent decision of the Supreme Court/High Court is available on the subject after the Appellate Tribunal's order

    (b) If an assessee apply for rectification of the Tribunal's order by raising fresh grounds before the Tribunal

    (c) If the omission or mistake is on the part of Appellate Tribunal

    (d) If the order is passed by the Appellate Tribunal under an erroneous impression of fact or law

    Codes :

    (1) (a), (b) and (c)

    (2) (b), (c) and (d)

    (3) (a), (c) and (d)

    (4) only (c) and (d)

- o O o -

UGC - NET JUNE 2015

ANSWER KEYS (PAPER III)

SUBJECT : 08 (Commerce)

Qus. No.	Ans.	Qus. No.	Ans.	Qus. No.	Ans.
1	1	26	4	51	2
2	4	27	3	52	4
3	2	28	1	53	2
4	3	29	4	54	3
5	1	30	2	55	2
6	3	31	2	56	4
7	3	32	3	57	1
8	3	33	3	58	*
9	3	34	1	59	3
10	4	35	2	60	2
11	3	36	2	61	3
12	2	37	3	62	1
13	3	38	4	63	2
14	4	39	3	64	4
15	1	40	1	65	2
16	3	41	1	66	3
17	2	42	2	67	3
18	2	43	3	68	2
19	4	44	4	69	3
20	1	45	4	70	1
21	4	46	3	71	4
22	1	47	1	72	4
23	1	48	1	73	3
24	4	49	3	74	*
25	3	50	1	75	3

* = No Option Is correct or The Question is Wrong

Note : This paper contains **fifty (50)** objective type questions of **two (2)** marks each. **All** questions are compulsory.

1. The responsibility of the organization to the workers includes :
   (i) The payment of fair wages
   (ii) Arrangement of proper training and education of the workers
   (iii) The installation of an efficient grievance handling system
   (iv) Welfare of family members
   (v) The provision of the best possible working conditions
   Identify the correct combination :
   (A) (i), (ii), (iii) and (v)   (B) (ii), (iii), (iv) and (v)
   (C) (i), (ii), (iii) and (iv)   (D) (i), (iii), (iv) and (v)

2. Match the items of List – I with List – II :

	List – I		List – II
a.	Industries Development Regulation Act	i.	1947
b.	Import and Export Control Act	ii.	1948
c.	Foreign Exchange Management Act	iii.	1951
d.	Factories Act	iv.	1999

   Identify the correct combination :
   Codes :

	a	b	c	d
(A)	i	iii	iv	ii
(B)	iii	i	ii	iv
(C)	iii	i	iv	ii
(D)	iii	iv	ii	i

3. Which among the following is not a correct sequential combination ?
   (A) Macro Environment → Economic Environment → National Income → Pattern of Income Distribution
   (B) Business Environment → Internal Environment → Business Ethics → Payment of Fair Wages
   (C) Business Environment → External Environment → Micro Environment → Suppliers
   (D) Macro Environment → External Environment → Customers → Prospects of Business Development

4. Which among the following is not a correct combination ?

   (A) Industrial Policy – 1948

   (B) Industrial Policy Statement – 1977

   (C) Industrial Policy Statement – 1980

   (D) Industrial Policy Statement – 1991

5. **Statement – I :** The industrial policy of the Government of India is aimed at increasing the tempo of industrial development.

   Statement – II : After the New Industrial Policy – 1991, the Balance of Trade for India has always been positive.

   Codes :

   (A) Statement (I) is correct, but (II) is incorrect.

   (B) Statement (II) is correct, but (I) is incorrect.

   (C) Both Statements (I) and (II) are correct.

   (D) Both Statements (I) and (II) are incorrect.

6. Current Ratio 2.5, Liquid Ratio 1.5 and Working Capital ₹ 60,000. What is Current Assets ?

   (A) ₹ 60,000   (B) ₹ 80,000

   (C) ₹ 1,00,000   (D) ₹ 1,20,000

7. X, Y, Z are sharing profits in the ratio of 6 : 5 : 3. A is admitted into partnership for $1/8^{th}$ share. The sacrificing ratio of X, Y and Z is

   (A) Equal   (B) 6 : 5 : 3

   (C) 5/14, 4/14, 5/14   (D) 4 : 5 : 5

8. Accounting information given by a company :

Total assets turnover	3 times
Net profit margin	10%
Total assets	₹ 1,00,000

   The net profit is

   (A) ₹ 10,000   (B) ₹ 15,000

   (C) ₹ 25,000   (D) ₹ 30,000

9. "Make sufficient provisions for future losses, but do not anticipate future profits." This statement is in accordance to the concept of :

(A) Matching

(B) Objectivity

(C) Conservatism

(D) Materiality

10. When a firm is dissolved, profit or loss on realisation is shared by the partners

(A) Equal

(B) In the ratio of their capital balances

(C) In the profit sharing ratio

(D) In the ratio laid down in Garner Vs. Murray

11. The inverse relationship between variations in the price and quantity demanded is not due to

(A) Income Effects

(B) Substitution Effects

(C) Future Expectations

(D) Law of Diminishing Marginal Utility

12. Consumer is said to be in equilibrium, maximizing his total utility, when

(A) the marginal utilities of the two goods consumed are equal.

(B) the proportions of the marginal utilities and respective prices are equal.

(C) the consumer gets full satisfaction from the consumption.

(D) the consumer feels satisfied with his expenditure on the various goods.

13. Match the items of the following two lists and suggest the correct code :

	List – I		List – II
a.	Zero Income Elasticity	i.	Substitute goods
b.	Unit Cross Elasticity	ii.	Complementary goods
c.	Positive Cross Elasticity	iii.	Indifferent goods
d.	Negative Cross Elasticity	iv.	Independent goods

Choose the correct option :

Codes :

	a	b	c	d
(A)	iii	ii	i	iv
(B)	ii	iii	iv	i
(C)	iii	iv	i	ii
(D)	iv	i	ii	iii

14. **Statement (A) :** The isoquant curves are drawn convex to the origin due to diminishing technical rate of substitution.

Statement (B) : The lesser the convexity of the isoquant curve the greater the possibility of the complementarity of the two inputs.

Codes :

(A) Statements (A) and (B) both are correct.

(B) Statement (A) is correct but (B) is incorrect.

(C) Statement (A) is incorrect but (B) is correct.

(D) Statements (A) and (B) both are incorrect.

15. Match the items of the List – I with those of List – II and suggest the correct code :

	List – I		**List – II**
a.	Constant average cost over a range of output	i.	Economic capacity
b.	Average cost becomes constant momentarily	ii.	Reserve capacity
c.	Normal average cost is a U-shaped curve	iii.	Production and Managerials costs effects
d.	Modern Long-run average cost is L-shaped	iv.	Economies and Diseconomies

Codes :

	a	b	c	d
(A)	i	ii	iii	iv
(B)	ii	iii	iv	i
(C)	iii	iv	ii	i
(D)	ii	i	iv	iii

16. Which one of the following is not probability sampling method ?

(A) Simple Random Sampling   (B) Cluster Sampling

(C) Judgemental Sampling   (D) Systematic Sampling

17. The research carried out to expand the knowledge of a particular field is known as

(A) Applied research   (B) Qualitative research

(C) Quantitative research   (D) Basic research

18. In univariate data analysis t-test is used when the data are in the form of

    (A) Metric data with one sample

    (B) Non-metric data

    (C) Non-metric data with independent variable

    (D) Metric data with independent two sample

19. To show the trend for a variable, which one of the presentation method is used ?

    (A) Histogram
    (B) Frequency polygon
    (C) Line graph
    (D) Scatter graph

20. Which one of the following objectives is not the objective of secondary data collection ?

    (A) Identify the problem

    (B) Test the hypotheses of the relevant present problem

    (C) Better define the problem

    (D) Interpret primary data more insightfully

21. The structure of an organisation in which there is separation of ownership and management is called

    (A) Sole proprietorship
    (B) Partnership
    (C) Company
    (D) Cooperative society

22. When a person transacts with a company on matters which is beyond the power of the company, the person will be governed by the Doctrine of

    (A) Management by Exception
    (B) Constructive Notice
    (C) Indoor Management
    (D) Self Management

23. **Assertion (A) :** MBO is effective way of planning and organizing the work.

    Reason (R) : Employees participate in setting the objectives.

    Codes :

    (A) Both (A) and (R) are true.

    (B) Both (A) and (R) are false.

    (C) (A) is true, but (R) is false.

    (D) (A) is false, but (R) is correct.

24. The appropriate sequence of the formation of a company are in the following order :

(A) Promotion, commencement of business and incorporation

(B) Promotion, incorporation, capital subscription and commencement of business

(C) Capital subscription, promotion, incorporation and commencement of business

(D) Incorporation, capital subscription, commencement of business and promotion

25. Delegation of authority makes the size of the organization :

(A) Smaller organization

(B) Larger organization

(C) Very big organization

(D) It does not affect the size of the organization

26. Managerial Grid suggests the following as the best leader behaviour :

(A) High structure and high consideration

(B) Low structure and low consideration

(C) High concern both for production and people

(D) Low concern both for production and people

27. Marketing strategy development is also known as

(A) Marketing Control   (B) Marketing Exercise

(C) Marketing Planning   (D) Situation Analysis

28. For most people, the purchase of cheese for daily use can be described as a

(A) Completely novel buy   (B) Modified re-buy

(C) Routine re-buy   (D) High involvement product

29. The promotion mix of a company consists of these –

(A) Marketing communication, promotion decisions

(B) Personal selling, product objectives

(C) Advertising, personal selling, sales promotion , publicity and public relations

(D) Consumer psychology, buyers motives, brand equity

30. Rational buying motives that determine purchase decisions are mostly based on

(A) Price factor   (B) Psychological factors

(C) Quality of product   (D) Advertisement

31. **Statement – I :** Capital structure refers to composition of long-term funds.

     Statement – II : These include equity share capital, preference share capital, debentures, all debts and all reserves.

(A) Both Statements I and II are correct.

(B) Statement I is correct but Statement II is incorrect.

(C) Statement I is incorrect but Statement II is correct.

(D) Both statements are incorrect.

32. Match the items of the following two lists and suggest the correct code :

	List – I		List – II
a.	Pay-back Rate of Return	i.	Discounted Cash Flow Technique
b.	Internal Rate of Return	ii.	Compounded values of investments and returns
c.	Benefit Cost Ratio	iii.	Crude method for project evaluation
d.	Net Terminal Value Method	iv.	Varying sized projects evaluation

Codes :

	a	b	c	d
(A)	ii	iii	i	iv
(B)	iii	i	iv	ii
(C)	i	iv	ii	iii
(D)	iv	ii	iii	i

33. Match the items of the following two lists and suggest the correct code :

	List – I		List – II
a.	Realised yield method	i.	Cost of equity share capital
b.	Taxation	ii.	Cost of equity capital
c.	Cost of total capital employed	iii.	Cost of debt capital
d.	Dividend growth is a consideration	iv.	Weighted cost of capital

Codes :

	a	b	c	d
(A)	iv	iii	ii	i
(B)	ii	iv	i	iii
(C)	ii	iii	iv	i
(D)	i	ii	iii	iv

34. Cash Flow Management involves :

I. Lock-box system

II. Marketable securities

III. Playing the float

IV. Concentration Bank Account

Codes :

(A) I, II and III only

(B) II, III and IV only

(C) I, III and IV only

(D) I, II and IV only

35. Dividend capitalisation model was developed by

(A) Ezra Solomon

(B) Myron J. Gordon

(C) James E. Walter

(D) Merton H. Miller and Franco Modigliani

36. The process of narrowing a large number of candidates to a smaller field is called

(A) Rushing

(B) Recruitment

(C) Selection

(D) Enrollment

37. According to which theory, people are motivated to the extent to which they expect that their actions will help in achievement of goals ?

(A) Vroom's Vector Valence Theory

(B) Need Theory

(C) Z Theory

(D) X Theory

38. Match the items of List – I with List – II and select the correct code :

	List – I		List – II
a.	Getting Effective Leadership in the Industrial Organization	i.	Dale Yoder
b.	The Nature of Leadership, Organization and Management	ii.	Alford and Beatty
c.	Industrial Management	iii.	Douglas McGregor
d.	Personnel Management	iv.	Chester I. Bernard

Codes :

	a	b	c	d
(A)	i	ii	iii	iv
(B)	iii	iv	ii	i
(C)	iii	iv	i	ii
(D)	iv	iii	ii	i

39. Match the items of List – I with List – II :

	List – I		List – II
a.	AITUC	i.	Indian National Congress
b.	BMS	ii.	Socialists
c.	INTUC	iii.	Rashtriya Swayamsevak Sangh
d.	CITU	iv.	Communist Party of India

Identify the correct combination :

Codes :

	a	b	c	d
(A)	iv	iii	ii	i
(B)	iv	i	ii	iii
(C)	iv	iii	i	ii
(D)	iv	i	iii	ii

40. The main characteristics of Weber's bureaucracy are :

(A) Specialization (B) Hierarchy of authority

(C) System of rules (D) All of the above

41. Match the items of List – I with List – II :

	List – I		List – II
a.	RBI Nationalization	i.	1964
b.	Imperial Bank Nationalization	ii.	1949
c.	Nationalization of 14 Commercial Banks	iii.	1955
d.	Establishment of IDBI	iv.	1969

Identify the correct combination :

Codes :

	a	b	c	d
(A)	i	ii	iii	iv
(B)	ii	iii	i	iv
(C)	iii	ii	iv	i
(D)	ii	iii	iv	i

42. As per the RBI Act, 1934, the following functions are described as the functions of a Central Bank :

(i)   Banking functions

(ii) Advisory functions

(iii) Supervisory functions

(iv) Promotional functions

Identify the correct combination :

(A) (i), (iii) and (iv)   (B) (i), (ii) and (iv)

(C) (ii), (iii) and (iv)   (D) Only (i) and (iii)

43. Phishing is an attempt to acquire :

(A) Loan from unauthorized firms

(B) Sensitive information such as username, password, etc.

(C) Personal information from banks

(D) None of the above

44. What is Call Money ?

(A) Money borrowed or lent for a day or overnight.

(B) Money borrowed for more than one day but upto 3 days.

(C) Money borrowed for more than one day but upto 7 days.

(D) Money borrowed for more than one day but upto 14 days.

45. The Regulatory Authority of Regional Rural Banks is

(A) NABARD   (B) Central Government

(C) State Government   (D) Sponsor Bank

46. Which of the following is not ensured to the consumer in the globalization ?

(A) Lower prices   (B) Better selection

(C) Clear origin of goods and services   (D) Improved services

47. In international trade which of the following is a non-tariff trade barrier ?

(A) Quotas

(B) Import bans

(C) Export controls

(D) Anti dumping laws

48. Match the items of List – I with items in List – II and select a correct code :

	List – I		List – II
a.	Current Account	i.	Official Capital
b.	Capital Account	ii.	Reserves from foreign countries
c.	Unilateral Payments	iii.	Reparations
d.	Official Statement Account	iv.	Visible Exports and Imports

Codes :

	a	b	c	d
(A)	i	iii	ii	iv
(B)	iv	i	ii	iii
(C)	iv	i	iii	ii
(D)	iii	ii	i	iv

49. Match the items of List – I with the items in List – II and select a correct code :

	List – I		List – II
a.	Vishesh Krishi Upaj Yojana	i.	Scheme intended to reduce difficulties of exporters
b.	EPCG	ii.	Duty Entitlement Pass Book
c.	DFRC	iii.	To boost exports of fruits, vegetables, flowers, minor forest produce etc.
d.	DEPB	iv.	Relating to import of duty free fuel

Codes :

	a	b	c	d
(A)	iv	i	ii	iii
(B)	iv	iii	i	ii
(C)	iii	iv	ii	i
(D)	iii	i	iv	ii

50. Which of the following is not the agency of World Bank ?

(A) MIGA

(B) ICSID

(C) ADB

(D) IDA

_____

UGC - NET DECEMBER 2014

ANSWER KEYS (PAPER II)

SUBJECT : 08 (Commerce)

Qus. No.	Ans.	Qus. No.	Ans.
1	A	26	C
2	C	27	C
3	D	28	C
4	D	29	C
5	A	30	B
6	C	31	B
7	B	32	B
8	D	33	C
9	C	34	C
10	C	35	B
11	C	36	C
12	B	37	A
13	C	38	B
14	B	39	C
15	D	40	D
16	C	41	D
17	D	42	A
18	D	43	B
19	C	44	B
20	B	45	A
21	C	46	C
22	B	47	B
23	A	48	C
24	B	49	D
25	B	50	C

COMMERCE
Paper – III

Note : This paper contains **seventy five (75)** objective type questions of **two (2)** marks each. **All** questions are compulsory.

1. Match the items of List – I with List – II :

	List – I (International Economic Groups)		List – II (Year of Establishment)
a.	European Union (EU)	i.	1973
b.	European Free Trade Association (EFTA)	ii.	1992
c.	Caribbean Community (CARICOM)	iii.	1985
d.	South Asian Association for Regional Cooperation (SAARC)	iv.	1960

   Codes :

	a	b	c	d
(A)	ii	iv	iii	i
(B)	ii	iv	i	iii
(C)	iv	ii	i	iii
(D)	iii	i	ii	iv

2. The important objectives of WTO are :
   (i) To improve the quality of technology in the member countries.
   (ii) To improve the standard of living of people in the member countries.
   (iii) To ensure full employment and broad increase in effective demand.
   (iv) To enlarge production and trade of goods.
   (v) To increase trade of services

   Codes :
   (A) (i), (ii), (iii) and (iv) (B) (ii), (iii), (iv) and (v)
   (C) (i), (ii), (iii) and (v) (D) (i), (iii), (iv) and (v)

3. **Assertion (A) :** The industrial growth in India has been hampered by the burden of many controls and regulations.

   Reason (R) : The New Industrial Policy seeks to liberate the industry from the shackles of Licensing System.

   Codes :
   (A) Assertion (A) is correct, but Reason (R) is not correct.
   (B) Assertion (A) is correct and Reason (R) is right explanation of (A).
   (C) Both Assertion (A) and Reason (R) are correct.
   (D) Both Assertion (A) and Reason (R) are incorrect.

4. Internal environment of a business includes :
   (i)   Business ethics and moral standards
   (ii)   Business and managerial policies
   (iii) Prospects of business development
   (iv)   Government rules and regulations
   (v)   Industrial relations
   Codes :
   (A)   (i), (ii), (iv) and (v)   (B)   (ii), (iii), (iv) and (v)
   (C)   (i), (ii), (iii) and (iv)   (D)   (i), (ii), (iii) and (v)

5. Identify the incorrect combination from the following :

	Finance Commission	Constituted (Year)	Report Submitted (Year)	Chairman
(A)	1st	1951	1953	K.C. Neogi
(B)	7th	1977	1978	J.M. Shelat
(C)	11th	1998	2000	N.K.P. Salve
(D)	13th	2007	2009	V.L. Kelkar

6. A flexible budget requires careful study and classification of expenses into
   (A)   Product expenses and period expenses
   (B)   Past and current expenses
   (C)   Administrative, selling and factory expenses
   (D)   Fixed, semi-variable and variable expenses

7. Responsibility accounting aims at collecting and reporting costing information
   (A)   Department-wise   (B)   Cost centre-wise
   (C)   Function-wise   (D)   Product-wise

8. Return on Investment (RoI) is computed as
   (A)   Net Profit Ratio × Capital Turnover Ratio
   (B)   Operating Net Profit Ratio × Shareholders Fund
   (C)   Net Profit / Sales
   (D)   Cost of Sales / Capital Employed

9. Margin of Safety is calculated by using
   (A) $\dfrac{\text{Profit}}{\text{P / V Ratio}}$ (B) $\dfrac{\text{Fixed Cost}}{\text{Contribution}}$
   (C) $\dfrac{\text{Break Even Sales}}{\text{Sales}}$ (D) $\dfrac{\text{Profit}}{\text{Sales}}$

10. Pre-acquisition profit in subsidiary company is considered as

(A) Revenue profit   (B) Capital profit

(C) Goodwill   (D) Minority interest

11. **Assertion (A) :** The financial statements prepared on historical cost basis result into an erosion of capital in the long run.

Reason (R) : Maintaining the books of accounts as per Current Purchasing Power Technique only may contain the inflationary pressure.

In the context of above two statements, which one of the following is correct one ?

(A) Both (A) and (R) are true and (R) is the correct explanation of (A).

(B) Both (A) and (R) are true, but (R) is not the correct explanation of (A).

(C) (A) is true, but (R) is false.

(D) (A) is false, but (R) is true.

12. Secondary market intermediaries for corporate securities in India are

I.   Investors   II.   Jobbers

III. Brokers and sub-brokers   IV.   Portfolio consultants

Codes :

(A) I, II and III only   (B) II, III and IV only

(C) II and III only   (D) III and IV only

13. The type of lease requiring an agreement between the financier and lessor is known as

(A) Financial lease   (B) Sale and lease back

(C) Leveraged lease   (D) Operating lease

14. Match the various stock exchanges in List – I with the years of their establishment in List – II as follows and suggest the correct code :

	List – I		List – II	
a.	National Stock Exchange (NSE)		i.	1875
b.	MCX Stock Exchange (MCX-SX)		ii.	1992
c.	Bombay Stock Exchange (BSE)		iii.	2000
d.	Interconnected Stock Exchange of India (ISEI)		iv.	2008

Codes :

	a	b	c	d
(A)	ii	iv	i	iii
(B)	ii	iii	iv	i
(C)	i	iii	ii	iv
(D)	iii	ii	iv	i

15. Monopolists prefer to sell the products in the markets with

(A) Elastic demand

(B) Unitary elastic demand

(C) Inelastic demand

(D) Absence of elasticity of demand

16. **Assertion (A) :** In long run under Perfect Competition all firms invariably get only normal profit.

Reason (R) : All firms incur minimum average cost and incur no selling cost due to absence of product differentiation.

Codes :

(A) Assertion (A) and Reason (R) both are correct.

(B) Assertion (A) is correct, but Reason (R) is incorrect.

(C) Assertion (A) is incorrect, but Reason (R) is correct.

(D) Assertion (A) and Reason (R) both are incorrect.

17. **Assertion (A) :** Differential pricing structure is designed to accommodate the various categories of buyers.

Reason (R) : It aims at increasing sales and revenues and driving the competitors out from the market.

Codes :

(A) Assertion (A) and Reasoning (R) both are correct.

(B) Assertion (A) is correct, but Reasoning (R) is incorrect.

(C) Assertion (A) is incorrect, but Reasoning (R) is correct.

(D) Assertion (A) and Reasoning (R) both are incorrect.

18. Cost-plus pricing is considered appropriate for :

I. Product Tailoring

II. Public Utility Pricing

III. Refusal Pricing

IV. Monopoly Pricing

Codes :

(A) I and II only

(B) I, II and III only

(C) II, III and IV only

(D) III and IV only

19. For promoting sales advertising endeavours may be made as per

I. Competitive parity

II. Objective and task

III. Tied sales

IV. All-one-can-Afford

Codes :

(A) I and II only

(B) II, III and IV only

(C) I, II and IV only

(D) III and IV only

20. In the hypothesis testing procedure a researcher may commit type II error in which of the following conditions ?
   (A) When the true null hypothesis is rejected.
   (B) When the alternative hypothesis is accepted.
   (C) When the false null hypothesis is accepted.
   (D) When the true null hypothesis is accepted.

21. Which one of the following tenets is not correct in the context of Central Limit Theorem ?
   (A) If a population from which a sample is drawn is normally distributed the sampling distribution of mean (SDM) will be normal for all sample sizes.
   (B) The mean of the SDM is the population mean.
   (C) If the population is not normal from which the sample is drawn, the SDM is not normal for any sample size.
   (D) If the population is not normal from which a sample is drawn, the SDM approaches normality as the sample size increases.

22. Which one of the following is not an example of tax evasion?
   (A) Submitting misleading documents.
   (B) Not maintaining proper accounts of income earned.
   (C) Suppression of facts.
   (D) Interpreting the tax law in ones own way to minimise tax liability.

23. Which one of the following is not the purpose of performance-monitoring research ?
   (A) To provide feedback for evaluation and control.
   (B) To indicate things that are not going as planned.
   (C) To help the organisation to plan various activities.
   (D) It is required to explain why something went wrong.

24. The transformation of raw data into a form that will make them easy to understand and interpret, rearranging and manipulating data to generate information is called
   (A) Descriptive research   (B) Descriptive analysis
   (C) Causal research   (D) Exploratory research

25. **Assertion (A)** : The span of management at the upper level is generally narrow while at the lower level span is wide.
   Reason (R) : The task allocated to subordinates at the lower level of management are more specific and precise and thus making supervision easy and simple.
   Suggest correct code :
   (A) (A) is correct, but (R) is wrong.
   (B) (A) is wrong, but (R) is correct.
   (C) Both (A) and (R) are correct.
   (D) Both (A) and (R) are wrong.

26. Match the following :

	List – I		List – II
a.	To check the quality of work	i.	Speed loss
b.	To see that work is completed in time	ii.	Inspector
c.	To check absenteeism of workers	iii.	Instruction and check
d.	To issue instructions regarding methods of work	iv.	Shop discipline

Select the code :

Codes :

	a	b	c	d
(A)	iii	ii	i	iv
(B)	ii	i	iv	iii
(C)	ii	i	iii	iv
(D)	iv	iii	i	ii

27. F.W. Taylor called "The Military type of Foreman" to

(A) Unity of Command   (B) Span of Control

(C) Delegated Legislature   (D) Department

28. Match the items of List – I with List – II :

	List – I		List – II
a.	Commentary Four Chambault	i.	F.W. Taylor
b.	Midvale Steel Works	ii.	Claud Henry Saint Simon
c.	Charleton Twist Company	iii.	Henry Fayol
d.	Credit Mobilier	iv.	Robert Owen

Codes :

	a	b	c	d
(A)	iii	ii	iv	i
(B)	i	ii	iii	iv
(C)	iii	i	ii	iv
(D)	iii	i	iv	ii

29. **Assertion (A) :** The risk condition exists when decision makers have absolutely no idea of what the results of an implemented alternative would be.

Reason (R) : When operating under complete uncertainty condition, decision makers usually find that sound decisions are a matter of chance.

In the context of the two statements, which one of the following is correct ?

Codes :

(A) Both (A) and (R) are correct.

(B) Both (A) and (R) are wrong.

(C) (A) is correct, but (R) is wrong.

(D) (A) is wrong, but (R) is correct.

30. **Assertion (A) :** In product concept, focus is on innovating and improving products.
Reason (R) : In selling concept, consumers are persuaded to buy products.
Codes :
(A) Both (A) and (R) are true. (B) (A) is true, but (R) is false.
(C) (A) is false, but (R) is true. (D) Both (A) and (R) are false.

31. Which of the following is not a method of segmenting a market ?
(A) Behavioural segmentation (B) Psychographic segmentation
(C) Benefits segmentation (D) Customer segmentation

32. Consumer attitudes and beliefs about diet, health and nutrition are influenced by
(A) Economic environment (B) Cultural environment
(C) Social environment (D) Natural environment

33. Select the phases of Product Life Cycle :
1. Initiation 2. Decline
3. Boom 4. Introduction
5. Maturity 6. Growth
Codes :
(A) 1, 3, 5, 6 (B) 1, 2, 3, 4
(C) 4, 6, 5, 2 (D) 2, 3, 5, 6

34. Which of the following is not a product-mix strategy ?
(A) Trading up (B) Alteration
(C) Simplification (D) Value addition

35. "Relationship" in marketing means
(A) Relation between buyer and seller
(B) Relation between sales person
(C) Relation between company and consumers
(D) All of the above

36. Match the items of List – I with the items of the List – II :

	List – I (Company Name)		List – II (Brand)
a.	HUL	i.	Cerelac
b.	ITC	ii.	Eclares
c.	Nestle	iii.	Vivel
d.	Cadbury	iv.	Sunsilk

Codes :

	a	b	c	d
(A)	iv	iii	i	ii
(B)	i	ii	iii	iv
(C)	iv	ii	iii	i
(D)	iv	iii	ii	i

37. The following are the steps in designing the market driven distribution :
    1. Know what customers want   2. Determine the costs
    3. Review assumptions   4. Decide on the outlet
    5. Compare alternatives   6. Implement changes
    Select the right sequence of the steps from the codes given below :
    (A) 1, 4, 2, 5, 3, 6   (B) 1, 2, 3, 5, 4, 6
    (C) 1, 3, 4, 5, 2, 6   (D) 2, 3, 4, 5, 6, 1

38. Which of the following are consumption values that customers look for in any product or service in a society ?
    1. Functional value
    2. Social value
    3. Money value
    4. Emotional value
    5. Maximum value
    Codes :
    (A) 1, 2, 3, 5   (B) 1, 3, 4, 5
    (C) 5, 4, 3, 2, 1   (D) 1, 2 and 4

39. Franchising is a practice of :
    (A) Leasing for a prescribed period of time, the right to use firm's successful business model and brand.
    (B) Selling out a successful business model and brand.
    (C) Hiring a firm's successful business model and brand.
    (D) None of the above.

40. Underwriters of the security issues are required to
    (A) Purchase the securities underwritten
    (B) Work as agent of the company for marketing the securities
    (C) Manage the issues of the securities
    (D) Take up securities not subscribed by investors

41. The optimum capital structure of a company is planned as per considerations of
    I. Profitability   II. Solvency
    III. Marketability of shares   IV. Control
    Codes :
    (A) I, II and IV only   (B) II, III and IV only
    (C) I and II only   (D) III and IV only

42. **Assertion (A) :** Investors in capital market seem to be inclined for fixed income securities.

Reason (R) : Debt instruments now have active secondary market.

Codes :

(A) Assertion (A) and Reason (R) both are correct and (R) is correct explanation of (A).

(B) Assertion (A) and Reason (R) both are correct, but (R) is not correct explanation of (A).

(C) Assertion (A) is correct, but Reason (R) is incorrect.

(D) Assertion (A) is not correct, but Reason (R) is correct.

43. Insufficient working capital in any enterprise may also result into

I. Failure to adapt to changes

II. Overcapitalisation

III. Reduced availability of trade and cash discounts

IV. Reduced volume of production and sales

Codes :

(A) I, II and III only   (B) I, III and IV only

(C) II and III only   (D) I and IV only

44. **Assertion (A) :** Arbitrage keeps the cost of capital constant despite change in the capital structure.

Reason (R) : It ensures compensating inverse change in cost of equity capital with a change in the cost of debt capital.

Codes :

(A) Assertion (A) and Reason (R) both are correct and (R) is correct explanation of (A).

(B) Assertion (A) and Reason (R) are correct, but (R) is not correct explanation of (A).

(C) Assertion (A) is correct, but Reason (R) is incorrect.

(D) Assertion (A) is not correct, but Reason (R) is correct.

45. **Assertion (A) :** High morale and high productivity go hand-in-hand.

Reason (R) : Workers do not have their own ways for relief from fatigue and monotony.

Codes :

(A) Both (A) and (R) are true.   (B) (A) is true, but (R) is false.

(C) (A) is false, but (R) is true.   (D) Both (A) and (R) are false.

46. Relationship at work is the source of

    (A)   Status anxiety
    (B)   Managerial stress

    (C)   Legitimate power
    (D)   Expert power

47. Match the group of words in List – I with the group of words in List – II :

	List – I		List – II
a.	Grievances	i.	Profit sharing
b.	Impact of technology	ii.	Effective planning
c.	Adjustment to technology	iii.	Index of low morale
d.	Morale improvement	iv.	Changes in occupation

Codes :

	a	b	c	d
(A)	i	ii	iii	iv
(B)	iv	iii	ii	i
(C)	iii	ii	iv	i
(D)	iii	iv	ii	i

48. **Assertion (A) :** Functional conflict is a type of institutionalised conflict.

    Reason (R) : Politics is a kind of emergent conflict.

    Codes :

    (A)   Both (A) and (R) are true.
    (B)   (A) is true, but (R) is false.

    (C)   (A) is false, but (R) is true.
    (D)   Both (A) and (R) are false.

49. Formal conflict is a kind of

    (A)   Goal Conflict
    (B)   Organisational Conflict

    (C)   Role Conflict
    (D)   Emergent Conflict

50. One of the objectives of organisational change is

    (A)   Increased motivation

    (B)   Greater innovation

    (C)   Solving inter-group problems

    (D)   Changes in an organisation's level of adaptation to its environment

51. **Assertion (A) :** Job design relates to the manner in which tasks are put together to form complete job.

    Reason (R) : The matrix organisation is a project organisation plus a functional organisation.

    Codes :

    (A)   Both (A) and (R) are true.
    (B)   (A) is true, but (R) is false.

    (C)   (A) is false, but (R) is true.
    (D)   Both (A) and (R) are false.

52. HRD as a total system includes the following major sub-systems :

1. Performance Appraisal
2. Career Planning
3. Role Analysis
4. ABC Analysis
5. Rewards

Select the correct answer from the codes.

Codes :

(A) 1, 2, 3, 4   (B) 1, 2, 3, 5

(C) 2, 3, 4, 5   (D) 1, 3, 4, 5

53. Which of the following is not true about employee grievances ?

(A) Grievance is a sign of employee's discontent with job or its nature.

(B) Grievance provides a downward channel of communication.

(C) Grievance arises only when an employee feels that injustice has been done to him.

(D) Grievance can be real or imaginary.

54. Which of the following is not a component of Job Analysis ?

(A) Job Description   (B) Role Analysis

(C) Job Summary   (D) Job Specification

55. As per the Master Circular on "Prudential Norms on Capital Adequacy – Basel I Framework", elements of Tier I capital include :

(i) Authorised Capital (Ordinary shares), statutory reserves, all other free reserves (disclosed), if any.

(ii) Paid-up capital (Preference shares).

(iii) Perpetual Non-Cumulative Preference Shares (PNCPS).

(iv) Innovative Perpetual Debt Instruments (IPDI).

Codes :

(A) (i) and (ii) only   (B) (ii) and (iii) only

(C) (i) and (iii) only   (D) (iii) and (iv) only

56. What is true about the Basel Committee on Banking Supervision (BCBS) ?

(i) BCBS is an Indian National Committee of banking supervisory authority.

(ii) BCBS was established by a group of 19 nationalized commercial banks.

(iii) BCBS was established in 1996.

(iv) It provides a forum for regular cooperation on banking supervisory matters.

Codes :

(A) (i) and (ii) only   (B) (ii) and (iii) only

(C) (iii) and (iv) only   (D) (iv) only

57. Under the Cooperative Bank structure, the apex institution is

    (A)   National Cooperative Bank   (B)   State Cooperative Bank

    (C)   District Cooperative Bank   (D)   IDBI Bank

58. What is SLR ratio of a bank ?

    (A)   Ratio of total deposits against total investments.

    (B)   Amount deposited by the bank with the Central Bank in the form of cash, gold and securities.

    (C)   Amount that commercial banks are required to maintain before providing credit to customers.

    (D)   Amount that commercial banks deposit with the foreign banks.

59. **Assertion (A) :** The USA remains the world's largest FDI recipient country.

    Reason (R) : The global economic crisis of 2009, causes a reduction of global FDI flows took place to USA.

    Select the correct code :

    Codes :

    (A)   Both (A) and (R) are correct and (R) is the correct explanation of (A).

    (B)   (A) is correct, but (R) is not correct.

    (C)   Both (A) and (R) are incorrect.

    (D)   Both (A) and (R) are correct, but (R) is not correct explanation of (A).

60. As per the South Asia Free Trade Agreement, 1993 of SAARC, the member countries have to bring their duties down to

    (A)   25 percent by 2006   (B)   15 percent by 2006

    (C)   10 percent by 2007   (D)   20 percent by 2007

61. Which of the following is the correct combination ?

    (i)   A GSA allows an MNE to enter into activities that might too costly and risky to pursue on its own.

    (ii)   A GSA does not allow a firm to enhance economics of scale.

    (iii)   A GSA does not allow a firm to bypass entry barriers into a target foreign country.

    (iv)   A GSA allows a firm to acquire partner knowledge.

    Codes :

    (A)   (i), (iv) are correct.   (B)   (i), (ii) are correct.

    (C)   (i), (ii), (iii) and (iv) are correct.   (D)   (ii) and (iii) are correct.

62. Which of the following are the outcomes of the Sixth Ministerial Conference of WTO which was held at Hong Kong in December 2005 ?

Select the correct combination :

(i) Resolve to complete the Doha Work Programme fully and to conclude negotiations in 2006.

(ii) Amendments to TRIPS agreement reaffirmed to address public health concerns of developing countries.

(iii) To continue export subsidies in agriculture upto 2018.

(iv) Duty free, quota free market access for all LDC's products to all developed countries.

Codes :

(A) (i), (ii) and (iv)   (B) (i), (ii), (iii) and (iv)

(C) (i) and (iii) only   (D) (ii) and (iv) only

63. Which of the following is not a function of Foreign Exchange Market ?

(A) Stabilization function   (B) Hedging function

(C) Credit function   (D) Transfer function

64. **Assertion (A) :** The impact of depreciating Indian Rupee leads to less competition for Indian firms from imports.

Reason (R) : The depreciating Indian Rupee results in downward pressure on inflation .

Select the correct code :

Codes :

(A) Both (A) and (R) are correct.

(B) (A) is false, but (R) is correct.

(C) Both (A) and (R) are false.

(D) (A) is true, but (R) is false.

65. In which of the following Stock Exchanges the GDR's are listed ?

(i)   London Stock Exchange

(ii) New-York Stock Exchange

(iii) Luxembourg Stock Exchange

(iv) Bombay Stock Exchange

(v)   Singapore Stock Exchange

(vi) Hong Kong Exchange

Identify the correct combination :

(A) (i), (ii) and (iii)   (B) (i), (iv), (v) and (vi)

(C) (iii), (iv), (v) and (vi)   (D) (i), (iii), (v) and (vi)

66. **Statement I :** FIIs do not invest in unlisted entities. They participate only through stock exchanges.

    Statement II : FIIs cannot invest at the time of initial allotment.

    Select the correct code :

    Codes :
    (A) Statements I and II are correct.
    (B) Statement I is true and II is false.
    (C) Statement I is false and II is correct.
    (D) Statements I and II are false.

67. ADRs' and GDRs' are an excellent means of investment to invest in India for
    (A) NRIs'   (B) Foreign nationals
    (C) Both (A) & (B)   (D) None of the above

68. Which of the following is not provided by EXIM Bank, for financing overseas investments ?
    (A) Term loans to Indian Companies upto 80% of their equity investment in overseas JV/WOS.
    (B) Term loans to Indian Companies towards upto 100% of loan extended by them to the overseas JV/WOS.
    (C) Term loan to overseas JV/WOS towards part financing.
    (D) Guarantee facility to the overseas JV/WOS for raising term loan/working capital

69. Under Section 271 C of the Income Tax Act, 1961 the amount of penalty for failure to deduct tax at source is
    (A) 10% of tax which is otherwise deductible under Section 194 C.
    (B) 100% of tax which is otherwise deductible under Section 194 C.
    (C) 200% of tax which is otherwise deductible under Section 194 C.
    (D) 300% of tax which is otherwise deductible under Section 194 C.

70. Match the following items of List – I and List – II and select the correct answer from the codes given below :

List – I (Sections)	List – II (Maximum Deduction)
a. Section 80C of I.T. Act	i. ₹ 10,000
b. Section 80D of I.T. Act	ii. ₹ 40,000
c. Section 80 DDB of I.T. Act	iii. ₹ 1,00,000
d. Section 80 TTA of I.T. Act	iv. ₹ 15,000

    Codes :

	a	b	c	d
(A)	iii	i	iv	ii
(B)	iii	iv	ii	i
(C)	iv	iii	ii	i
(D)	ii	iii	i	iv

71. In which of the following cases, income of previous year is assessable in the previous year itself ?

   (A) A person in employment.

   (B) A person engaged in illegal business.

   (C) A person who is running charitable business.

   (D) A person leaving India permanently.

72. Long term capital loss can be set off from which of the following ?

   (A) Short term capital gain only

   (B) Long term capital gain only

   (C) Income from business and profession

   (D) Capital gain head of income

73. In which of the following long term assets, cost indexation benefit is allowed ?

   (A) Debentures issued by a company

   (B) Self generated goodwill of a business

   (C) Bonus shares allotted on 1-4-2000

   (D) Jewellery

74. Calculate the Gross Annual Value from the following details :

   Municipal Value   –   ₹ 45,000

   Fair Rental Value   –   ₹ 50,000

   Standard Rent   –   ₹ 48,000

   Actual Rent   –   ₹ 42,000

   (A) ₹ 50,000   (B) ₹ 48,000

   (C) ₹ 45,000   (D) ₹ 42,000

75. Minimum Alternate Tax (MAT) is imposed on

   (A) All companies

   (B) Public Limited Companies only

   (C) Private Limited Companies only

   (D) Partnership Firms and Companies

UGC - NET DECEMBER 2014

ANSWER KEYS (PAPER III)

SUBJECT : 08 (Commerce)

Qus. No.	Ans.	Qus. No.	Ans.	Qus. No.	Ans.
1	B	26	B	51	A
2	B	27	A	52	B
3	A	28	D	53	B
4	D	29	D	54	C
5	C	30	A	55	D
6	D	31	D	56	D
7	B	32	B	57	B
8	A	33	C	58	C
9	A	34	D	59	A
10	B	35	C	60	D
11	B	36	A	61	A
12	B	37	A	62	A
13	C	38	D	63	A
14	A	39	A	64	D
15	A	40	D	65	D
16	C	41	B	66	D
17	B	42	C	67	C
18	B	43	B	68	B
19	C	44	A	69	B
20	C	45	D	70	B
21	C	46	B	71	D
22	D	47	D	72	B
23	C	48	A	73	D
24	B	49	B	74	B
25	C	50	D	75	A

COMMERCE
Paper – II

Note : This paper contains **fifty (50)** objective type questions of **two (2)** marks each. **All** questions are compulsory.

1. There is acute shortage of electricity in some of the states in India. This reflects a problem in which type of business environment ?
   (A) Economic
   (B) Demographic
   (C) Politico-legal
   (D) Socio-cultural

2. Match the items given in List-I and List-II.

List – I	List – II
(a) Economic liberalisation	(i) IT-enabled services
(b) Out sourcing	(ii) SFIO
(c) Corporate frauds	(iii) Macro economic stability
(d) Second generation reforms	(iv) Increased competition

   Indicate the correct combination :
   Codes :

	(a)	(b)	(c)	(d)
(A)	(i)	(ii)	(iii)	(iv)
(B)	(i)	(iii)	(ii)	(iv)
(C)	(ii)	(iii)	(iv)	(i)
(D)	(iv)	(i)	(ii)	(iii)

3. Which of the following is true ?
   (A) A consumer court setup under the Consumer Protection Act, does not have the power to punish for its contempt.
   (B) Professional services are outside the purview of the CPA.
   (C) A consumer court cannot force a person indulging in misleading advertising to confess his quit.
   (D) None of the above.

4. Match the items/terms given in List-I with those given in and List-II.

List – I	List – II
(a) BIS	(i) Print Media
(b) CERC	(ii) Minimum support price for agricultural products.
(c) CACP	(iii) Quality of manufactured products.
(d) PCI	(iv) Comparative product testing.

   Indicate the correct answer :
   Codes :

	(a)	(b)	(c)	(d)
(A)	(iv)	(iii)	(ii)	(i)
(B)	(i)	(ii)	(iii)	(iv)
(C)	(iii)	(iv)	(ii)	(i)
(D)	(ii)	(iii)	(iv)	(i)

5. Which one among the following is not the salient feature of industrial policy since 1991 ?
   (A) Enormous expansion of the private sector.
   (B) Redefining the role of public sector.
   (C) Limited exposure of Indian industry to foreign competition.
   (D) Pruning of the list of items reserved for SSI units.

6. A, a partner in a firm, is drawing ₹ 500 regularly on the 16th of every month. He will have to pay interest at the given rate in a year on ₹ 6000 for the total period of
   (A) 5 months   (B) 6 months
   (C) 7 months   (D) 12 months

7. Subsequent expenditures that extend the useful life, improve the quality of output, or reduce operating costs of an existing asset beyond their originally estimated levels are
   (A) Capital expenditures
   (B) Revenue expenditures
   (C) Deferred Revenue expenditures
   (D) None of the above

8. Marginal-costing technique is useful for
   (A) Make or Buy decisions
   (B) Profit planning
   (C) Shut-down decisions
   (D) All of the above

9. Which one is not a feature of budgetary control ?
   (A) A tool for management control.
   (B) An instrument of delegation and authority.
   (C) An instrument for evaluating the overall performance.
   (D) A statement of budget and forecasts.

10. The Debt-Equity Ratio of a company is 2 : 1. In this relation, match the following :

List – I		List – II	
(a)	Issue of equity shares	1.	No change on the ratio
(b)	Cash received from debtors	2.	Reduce the ratio
(c)	Redemption of debentures	3.	No change on the ratio
(d)	Purchased goods on credit	4.	Reduce the ratio

Codes :

	(a)	(b)	(c)	(d)
(A)	1	2	3	4
(B)	2	3	4	1
(C)	1	3	4	2
(D)	2	4	1	3

11. Which one of the following does not explain the basic nature of Business economics ?
    (A) Behaviour of firms in theory and practice.
    (B) Distribution theories like rent, wages and interest along with the theory of profit.
    (C) Use of the tools of economic analysis in clarifying problems in organising and evaluating information and in comparing alternative courses of action.
    (D) Integration of economic theory with business practices for the purpose of facilitating decision-making.

12. At a point of satiety for a commodity the marginal utility is
    (A) Negative
    (B) Positive
    (C) Zero
    (D) Highly positive

13. A rectangular hyperbola shaped demand curve on all its points has
    (A) Equal slopes and equal point elasticities.
    (B) Unequal slopes and unequal point elasticities.
    (C) Unequal slopes and equal point elasticities.
    (D) Equal slopes and unequal point elasticities.

14. **Assertion (A)** : A perfectly competitive firm is not a price-maker but is a price-taker.
    Reason (R) : The firm is interested in deciding the level of output only.
    Codes :
    (A) Both (A) and (R) are true.
    (B) Both (A) and (R) are false.
    (C) (A) is false, while (R) is true.
    (D) (A) is true, but (R) is not a correct explanation of (A).

15. Match the items of List-I with the items of List-II.

List – I	List – II
(a) A market having high price elasticity.	I. Skimming pricing
(b) A market having high price inelasticity	II. Differential pricing
(c) A market having several segments differing prominently with regard to price elasticities of their demand.	III. Penetrating pricing

Codes :

	I	II	III
(A)	(b),	(c),	(a)
(B)	(a),	(b),	(c)
(C)	(b),	(a),	(c)
(D)	(a),	(c),	(b)

16. Which one of the following options deals with the process of making estimates, predictions and decisions ?

(A) Descriptive statistics

(B) Inferential statistics

(C) Probability theory

(D) None of the above

17. A hypothesis test is being performed for a process in which a Type-I error will be very costly, but a Type-II error will be relatively inexpensive and unimportant. Which of the following would be the best choice for alpha (α) in this test ?

(A) 0.10

(B) 0.05

(C) 0.01

(D) 0.50

18. If the dependent variable increases as the independent variable increases in an estimating equation, the coefficient of correlation will be in the range

(A) 0 to (–) 1

(B) 0 to (–) 0

(C) 0 to (–) 0.05

(D) 0 to 1

19. **Assertion (A) :** When there is an evidence of a linear relationship between two variables, it may not always mean an independent-dependent relationship between the two variables.

Reason (R) : The causal relationship between the two variables may not imply a reasonable theoretical relationship between the two.

Choose the right answer from the following statements :

Codes :

(A) Both (A) and (R) are true and (R) is the correct explanation.

(B) Both (A) and (R) are true, but (R) is not the correct explanation.

(C) (A) is true, but (R) is false.

(D) (A) is false, but (R) is true.

20. **Assertion (A) :** User interface is most critical task in DSS design

Reason (R) : DSS is used by outside Customers frequently.

(A) (A) is correct, but (R) is wrong.

(B) Both (A) and (R) are wrong.

(C) (A) is wrong, but (R) is correct.

(D) Both (A) and (R) are correct.

21. Which of the following is not true about Matrix Organisation ?

(A) It is relatively permanent.

(B) Its project managers authority is distributed reasonably.

(C) There is slow information processing.

(D) Its project heads have to share resources with functional heads.

22. Consider the following leadership styles :

1. Telling   2. Autocratic
3. Selling   4. Motivating
5. Participating 6. Delegating
7. Charismatic

Select the four styles of leadership explained by Hersey and Blauchard.

(A) 1, 2, 6 and 7   (B) 2, 3, 4 and 5

(C) 1, 3, 5 and 6   (D) 4, 5, 6 and 7

23. Given below are two statements, one labelled as Assertion (A), and the other labelled as Reason (R).

Assertion (A) : Classical organisations believed in the use of authority to achieve coordination.

Reason (R) : Classical thinkers consider organisation is an open system.

Codes :

(A) (A) is correct, but (R) is incorrect.

(B) Both (A) and (R) are correct.

(C) (A) is incorrect, but (R) is correct.

(D) Both (A) and (R) are incorrect.

24. Who has modified Maslow's Hierarchical levels of needs and developed ERG model ?

(A) Frederick Herzberg

(B) David C. McClelland

(C) Douglas McGregor

(D) Clayton Alderfer

25. Taylor's differential piece work plan provides that

(A) All labourers should be assigned different amount of work.

(B) All labourers should be put in different time-period.

(C) Those who produce above standard should receive higher wages than those producing below standard.

(D) Payment should be the same on a fixed standard.

26. Which one of the following stages of the marketing research process is most expensive ?

(A) Data analysis

(B) Data collection

(C) Developing the research plan

(D) Report writing

27. The people to adopt a new product first are called

(A) Early adopters

(B) First users

(C) Initial adopters

(D) Innovators

28. A concept in retailing that helps explain the emergence of new retailers is called the _____ hypothesis.

(A) Product life cycle

(B) Service assortment

(C) Retail life cycle

(D) 'Wheel-of-retailing'

29. Manufacturers of cars and motor cycles typically seek_____ distribution.

(A) selective

(B) intensive

(C) exclusive

(D) restrictive

30. Which method of setting advertising budget is most scientific and logical ?

    (A) All-you-can afford method

    (B) Competitive parity method

    (C) Objective-and-task method

    (D) Percentage-of-sales method

31. **Assertion (A) :** Weighted average cost of capital should be used as a hurdle rate for accepting or rejecting a capital budgeting proposal.

    Reason (R) : It is because by financing in the proportions specified and accepting the project, yielding more than the weighted average required return, the firm is able to increase the market price of its stock.

    Codes :

    (A) Both (A) and (R) are false.

    (B) Both (A) and (R) are true.

    (C) (A) is true, while (R) is false.

    (D) (A) is false, while (R) is true.

32. A firm wants to know the Degree of Operating Leverage (DOL) with the following information :

    Current level of sales   : 6000 units

    Break-even point sales : 4000 units

    What would be the DOL ?

    (A) 1.50

    (B) 0.67

    (C) 3.00

    (D) None of the above

33. **Assertion (A) :** When two or more investment proposals are mutually exclusive, ranking the proposals on the basis of IRR, NPV and PI methods may give contradictory results.

    Reason (R) : The contradictory results in the ranking are due to differing dimensions relating to the scale of investments, cash flow patterns and project lives.

    Indicate the correct answer :

    Codes :

    (A) Both (A) and (R) are true.

    (B) (A) is true, but (R) is a necessary condition, but not a sufficient condition.

    (C) Both (A) and (R) are false.

    (D) Both (A) and (R) are true and (R) explains the reason sufficiently.

34. Which one of the following assumptions is not covered in the Walter's Model of the dividend policy ?

    (A) All financing is done through retained earnings.

    (B) Firm's business risk does not change due to additional investments.

    (C) The firm has an infinite life.

    (D) The key variables like EPS and DPS keep on changing.

35. Which one of the following emphasizes the qualitative aspects of working capital management ?

    (A) Gross working capital

    (B) Quick working capital

    (C) Net working capital

    (D) None of the above

36. Which of the following training methods exposes the newly recruited employee to the various business functions, divisions and departments ?

(A) Orientation

(B) Vestibule Training

(C) Transition Analysis

(D) Role playing

37. Match the names of the Authors given below with the motivational theories they are associated with

List-I	List-II
1. Herzberg	a. ERG Theory
2. McGregor	b. Three-need theory
3. Alderfer	c. Theory X and Theory Y
4. David McClelland	d. Two-factor theory

Codes :

	1	2	3	4
(A)	a	b	c	d
(B)	d	c	b	a
(C)	b	a	d	c
(D)	d	c	a	b

38. Who was closely associated with industrial relations in India ?

(A) B. Kurien

(B) Gadgil

(C) V.V. Giri

(D) Vinoba Bhave

39. Under the Trade Union Act 1926, how many minimum number of members are required for a trade union to be registered ?

(A) 5   (B) 7

(C) 9   (D) 11

40. The idea that a manager tends to be promoted to a level of his incompetence is referred to as

(A) the advancement principle

(B) the Paul principle

(C) the Peter principle

(D) the job design principle

41. Which of the following committees is intended to review the working of the monetory system in India ?

(A) Narasimham Committee

(B) Tandon Committee

(C) Sukhamoy Chakravarty Committee

(D) Deheja Committee

42. Match the items of List-I with those in List-II and select the correct answer.

List-I	List-II
(a) Bank Rate Policy	1. Involving the shortening of the currency of bills eligible for rediscount.
(b) Credit Rationing	2. Involving the Purchase and sale of securities in the open market.
(c) Variable Reserve System	3. Involving the alteration of discount rate.
(d) Open Market Operations	4. Involving the variation of the minimum reserves

Codes :

	(a)	(b)	(c)	(d)
(A)	1	4	2	3
(B)	2	1	3	4
(C)	4	2	1	3
(D)	3	1	4	2

43. Match the items of List-I with the items of List-II and select the correct answer using the codes given below the lists.

	List-I		List-II
(a)	Rural Industries Programme	(i)	Meant for various target groups like Rural youth, Ex-serviceman, women and Scheduled Castes/Tribes
(b)	Mahila Vikas Nidhi Scheme	(ii)	Aim at ensuring flow of credit to the dis-advantaged sections of the society.
(c)	Entre-preneurship Development Programme	(iii)	Commercial exploitation of local resources.
(d)	Micro Credit Scheme	(iv)	Provides assistance to voluntary organizations for the benefit of women.

Codes :

	(a)	(b)	(c)	(d)
(A)	(i)	(iii)	(ii)	(iv)
(B)	(ii)	(iv)	(i)	(iii)
(C)	(iv)	(ii)	(iii)	(i)
(D)	(iii)	(iv)	(i)	(ii)

44. According to the FDI Policy of the Government of India (2012), the FDI in banks is limited to
   (A) 20% in Nationalised Banks and 74% in Private Sector Banks.
   (B) 20% in Nationalised Banks and 49% in Private Sector Banks.
   (C) 16% in Nationalised Banks and 74% in Private Sector Banks.
   (D) 49% in Nationalised Banks and 51% in Private Sector Banks.

45. According to the recent guidelines (2013) of the Reserve Bank of India the Private Sector Banks are required to have a minimum paid up equity capital of
   (A) ₹ 300 crores   (B) ₹ 200 crores
   (C) ₹ 400 crores   (D) ₹ 500 crores

46. International trade theory which provides that capital intensive country should export labour-intensive goods and import capital goods is referred to as
   (A) Leontief Paradox
   (B) Heckscher-Ohlin Theory
   (C) Mercantilism Theory
   (D) Theory of Comparative Advantage

47. Which of the following is not a form of economic integration in the context of intra-regional trade ?
   (A) Customs Union
   (B) European Union
   (C) Economic Union
   (D) African Union

48. 'Crawling Peg System' means
   (A) Fixed Exchange Rate System.
   (B) Floating Exchange Rate System.
   (C) Hybrid of Fixed and Floating Exchange System.
   (D) None of the above.

49. From the following modes of international business, identify the mode which involves strategic alliance
   (A) Franchising
   (B) Leasing
   (C) Turnkey Project
   (D) Joint venture

50. Which of the following expressions amount to the import restriction measures ?
   (i) Currency control
   (ii) Establishment of EPZs
   (iii) Tariff cuts
   (iv) Imposition of tariffs
   (v) Imposition of non-tariff barriers

Codes :
   (A) (i), (ii) and (iii)
   (B) (i), (iv) and (v)
   (C) (iii), (iv) and (v)
   (D) (ii), (iii) and (v)

UGC - NET JUNE 2014

ANSWER KEYS (PAPER II)

SUBJECT : 08 (Commerce)

Qus. No.	Ans.	Qus. No.	Ans.
1	A	26	B
2	D	27	D
3	A	28	D
4	C	29	D
5	C	30	C
6	B	31	B
7	A	32	C
8	D	33	B
9	D	34	D
10	B	35	C
11	B	36	A
12	C	37	D
13	C	38	C
14	D	39	B
15	A	40	C
16	B	41	C
17	C	42	D
18	D	43	D
19	A	44	A
20	A	45	D
21	C	46	A
22	C	47	D
23	A	48	C
24	D	49	D
25	A	50	B

June-2014

COMMERCE
Paper – III

Note : This paper contains **seventy five (75)** objective type questions of **two (2)** marks each. **All** questions are compulsory.

1. The Competition Act, 2002, seeks to regulate
   - (A) Anti-competitive agreements
   - (B) Mergers and amalgamation
   - (C) Unfair trade practices
   - (D) (A) and (B) above

2. Indicate the true statement :
   - (A) Large industrial houses are outside the purriew of the Competition Act, 2002
   - (B) There is no provision for curbing frivolous complaints under the CPA.
   - (C) The Trade Marks Act, 1999 does not apply to services.
   - (D) All of the above are true.

3. The time limit for filing a complaints before the District forum under the Consumer Protection Act, 1986 is
   - (A) one year
   - (B) two years
   - (C) three years
   - (D) There is no such time limit.

4. The Foreign Investment Promotion Board (FIPB) revamps the rules and regulations pertaining to
   - (A) Accounting of Foreign Investment
   - (B) Investment by NRIs
   - (C) Foreign investments
   - (D) All of the above

5. Which of the legislation(s) do (does) not form part of the legal environment of business in India ?
   - (A) The Drugs and Cosmetics Act, 1940
   - (B) The Prevention of Food Adulteration Act, 1954
   - (C) The Monopolies and Restrictive Trade Practices Act, 1969
   - (D) Both (B) and (C) above

6. What is the underlying concept that support the immediate recognition of an estimated loss ?
   - (A) Substance over form
   - (B) Consistency
   - (C) Matching
   - (D) Prudence

7. Which is not the limitation of budgetary control ?
   - (A) Budgets are based on forecasts which may not be true
   - (B) Installation and operation of a system of budgetary control is costly.
   - (C) Budget is a tool of management and not a substitute of management
   - (D) Budgets do not pinpoint the lack of efficiency or the presence of it.

8. Profit volume ratio of an enterprise is 40%. To offset 10% decrease in selling price, how much sales must be increased ?
   - (A) 10%   (B) 20%
   - (C) 25%   (D) 40%

9. If debt is ₹ 220, cash balance is ₹ 20 and equity is ₹ 300, then the gearing ratio is
   - (A) 20%   (B) 40%
   - (C) 50%   (D) 30%

10. Responsibility accounting aims to
    - (A) ensure that a manager is punished if things go wrong.
    - (B) ensure that costs become the responsibility of a specific manager.
    - (C) allocate costs to all areas of a business.
    - (D) reduce the costs that a department incurs.

11. Find the correct matching of the items of List – I with the items of List – II given below :

List – I		List – II
(a) Normal Profit	(I)	Excess of total revenue over total explicit cost
(b) Economic profit	(II)	Total revenue equals total economic cost
(c) Accounting profit	(III)	Excess of total revenue over total of explicit and implicit costs and a normal rate of return

Codes :

	(I)	(II)	(III)
(A)	(c)	(a)	(b)
(B)	(b)	(a)	(c)
(C)	(a)	(b)	(c)
(D)	(a)	(c)	(b)

12. **Assertion (A) :** A monopoly firm's revenue curve is downward sloping from left to right.

   Reason (R) : The monopoly firm does not simultaneously enjoy the freedom to determine both price and quantity to be sold according to its whims and fancy.

   Codes :
   (A) Both (A) and (R) are true.
   (B) Both (A) and (R) are false.
   (C) (A) is true, but (R) is false.
   (D) (A) is false, but (R) is true.

13. The equilibrium level of output for a perfect competitive firm is given by the point where :
   (A) MR = MC
   (B) MR < MC
   (C) MR > MC
   (D) MR = MC, and MC starts rising.

14. Match the following :

List – I		List – II
(i) Dumping	(a)	Monopolistic competitive firm
(ii) Kinked Revenue Curve	(b)	Oligopoly firm
(iii) Horizontal straight line revenue curve	(c)	Perfectly competitive firm
(iv) Large number of buyers and sellers with differentiated products	(d)	Discriminatory monopoly

Codes :

	(i)	(ii)	(iii)	(iv)
(A)	(a)	(d)	(c)	(b)
(B)	(b)	(d)	(a)	(c)
(C)	(d)	(b)	(c)	(a)
(D)	(a)	(b)	(c)	(d)

15. Penetrating pricing strategy is appropriate when
   (A) price elasticity of demand in the market is highly inelastic.
   (B) price elasticity of demand in the market is uncertain.
   (C) price elasticity of demand in the market is highly elastic.
   (D) income elasticity of demand in the market is negatively elastic.

16. **Assertion (A) :** The expected values should be atleast 5 to apply the chi-square test.
Reason (R) : The chi-square distribution provides an adequate approximation of the sampling distribution.
Indicate the correct answer from the following :
Codes :
(A) Both (A) and (R) are true, and (R) is the right explanation.
(B) Both (A) and (R) are true, but (R) is not the correct explanation.
(C) (A) is true, but (R) is false.
(D) (A) is false, but (R) is true.

17. In a decision problem having four possible alternative decisions and six possible states of nature, the pay-off table will include
(A) Four payoffs
(B) Six payoffs
(C) Twenty four payoff
(D) Ten payoff

18. The mathematical formula for joint probabilities $P(AB) = P(A/B) \times P(B)$, holds when
(A) The events are statistically independent.
(B) The events are statistically dependent.
(C) The event is either independent or dependent.
(D) None of the above

19. Which one of the following statements is the correct interpretation of P-value of less than 0.01 in hypothesis testing ?
(A) There is <u>overwhelming</u> evidence to infer that the alternative hypothesis is true.
(B) There is <u>strong</u> evidence to infer that the alternative hypothesis is true.
(C) There is <u>weak</u> evidence to indicate that the alternative hypothesis is true.
(D) There is <u>no</u> evidence to infer that the alternative hypothesis is true.

20. Two lists of items are given below :

List – I	List – II
(i) Charles Babbage	(a) Mossai
(ii) Herbert A. Simon	(b) HTML
(iii) Tim Berners Lee	(c) Computer Design
(iv) Maarc Andreessen	(d) Decision model

Which one of the following is the correct match ?
Codes :

	(i)	(ii)	(iii)	(iv)
(A)	(c)	(b)	(a)	(d)
(B)	(a)	(c)	(d)	(b)
(C)	(b)	(a)	(c)	(d)
(D)	(c)	(d)	(b)	(a)

21. Which of the following statements are true about informal organization ?
1. It arises spontaneously.
2. It reflects individual and group goals.
3. It tends to be permanent and stable.
4. It tends to be small and manageable.
5. Its basic purpose is to improve human relations.
6. Its basic purpose is to achieve organisation's goals.
Codes :
(A) 1, 2, 3 and 5
(B) 1, 2, 4 and 6
(C) 1, 2, 4 and 5
(D) 2, 3, 5 and 6

22. Which of the following is not true about an employee-centered leader as identified by Michigan researchers ?

(A) Treats subordinates as human beings.

(B) Shows concern for their well being.

(C) Focuses on work standards and close supervision.

(D) Encourages and involves them in goal setting.

23. According to Talcott Parson, organizations can be classified primarily into four categories, based on functions. Which of the following is not an organization in Parson's scheme ?

(A) Political organisations

(B) Integrative organisations

(C) Pattern maintenance organisations

(D) Commercial organisations

24. An MBO programme usually involves the following steps :

1. Establishing unit's objectives
2. Establishing organisational goals
3. Negotiating or agreeing
4. Reviewing the performance
5. Creating action plans

Indicate the correct sequence of the above steps from the following codes :

(A) 1, 2, 3, 4, 5

(B) 2, 1, 3, 5, 4

(C) 2, 3, 1, 4, 5

(D) 5, 4, 3, 2, 1

25. Match the following :

List – I	List – II
(a) Fayol	(1) Economy and Society
(b) Taylor	(2) General and Industrial Administration
(c) Weber	(3) Principles of Organization
(d) Mooney and Reilly	(4) Shop Management

Codes :

	(a)	(b)	(c)	(d)
(A)	(3)	(4)	(1)	(2)
(B)	(2)	(4)	(1)	(3)
(C)	(1)	(3)	(2)	(4)
(D)	(4)	(3)	(2)	(1)

26. A primary group influencing the buyer behaviour is a

(A) Family

(B) Professional association

(C) Religious group

(D) Trade Union

27. After conducting the business analysis for developing a new product, a company must do

(A) Idea generation

(B) Product positioning

(C) Product development and testing

(D) Test marketing

28. Match the items in List – I with those in List – II :

	List – I		List – II
(a)	Post purchase behaviour	(i)	AIDA
(b)	Personal selling	(ii)	ACMEE
(c)	Everitt M. Rogers	(iii)	Diffusion of Innovation
(d)	Salesperson training	(iv)	Cognitive dissonance

Indicate the correct matching :

Codes :

	(a)	(b)	(c)	(d)
(A)	(i)	(ii)	(iii)	(iv)
(B)	(iv)	(ii)	(iii)	(i)
(C)	(iii)	(ii)	(i)	(iv)
(D)	(iv)	(i)	(iii)	(ii)

29. Which type of retail stores generally has the highest operating costs ?

(A) Department store

(B) Supermarket

(C) Chain store

(D) Co-operative Store

30. Indicate the correct statement :

(A) India has been a pioneer in social marketing.

(B) Advertising Standards Council of India is a statutory body set up by the government of India.

(C) Both (A) and (B) are incorrect.

(D) Both (A) and (B) are correct.

31. Match the items of List – I with the items of List – II :

	List – I		List – II
(a)	Trade credit and other payables that arise in the firm's day today operations	(i)	Maturity Financing
(b)	Financing and asset needs over time	(ii)	Factoring
(c)	A tool for accelerating the collection from the customers	(iii)	Spontaneous financing
(d)	Seeking financial service to finance on its debtors' balances	(iv)	Lockbox system

Codes :

	(a)	(b)	(c)	(d)
(A)	(iv)	(iii)	(ii)	(i)
(B)	(iii)	(ii)	(iv)	(i)
(C)	(ii)	(iv)	(i)	(iii)
(D)	(i)	(ii)	(iii)	(iv)

32. Indicate the cost of equity capital, based on capital asset pricing model, with the following information :

Beta coefficient – 1.40

Risk-free rate of interest – 9%

Expected Rate of Return on equity in the market – 16%

(A) 9.8%   (B) 18%

(C) 18.8%   (D) 16%

33. The degree of super-leverage would be calculated by :

(A) Adding DOL (Degree of Operating Leverage) and DFL (Degree of Financial Leverage)

(B) Dividing DOL with DFL

(C) Multiplying DOL and DFL

(D) Subtracting DOL from DFL

34. Interim cash inflows are reinvested at a rate of return equal to the internal rate of return is the built-in-mechanism for

(A) Net Present Value Method

(B) Internal Rate of Return Method

(C) Profitability Index Method

(D) None of the above

35. Who formulated the following model for estimating the market price of equity share ?

$$P = \frac{D + \dfrac{R_a}{R_c}(E - D)}{R_c}$$

Where, P = Market price of equity share

D = DPS

E = EPS

E – D = Retained earning per share

R_a = Internal rate of return on investment

R_c = Cost of capital

(A) Modigliani-Miller

(B) Myron-Gordon

(C) James E. Walter

(D) Clarkson and Elliot

36. Indicate the quantitative methods of job evaluation

(A) Ranking methods and Job comparison method

(B) Point rating method and Factor comparison method

(C) Grading method and Job classification method

(D) Factor comparison method and Ranking method

37. Match the items of List – I with those List – II :

List – I	List – II
(1) Career goals	(a) The process where in an executive serves as a guide
(2) Career path	(b) The future positions one strives to reach as part of career
(3) Career counseling	(c) The sequential pattern of jobs that form a career
(4) Mentoring	(d) Guiding people on their possible career path

Codes :

	(1)	(2)	(3)	(4)
(A)	(b)	(c)	(d)	(a)
(B)	(a)	(b)	(c)	(d)
(C)	(d)	(c)	(b)	(a)
(D)	(c)	(b)	(a)	(d)

38. The process of receiving and welcoming an employee when he first joins a company and giving him the basic information he needs to settle down quickly and happily and starts working, is referred to as
   (A) Placement
   (B) Orientation
   (C) Job Rotation
   (D) Counseling

39. Which is not relevant of succession planning ?
   (A) Analysis of the demand for managers
   (B) Review of existing executives
   (C) Planning individuals career paths
   (D) Recruitment to meet immediate needs

40. Where does recognition of an Employee fall in Maslow's hierarchy of needs theory ?
   (A) Self-actualisation
   (B) Security needs
   (C) Social needs
   (D) Esteem needs

41. The profitability of public-sector banks is low due to
   (i) Over-cautions approach to lending
   (ii) Reserve Bank Policies
   (iii) High Overhead Costs
   (iv) Social-sector lending
   Identify the correct code :
   Codes :
   (A) (i) and (ii)
   (B) (i) and (iv)
   (C) (i), (iii) and (iv)
   (D) (ii) and (iii)

42. Match the items of List – I with those List – II and select correct answer :

List – I	List – II
(1) Narasimham Committee	(a) Lending under consortium arrangement
(2) Shetty Committee	(b) Frauds and Malpractices in banks
(3) Ghosh Committee	(c) Securities operations of banks and financial institutions
(4) Janakiraman Committee	(d) Financial system in India

   Codes :

	(a)	(b)	(c)	(d)
(A)	(3)	(4)	(2)	(1)
(B)	(2)	(3)	(4)	(1)
(C)	(4)	(2)	(3)	(1)
(D)	(3)	(4)	(1)	(2)

43. Which of the following financial institutions is not with in the supervisory Purview of Reserve Bank of India ?
   (A) Foreign Commercial Banks Operating in India
   (B) Regional Rural Banks
   (C) Mutual Funds
   (D) State Co-operative Banks

44. The Repo and Reserve Repo rates are resorted to by the RBI as a tool of
   (A) Credit Control
   (B) Settlement Systems
   (C) Currency Management
   (D) Liquidity Control

45. Which one of the following institutions is promoted by the IFCI :

(A) Credit Analysis and Research Ltd (CARE)

(B) Rashtriya Gramin Vikas Nidhi (RGVN)

(C) Clearing Corporation of India Ltd (CCIL)

(D) Small Industries Development Bank of India (SIDBI)

46. Indicate the right sequence of the stages of internationalization :

(i) Multinational Company

(ii) Global Company

(iii) Transnational Company

(iv) International Company

Codes :

(A) (i) (iv) (ii) (iii)

(B) (iv) (i) (iii) (ii)

(C) (i) (iv) (iii) (ii)

(D) (iv) (i) (ii) (iii)

47. Which of the following is <u>not</u> one of the components of 'International Reserve' ?

(A) Special Drawing Rights

(B) Reserve Position in IMF

(C) Monetary Gold

(D) Money Market Instruments

48. Match the items given in List – I with the most appropriate items in List – II :

List – I	List – II
(a) UNCTAD	(i) Foreign investment
(b) WTO	(ii) Developing Countries
(c) TRIMS	(iii) UNDP
(d) ITC	(iv) General Council

Codes :

	(a)	(b)	(c)	(d)
(A)	(ii)	(iv)	(i)	(iii)
(B)	(iii)	(iv)	(i)	(ii)
(C)	(iv)	(ii)	(i)	(iii)
(D)	(iii)	(ii)	(i)	(iv)

49. Duty levied on the value of goods imported is referred to as

(A) Ad valorem Duty

(B) Compound Duty

(C) Specific Duty

(D) Import Duty

50. Which of the following can be included in the current account of the balance of payments ?

(i) Purchase of goods from abroad

(ii) Sale of services abroad

(iii) Workers' remittances from aboard

(iv) Sale of copyright to foreigners

(v) Direct investment in equity capital

Codes :

(A) (i), (ii) and (iii)

(B) (i), (ii) and (iv)

(C) (i), (ii), (iii) and (v)

(D) (i), (ii), (iii) and (iv)

51. Which of the following items would be specifically included in the statement of cash flows constructed in compliance with AS-3 ?
   (A) Conversion of debt to equity
   (B) Acquiring an asset through lease
   (C) Operating and non-operating cash flow information
   (D) Purchasing a building by giving a mortgage to the seller

52. Fixing the value of an employee depending upon his productivity, promotability, transferability and retainability is the core of the
   (A) Certainty equivalent model
   (B) Stochastic Reward Valuation model
   (C) Human asset multiplier model
   (D) Present value of future earnings model

53. Which of the following refers to a situation in which the merger of companies results in over 25% of the market in the hands of the merged companies ?
   (A) 'Gateway' condition
   (B) Restrictive practice
   (C) 'Share of supply' test
   (D) 'Asset' test

54. Which of the following is true ?
   (A) Systematic risk is diversifiable but unsystematic risk is non-diversifiable.
   (B) Systematic risk is non-diversifiable but unsystematic risk is diversifiable.
   (C) Both systematic and unsystematic risks are diversifiable.
   (D) Both systematic and unsystematic risks are non-diversifiable.

55. Match the following :

List – I (Explanation)	List – II (Term)
(a) It involves using the version of master file and the update transactions used to create the current file to re-create the current master file if it becomes damaged.	(1) Audit Trail Controls
(b) It involves copying the whole or a portion of the database to some back up medium, typically magnetics tape.	(2) Dumping
(c) It stores current and historical data extracted from various operations systems and consolidates for management reporting and analysis.	(3) Grandfather, Father, Son
(d) It maintains the chronology of events that occur either to the database definition or the database itself.	(4) Data warehouse for Accounting

Codes :

	(a)	(b)	(c)	(d)
(A)	(3)	(2)	(4)	(1)
(B)	(3)	(1)	(2)	(4)
(C)	(1)	(3)	(2)	(4)
(D)	(4)	(3)	(2)	(1)

56. Which one is not a major component of holistic marketing ?
(A) Relationship marketing
(B) Integrated marketing
(C) Internal marketing
(D) Socially responsible marketing

57. The final step in target marketing is
(A) Market Analysis
(B) Market Positioning
(C) Market Segmentation
(D) Market Targeting

58. The most recent consideration in product packaging is
(A) Cost effectiveness
(B) Product protection
(C) Product promotion
(D) Economy

59. Distribution logistics (also termed as 'market logistics') does not include
(A) Distribution channel
(B) Inventory
(C) Transportation
(D) Warehouses

60. Most of the money spent in measuring the effectiveness of advertising is spent on
(A) Communication-response research
(B) Pre-testing the advertisements
(C) Post-testing the advertisements
(D) Sales-response research

61. Which of the following is not included in the model of the systems approach to human resource management ?
(A) Departmentation
(B) Recruitment
(C) Performance Appraisal
(D) Promotion

62. Which one of the following is not an example of Herzberg's hygiene factors ?
(A) Advancement
(B) Interpersonal relations
(C) Job security
(D) Work conditions

63. Which of the following two forms of collective bargaining were identified by Chamberlain and Kuhn ?
(A) Integrative Bargaining and Distributive Bargaining
(B) Conjunctive Bargaining and Cooperative Bargaining
(C) Integrative Bargaining and Cooperative Bargaining
(D) Distributive Bargaining and Conjunctive Bargaining

64. Who observed that a worker's behaviour and sentiments are closely related ?
(A) Peter Drucker (B) Elton Mayo
(C) F.W. Taylor (D) Dale Yoder

65. What is not an operative function of HRM ?
(A) Procurement
(B) Development
(C) Organising
(D) Integration

66. The total number of Special Economic Zones notified by the Government of India till March 2011 under the SEZ Act, 2005 is
(A) 154 (B) 184
(C) 286 (D) 386

67. The different forms of IMF assistance are given below. Identify the one which is mainly meant for Less Developed Countries (LDCs)
(A) Credit Tranche Drawing
(B) Extended Fund Facility
(C) Compensatory Financing Facility
(D) Structural Adjustment Facility

68. In the context of globalization, 'Levitt Thesis' means

(A) Standardisation strategy to respond to the worldwide homogenised market and expand the market through aggressive low pricing

(B) Customise products to regional markets

(C) Customise products to meet the national market

(D) None of the above

69. Which one of the following is an internal hedging technique ?

(A) Leading

(B) Netting

(C) Both (A) and (B) above

(D) Swap

70. Business conglomerates have different names in different countries. Which country's conglomerates are called 'Chaebols' ?

(A) Japan

(B) South Korea

(C) Germany

(D) China

71. Mr. X, a non-resident, earned ₹ 36,000 as interest on German Development Bonds. Of this, he received one-sixth in India. The amount to be included as interest for the computation of his Gross Total Income is

(A) ₹ 36,000   (B) ₹ 30,000

(C) ₹ 6,000   (D) Nil

72. Consider the following problem relating to a let-out house property :
Municipal value – ₹ 60,000
Fair rent – ₹ 68,000
Standard rent under the Rent Control Act – ₹ 62,000
Annual Rent received – ₹ 65,000
The Gross Annual Value of the property will be

(A) ₹ 68,000   (B) ₹ 62,000

(C) ₹ 65,000   (D) ₹ 60,000

73. From the following, identify by the web-based financial software :

(A) Private Equity Software

(B) Share Accounting Software

(C) Wealth Management Software

(D) WINGS 2013

74. Which of the following are true in tax planning ?

(i) It is futuristic in its approach.

(ii) It has limited scope compared to tax management.

(iii) The benefits arising from it are limited particularly in the short run.

(iv) Its main objective is to reduce the tax liability.

Codes :

(A) (i), (ii) and (iii)

(B) (i) and (ii)

(C) (i) and (iv)

(D) (ii), (iii) and (iv)

75. The benefits of debt financing over equity financing are likely to be highest in which of the following situations ?

(A) High marginal tax rates and low non-interest tax benefits

(B) Low marginal tax rates and low non-interest tax benefits

(C) High marginal tax rates and high non-interest tax benefits

(D) Low marginal tax rates and high non-interest tax benefits.

UGC - NET JUNE 2014

ANSWER KEYS (PAPER III)

SUBJECT : 08 (Commerce)

Qus. No.	Ans.	Qus. No.	Ans.	Qus. No.	Ans.
1	D	26	A	51	C
2	C	27	C	52	B
3	B	28	D	53	C
4	C	29	A	54	B
5	D	30	A	55	A
6	D	31	C	56	C
7	D	32	C	57	B
8	B	33	C	58	C
9	B	34	B	59	A
10	B	35	C	60	B
11	A	36	B	61	A
12	A	37	A	62	A
13	D	38	B	63	B
14	C	39	D	64	B
15	C	40	D	65	C
16	A	41	C	66	D
17	C	42	B	67	C
18	B	43	C	68	A
19	A	44	D	69	C
20	D	45	B	70	B
21	C	46	D	71	C
22	C	47	D	72	C
23	D	48	A	73	D
24	B	49	A	74	C
25	B	50	A	75	A

Dec-2013
COMMERCE
Paper – II

Note : This paper contains **fifty (50)** objective type questions of **two (2)** marks each. **All** questions are compulsory.

1. Who is the fiscal agent and advisor to Government in monetary and financial matters ?
   (A) NABARD
   (B) SBI
   (C) RBI
   (D) None of the above

2. Match the items of List – I with the items of List – II :

	List – I		List – II
(a)	National Manufacturing Competitiveness Council (NMCC)	(i)	Industrial Licensing Policy
(b)	National Investment Fund (NIP)	(ii)	Eleventh Five Year Plan
(c)	The Industries (Development and Regulation) Act (IDRA), 1951	(iii)	The Competition Act, 2002
(d)	Increase in Employment	(iv)	Public Sector Undertakings

   Codes :

	(a)	(b)	(c)	(d)
(A)	(iv)	(i)	(ii)	(iii)
(B)	(iii)	(iv)	(i)	(ii)
(C)	(i)	(ii)	(iii)	(iv)
(D)	(iv)	(iii)	(ii)	(i)

3. Kyoto Protocol pertains to
   (A) Capital formulation
   (B) Globalisation
   (C) Environmental protection
   (D) Unemployment reduction

4. Uruguay Round pertains to
   (A) WTO
   (B) IMF
   (C) GATT
   (D) World Bank

5. Which of the following are outside the scope of the Consumer Protection Act, 1986 ?
   (A) Newspaper industry
   (B) Services provided under contract of personal service
   (C) Banking industry
   (D) Both (A) and (B)

6. Which of the following is 'true' regarding the Prudence Principle of Accounting ?
   (A) Taking care of the future losses
   (B) Taking care of the future profits
   (C) Taking care of bad debts
   (D) Taking care of inventory and depreciation

7. Which of the following is a non-operating expense ?
   (A) Salary of Managing Director
   (B) Depreciation
   (C) Advertisement expenditure
   (D) Interest on loan

8. A and B are partners sharing profits in the ratio of 3 : 2. Their books showed goodwill at ₹ 3,000. C is admitted with $\frac{1}{4}$th share of profits and brings ₹ 10,000 as his capital. But he is not able to bring in cash for his share of goodwill ₹ 3,000. How will you treat this ?
   (A) Goodwill is raised by ₹ 12,000
   (B) C will remain as debtor for ₹ 3,000
   (C) C's A/c. is debited for ₹ 3,000
   (D) Goodwill is raised by ₹ 9,000

9. If there is mutual indebtedness between the transferor company and the transferee company in business combination, which of the following is correct ?
   (A) No adjustment is required in the books of the transferor company.
   (B) Adjustment is required in the books of the transferor company.
   (C) No adjustment is required in the books of the transferee company.
   (D) None of the above

10. Improvement of profit-volume ratio can be done by
    (A) Increasing selling price
    (B) Altering sales mixture
    (C) Reducing variable cost
    (D) All of the above

11. Business Economics is a subject which
    (A) studies economic relationships
    (B) studies economic activities at the aggregate level
    (C) deals with the tools of economics used for decision making in business
    (D) studies optimum allocation of limited resources

12. Match List – I with List – II and select the correct code for the answer :

List – I	List – II
(a) Cross elasticity is zero	(i) Price = AVC
(b) Shut-down point	(ii) Two commodities are independent
(c) Slutsky theorem	(iii) Trans-formation line
(d) Production Possibility Curve	(iv) Substitution effect

    Codes :

	(a)	(b)	(c)	(d)
(A)	(ii)	(iv)	(i)	(iii)
(B)	(iii)	(ii)	(iv)	(i)
(C)	(i)	(iii)	(ii)	(iv)
(D)	(ii)	(i)	(iv)	(iii)

13. **Assertion (A) :** The demand curve has negative slope showing inverse relationship between price and the quantity demanded.
    Reason (R) : This applies only to Giffen goods.
    Codes :
    (A) Both (A) and (R) are true.
    (B) (A) is true, but (R) is false.
    (C) (A) is false, but (R) is true.
    (D) Both (A) and (R) are false.

14. The consumer is said to be in equilibrium when he plans his expenditure on x, y and z commodities in such a way that he ultimately attains :
    (A) $MU_x = MU_y = M_z$
    (B) $\dfrac{MU_x}{P_x} = \dfrac{MU_y}{P_y} = \dfrac{MU_z}{P_z}$
    (C) $\dfrac{MU_x}{P_x} = \dfrac{MU_y}{P_y} = \dfrac{MU_z}{P_z} = MU_m$
    (D) $\dfrac{MU_x}{P_x} < \dfrac{MU_y}{P_y} < \dfrac{MU_z}{P_z} < MU_m$

15. Match the items in List – I with those in List – II and select the correct code for the answer :

	List – I		List – II
(a)	Monopoly	(i)	Price Taker
(b)	Monopolistic competition	(ii)	Homo-geneous product's price maker
(c)	Perfect competition	(iii)	Hetero-geneous product
(d)	Oligopoly	(iv)	Price Rigidity

Codes :

	(a)	(b)	(c)	(d)
(A)	(ii)	(iii)	(i)	(iv)
(B)	(i)	(ii)	(iv)	(iii)
(C)	(iii)	(iv)	(ii)	(i)
(D)	(iv)	(i)	(iii)	(ii)

16. Match the following items in List – I with most suitable options in List – II :

	List – I		List – II
(a)	Fisher	(i)	Inverse probability
(b)	Karl Pearson	(ii)	Normal Distribution
(c)	Thomas Baye's	(iii)	Correlation Coefficient
(d)	Karl Gauss	(iv)	Index Numbers

Codes :

	(a)	(b)	(c)	(d)
(A)	(iv)	(iii)	(ii)	(i)
(B)	(iv)	(iii)	(i)	(ii)
(C)	(iv)	(ii)	(iii)	(i)
(D)	(iv)	(ii)	(i)	(iii)

17. The law of statistics, which says 'Moderately large number of items chosen at random from a large group possess the characteristics of the large group', is referred to as :
(A) The Central Limit Theorem
(B) The Law of Statistical Regularity
(C) The Law of Inertia of Large Numbers
(D) None of the above

18. A distribution, where the value of arithmetic mean is maximum as compared to median and mode, is
(A) Normal distribution
(B) Positively-skewed distribution
(C) Negatively-skewed distribution
(D) None of these

19. The most appropriate average to be used to compute the average rate of growth in population is
(A) Arithmetic mean
(B) Median
(C) Geometric mean
(D) Harmonic mean

20. "The life expectancy of people in Kerala is more than that of Tamil Nadu." This statement is an example of
(A) Descriptive Hypothesis
(B) Causal Hypothesis
(C) Correlational Hypothesis
(D) None of the above

21. Match the items of List – I with the items of List – II and choose the correct answer :

	List – I		List – II
(a)	Intrapersonal communication	(i)	Information sharing
(b)	Element of a communication event	(ii)	Development of 'will' to work
(c)	Objective of organisational communication	(iii)	Thinking
(d)	Goals of organisational communication	(iv)	Purpose

Codes :

	(a)	(b)	(c)	(d)
(A)	(i)	(ii)	(iii)	(iv)
(B)	(iii)	(iv)	(ii)	(i)
(C)	(ii)	(iii)	(i)	(iv)
(D)	(iv)	(iii)	(ii)	(i)

22. According to the Boston Consulting Group, a business which has a high growth rate but a weak market share is referred to as a

   (A) Cash Cow

   (B) Dog

   (C) Question Mark

   (D) Star

23. 'No ideas are ever criticized' and 'the more radical the ideas are the better' – are the rules of which decision making process ?

   (A) Programmed decision-making

   (B) Non-programmed decision making

   (C) Brainstorming

   (D) Group discussion

24. According to McClelland's Needs Theory, which of the following is not a motivating need ?

   (A) Need for Power

   (B) Need for Security

   (C) Need for Achievement

   (D) Need for Affiliation

25. In the managerial grid, developed by Blake and Mouton, a manager who has high consideration for production but little concern for people is known as

   (A) 1.1 Management

   (B) 1.9 Management

   (C) 9.1 Management

   (D) 5.5 Management

26. Which of the following is not the major component of holistic marketing ?

   (A) Relationship marketing

   (B) Integrated marketing

   (C) Customer satisfaction

   (D) Socially-responsible marketing

27. Which of the legislations listed below do not form part of the marketing environment of India ?

   (A) The Drugs and Cosmetics Act, 1940

   (B) The Prevention of Food and Adulteration Act, 1954

   (C) The Monopolies and Restrictive Trade Practices Act, 1969

   (D) Both (B) and (C)

28. The set of all actual and potential buyers of a product is known as

   (A) Customer group

   (B) Industry

   (C) Market

   (D) None of the above

29. In the model of consumer behaviour given by Philip Kotler, what constitutes the marketing stimuli ?

   (A) Marketing environment

   (B) Four P's of marketing

   (C) Consumer needs and wants

   (D) None of the above

30. The factor that exerts the broadest and deepest influence on consumer behaviour is

   (A) Culture

   (B) Sub-culture

   (C) Social class

   (D) Income

31. Which one of the following is not among the assumptions of the Modigliani-Miller model ?
- (A) Perfect capital market
- (B) Equivalent risk classes
- (C) Unity for dividend payout ratio
- (D) Absence of taxes

32. The most suitable coverage ratio for deciding the debt capacity of a firm is
- (A) Interest Coverage Ratio
- (B) Cash Flow Coverage Ratio
- (C) Debt Service Coverage Ratio
- (D) Fixed Assets Coverage Ratio

33. Which one of the following is the most popular method for estimating the cost of equity ?
- (A) Capital asset pricing model
- (B) Dividend yield method
- (C) Gordon's dividend discount model
- (D) Earnings yield method

34. Which one of the following is not the internal factor affecting the weighted average cost of capital of a firm ?
- (A) Investment policy of the firm
- (B) Capital structure of the firm
- (C) Dividend policy followed
- (D) Market risk premium for the firm

35. Most common approach for analysing the capital structure of a firm is
- (A) Ratio Analysis
- (B) Cash Flow Analysis
- (C) Comparative Analysis
- (D) Leverage Analysis

36. Who propounded "Theory Z" ?
- (A) William Ouchi
- (B) Peter F. Drucker
- (C) Joseph H. Jurau
- (D) Douglas McGregor

37. Another name for MATRIX organisation is
- (A) Flexible organisation
- (B) Geographic organisation
- (C) Project organisation
- (D) None of the above

38. Which of the following are methods of on-the-job training ?
- (i) Coaching
- (ii) Vestibule training
- (iii) Demonstration
- (iv) Role-playing
- (v) Apprenticeship training

Select the right answer from the following codes :
- (A) (i), (ii), (iii), (iv)
- (B) (i), (iii), (v)
- (C) (ii), (iii), (iv)
- (D) (i), (ii), (iii), (iv), (v)

39. The idea that a manager tends to be promoted to the level of his incompetence is referred to as
- (A) The advancement principle
- (B) The Parkinson's law
- (C) The Peter principle
- (D) The job design principle

40. Assertion (A): The emphasis in industrial psychology has shifted from the studies of the isolated individual and the physical environment to the consideration of motivation and morale.

Reason (R) : A motivated employee with a high morale will always give high productivity.

Codes :

(A) Both (A) and (R) are correct, and (R) is the right explanation of (A).

(B) (A) is correct, but (R) is not correct.

(C) Both (A) and (R) are incorrect.

(D) Both (A) and (R) are correct, but (R) is not the right explanation of (A).

41. Match the following items of List – I and List – II in terms of functions of commercial banks :

List – I	List – II
(a) Letter of reference	(i) Advancing loans
(b) Sale of gold coins	(ii) Receiving deposits
(c) Recurring Account	(iii) Non-banking function
(d) Overdrafts	(iv) Agency function

Codes :

	(a)	(b)	(c)	(d)
(A)	(i)	(ii)	(iii)	(iv)
(B)	(iv)	(iii)	(ii)	(i)
(C)	(iv)	(ii)	(iii)	(i)
(D)	(i)	(iii)	(ii)	(iv)

42. Which of the following are included under representation functions of a bank ?

(i) Payment of cheques and bills

(ii) Providing remittance facilities

(iii) Underwriting of securities

(iv) Advancing clean credit

(v) Allowing overdrafts on current account

(vi) Purchase and sale of securities

Codes :

(A) (i), (ii), (iii) and (iv)

(B) (iii), (iv), (v) and (vi)

(C) (i), (ii), (iii) and (vi)

(D) (ii), (iii), (v) and (vi)

43. Call money rate is applicable for a very short period to

(A) Inter bank advances

(B) Bank to Reserve Bank advances

(C) Reserve Bank to Bank advances

(D) Commercial Banks to Industrial Banks advances

44. Match the following List – I with List – II :

List – I (Name of Securities)	List – II (Type of Securities)
(a) Bonds of Land Development Banks	(i) Semi-Government Securities
(b) Treasury Bills	(ii) First Order Securities
(c) Shares of a Public Ltd. Co.	(iii) Personal Securities

Codes :

	(a)	(b)	(c)
(A)	(i)	(ii)	(iii)
(B)	(ii)	(i)	(iii)
(C)	(iii)	(ii)	(i)
(D)	(i)	(iii)	(ii)

45. Reserve Bank of India controls the activities of some of the following banks in India :

(i) Commercial Banks

(ii) Cooperative Banks

(iii) Foreign Banks

(iv) Rural Banks

Codes :

(A) (i), (ii) and (iii)

(B) (i), (iii) and (iv)

(C) (ii), (iii) and (iv)

(D) (i), (ii), (iii) and (iv)

46. Match the following List – I with List – II and select the correct answer:

List – I		List – II
(a) Comparative Cost Theory of International Trade	(i)	Gottfried Haberler
(b) International Trade Theory of Opportunity Cost	(ii)	J.S. Mill
(c) Factor Endowment Theory of International Trade	(iii)	David Ricardo
(d) Doctrine of Reciprocal Demand	(iv)	Hecksher-Ohlin

Codes :

	(a)	(b)	(c)	(d)
(A)	(iii)	(ii)	(iv)	(i)
(B)	(i)	(iii)	(ii)	(iv)
(C)	(iii)	(i)	(iv)	(ii)
(D)	(ii)	(i)	(iv)	(iii)

47. Identify the one, from the following, which is not a type of disequilibrium in the balance of payments of a country :

(A) Cyclical disequilibrium

(B) Secular disequilibrium

(C) Structural disequilibrium

(D) Sectoral disequilibrium

48. The participants who take advantage of different exchange rates in different markets are

(A) Speculators

(B) Arbitrageurs

(C) Hedgers

(D) Investors

49. **Assertion (A) :** The liability of the option buyer is limited in the currency options market.

Reason (R) : Option buyer need not exercise the option if the exchange rate is not favourable for him.

Codes :

(A) (R) is correct and (A) is wrong.

(B) (A) is correct and (R) is wrong.

(C) Both (A) and (R) are correct.

(D) Both (A) and (R) are wrong.

50. An MNC that maintains a balance between the home market and host market oriented policies is

(A) Ethnocentric firm

(B) Polycentric firm

(C) Geocentric firm

(D) None of the above

UGC - NET DECEMBER 2013

ANSWER KEYS (PAPER II)

SUBJECT : 08 (Commerce)

Qus. No.	Ans.	Qus. No.	Ans.
1	C	26	C
2	B	27	D
3	C	28	C
4	C	29	B
5	B	30	A
6	A	31	C
7	D	32	B
8	D	33	A
9	A	34	D
10	D	35	C
11	C	36	A
12	D	37	C
13	B	38	B
14	C	39	C
15	A	40	B
16	B	41	B
17	B	42	C
18	B	43	A
19	C	44	A
20	C	45	D
21	B	46	C
22	C	47	D
23	C	48	B
24	B	49	C
25	C	50	C

Dec-2013

COMMERCE
Paper – III

Note : This paper contains **seventy five (75)** objective type questions of **two (2)** marks each. **All** questions are compulsory.

1. The present regime of subsidies can be improved by focussing on

   (i) Reducing the overall scale of subsidies.

   (ii) Making subsidies as transparent as possible.

   (iii) Giving a specific amount to the Member of Parliament for subsidies.

   (iv) Setting clear limits on duration of any new subsidy scheme.

   (v) Eliminating system of periodic review of subsidies

   (vi) Using subsidies for well-defined economic objectives.

   Codes :

   (A) (i), (ii), (iii) and (iv)

   (B) (ii), (iii), (iv) and (v)

   (C) (i), (iii), (iv) and (vi)

   (D) (i), (ii), (iv) and (vi)

2. Which of the following is not regulated by The Competition Act, 2002 ?

   (A) Abuse of dominant position

   (B) Anti-competitive agreements

   (C) Medical negligence

   (D) Predatory pricing

3. The freedom of private enterprise is the greatest in the free market economy. This is characterized by which of the following assumptions ?

   (i) The factors of production (labour, land, capital) are privately owned and production occurs at the initiative of the private enterprise.

   (ii) Income is received in monetary form by the sale of services of the factors of production and from the profits of the private enterprise.

   (iii) Members of the free market economy have freedom of choice in so far as consumption, occupation, savings and investments are concerned.

   (iv) The free market economy is not planned, controlled or regulated by the government.

   (v) The free market economy is prone to corrupt practices.

   Codes :
   (A) (i), (ii) and (iii)
   (B) (i), (ii), (iii) and (iv)
   (C) (i), (ii), (iii), (iv) and (v)
   (D) (ii), (iii), (iv) and (v)

4. The important responsibilities of a business to the customers are
   (i) To ensure family welfare of the customers.
   (ii) To understand customer needs and to take the necessary measures to satisfy these needs.
   (iii) To ensure health condition of the customers.
   (iv) To ensure that the product supplied has no adverse effect on the customer.
   (v) To provide an opportunity for being heard and to redress genuine grievances.
   Codes :
   (A) (i), (ii), (iii), (iv) and (v)
   (B) (i), (ii), (iii) and (iv)
   (C) (ii), (iv) and (v)
   (D) (ii), (iii), (iv) and (v)

5. The rationale of expanding role of the public sector stems mainly from which of the following factors ?
- (i) The failure of the private sector in certain crucial areas
- (ii) The exploitation of the society by the private sector
- (iii) The revenue need of the Central Government
- (iv) The demand of economic justice
- (v) The need for accelerating the pace of economic growth

Codes :
- (A) (i), (ii), (iii) and (iv)
- (B) (ii), (iii), (iv) and (v)
- (C) (i), (iii), (iv) and (v)
- (D) (i), (ii), (iv) and (v)

6. Which of the following factors may lead to a sick industrial unit ?
- (i) Shortage of funds and faulty financial management
- (ii) Investment by the FIIs in Indian industries
- (iii) Unauthorized FDI in Indian industries
- (iv) Lack of experience on the part of promoters
- (v) Technological factors including obsolete or improper technology

Codes :
- (A) (i), (ii), (iii) and (iv)
- (B) (ii), (iii), (iv) and (v)
- (C) (i), (iv) and (v)
- (D) (i), (ii) and (iii)

7. Indicate what is <u>not</u> correct in respect of the Consumer Protection Act, 1986.
- (A) No complaint can be entertained in respect of a product purchased more than 2 years back.
- (B) A complaint against medical negligence can be filed by legal heir or representative of the deceased.
- (C) A complaint involving a claim of ₹ 15 lakhs is to be filed before the State Commission.
- (D) Both (A) and (C)

8. If bonus shares are issued out of pre-acquisition profit, it will have
- (A) Direct effect on the Consolidated Balance Sheet
- (B) No effect on the Consolidated Balance Sheet
- (C) No effect on Net Profit
- (D) None of the above

9. The present value of the future contributions of employees is one of the methods of
- (A) HR Accounting
- (B) Inflation Accounting
- (C) Social Accounting
- (D) Responsibility Accounting

10. A standard which can be attained under the most favourable working conditions is called
- (A) Attainable Standard
- (B) Basic Standard
- (C) Current Standard
- (D) Ideal Standard

11. Which of the following ratios are taken into consideration by a banker before sanctioning the loan ?
- (A) Proprietory Ratio
- (B) Stock-Turnover Ratio
- (C) Debt-Equity Ratio
- (D) All of the above

12. Match the items of the following two lists :

	List – I		List – II
(i)	Zero-base Budgeting	(a)	Internal Reconstruction
(ii)	Goodwill or Capital Reserve	(b)	Earnings Per Share
(iii)	Reduction of Capital	(c)	Control of Expenditure
(iv)	Basic & Diluted	(d)	Business Combination

Codes :

	(i)	(ii)	(iii)	(iv)
(A)	(c)	(d)	(b)	(a)
(B)	(d)	(c)	(a)	(b)
(C)	(d)	(a)	(c)	(b)
(D)	(c)	(d)	(a)	(b)

13. **Assertion (A) :** Dividend paid out of pre-acquisition profit by the subsidiary company to the holding company is deducted from the cost of investment.

   Reason (R) : Dividend paid out of pre-acquisition profit by the subsidiary company should be treated as a return of capital to the holding company.

   Which one of the following is correct ?
   (A) Both (A) and (R) are correct.
   (B) (A) is correct, but (R) is wrong.
   (C) (A) is wrong, but (R) is correct.
   (D) Both (A) and (R) are wrong.

14. Given below are two statements, one labelled as Assertion (A) and the other labelled as Reason (R) :

   Assertion (A) : Increasing the value of closing inventory increases profit.

   Reason (R) : Increasing the value of closing inventory reduces cost of goods sold.

   In the context of the above two statements, which of the following is correct ?
   Codes :
   (A) Both (A) and (R) are correct.
   (B) Only (A) is correct.
   (C) Only (R) is correct.
   (D) Both (A) and (R) are wrong.

15. Match the items of List – I with the items of List – II and select the correct code for the answer :

	List – I		List – II
(a)	Multiple plants	(i)	$MRP_T = MC = MRP_X = MRP_{PY}$
(b)	Cost-plus pricing	(ii)	$MRT = MC = MR_1 = MR_2$
(c)	Multiple markets	(iii)	$MR = MC_T = MC_A = MC_B$
(d)	Multiple products	(iv)	$P = (1 + m) ATC$

   Codes :

	(a)	(b)	(c)	(d)
(A)	(iv)	(ii)	(i)	(iii)
(B)	(i)	(iii)	(iv)	(ii)
(C)	(ii)	(i)	(iii)	(iv)
(D)	(iii)	(iv)	(ii)	(i)

16. A measure of the responsiveness of quantity demanded to changes in the price of a related good is known as
   (A) Cross Elasticity of Demand
   (B) Substitution Elasticity of Demand
   (C) Complementary Elasticity of Demand
   (D) Price Elasticity of Demand

17. If the total cost is ₹ 260 and the total variable cost is ₹ 60, what will be total fixed cost if output is (a) 100 units and (b) 200 units ?
   (A) ₹ 200 and ₹ 200
   (B) ₹ 100 and ₹ 200
   (C) ₹ 260 and ₹ 100
   (D) ₹ 160 and ₹ 100

18. Optimal input combination to minimize the cost for a given output will be at the point where :
   (A) Isocost is tangent to Isoquant
   (B) MRTS between inputs is equal
   (C) Any movement from optimum point will lead to low level of output
   (D) All the above conditions are fulfilled.

19. What kinds of actions can be taken to put the rivals at a disadvantageous position under oligopoly market ?
   (A) Commitments
   (B) Threats
   (C) Promises
   (D) All the above

20. There is no exceptions to the law of demand in the case of
   (A) Giffen goods
   (B) Normal goods
   (C) Articles of conspicuous consumption
   (D) Ignorance of the buyer

21. What is the degree of elasticity of demand in case the demand is represented by a straight line parallel to the x-axis ?
    (A) $e > 1$
    (B) $e = 0$
    (C) $e = \infty$
    (D) $e < 1$

22. If a chi-square test is to be performed on a contingency table with 3 rows and 4 columns, how many degrees of freedom should be used ?
    (A) 6
    (B) 12
    (C) 8
    (D) 9

23. **Assertion (A)** : If regression co-efficient of X on Y is greater than one, regression co-efficient of Y on X must be less than one.
    Reason (R) : The geometric mean between two regression coefficients is the co-efficient of correlation.
    On the basis of the above, choose the appropriate answer :
    (A) (A) and (R) are correct.
    (B) (A) is correct, but (R) is not correct.
    (C) (A) is not correct, but (R) is correct.
    (D) Both (A) and (R) are not correct.

24. If the sum of squares of deviations within samples is 140 with 12 degrees of freedom and the sum of squares of deviations between samples is 190 with 2 degrees of freedom, the test statistic will be
    (A) 81.4
    (B) 12.28
    (C) 8.14
    (D) 1.22

25. The regression equation of profits (X) on sales (Y) of a firm is given as : $3Y - 5X + 110 = 0$. If the sales of the firm is ₹ 44,000, the profit will be
    (A) ₹ 23,370   (B) ₹ 26,422
    (C) ₹ 24,422   (D) ₹ 21,370

26. Cricketer 'A' scores on an average 40 runs with a standard deviation of 5. Scores of players 'B' and 'C', on an average, are 75 and 90 with standard deviations 10 and 18 respectively. Arrange the players in the descending order of consistency :
    (A) A, B and C
    (B) C, B and A
    (C) B, A and C
    (D) C, A and B

27. Among the following, choose the most suitable 'test' that can be applied to examine the influence of one factor on different groups :
    (A) 't' test
    (B) 'F' test
    (C) 'Chi-square' test
    (D) None of the above

28. A machine produced 20 defective articles in a batch of 400. After overhauling, it produced 10% defectives in a batch of 300. Which test of hypothesis can be applied to the above situation to examine whether the machine has improved ?
    (A) Test of significance of a sample proportion (two-tail test)
    (B) Test of significance of a sample proportion (one-tail test)
    (C) Test of significance of difference between two sample proportion (two-tail test)
    (D) Test of significance of difference between two sample proportion (one-tail test)

29. Strategies and policies
    (A) are not closely related
    (B) give direction
    (C) are the framework for performance appraisal
    (D) both (A) and (B)

30. According to Vroom's Expectancy Theory of Motivation,
    (A) Force = valence divided by expectancy
    (B) Force = valence × expectancy
    (C) Force = strength of an individual preference for an outcome
    (D) Valence = probability that a particular action shall lead to a desired outcome

31. In the managerial grid, the managers who have little or no concern for production but are concerned only for people are known as what type of managers ?
    (A) 1.1 Management
    (B) 5.5 Management
    (C) 9.1 Management
    (D) 1.9 Management

32. According to the Boston Consulting group, a business, which has a strong market share in a low growth industry is referred to as a
    (A) Dog
    (B) Cash Cow
    (C) Star
    (D) Question mark

33. Which of the following are major principles of leading ?
    (i) Principle of motivation
    (ii) Principle of continuous development
    (iii) Principle of harmony of objectives
    (iv) Principle of open competition
    (v) Principle of communication clarity
    Select the correct answer from the codes given below :
    Codes :
    (A) (i), (ii), (iii), (v)
    (B) (i), (ii), (iii), (iv), (v)
    (C) (i), (iii), (iv), (v)
    (D) (i), (iii), (v)

34. The following are the steps of management control process :
    (i) Taking corrective action from standards
    (ii) Establishing standards
    (iii) Measuring actual performance
    (iv) Comparing performance against standard
    Select the correct sequence of these steps from the codes given below :
    Codes :
    (A) (i), (ii), (iii), (iv)
    (B) (ii), (iii), (iv), (i)
    (C) (iii), (iv), (i), (ii)
    (D) (ii), (iv), (i), (iii)

35. Consider the following :
    (i) Planning is today's action for tomorrow's decision.
    (ii) Planning is forward looking while controlling is looking back.
    (iii) Motivation is about getting voluntary willingness of subordinates for action.
    (iv) Line and staff organisation is the oldest form of organisation.
    Select the correct statements from the codes given below :
    Codes :
    (A) (ii) and (iii) are correct.
    (B) (i), (ii) and (iv) are correct.
    (C) (i), (iii) and (iv) are correct
    (D) All are correct.

36. Which is not one of the stages in the consumer buying-decision process ?
    (A) Purchase decision
    (B) Post-purchase behaviour
    (C) Problem recognition
    (D) Cultural factors

37. At which stage of product-life-cycle are the pricing decisions most complex ?
    (A) Decline
    (B) Growth
    (C) Introduction
    (D) Maturity

38. Which one is not an element of market logistics ?

(A) Inventory

(B) Order-processing

(C) Warehousing

(D) Supply chain management

39. Under which legislation, the manufacturers and distributors are required to declare Maximum Retail Price (MRP) on packaged commodities ?

(A) The Bureau of Indian Standards Act, 1986

(B) The Consumer Protection Act, 1986

(C) The Standards of Weights and Measures Act, 1976

(D) The Essential Commodities Act, 1955

40. In modern marketing, which of the following functions of a distribution middleman is gaining maximum importance ?

(A) Making persuasive communication

(B) Price negotiation

(C) Keeping adequate inventory

(D) Gathering market information

41. Which method of setting the advertising budget of a company is considered to be the most scientific ?

(A) All-you-can-afford method

(B) Percentage of sales method

(C) Competitive-parity method

(D) Objectives and tasks method

42. Match the items of List – I with those of List – II and indicate the correct combination from the codes given below :

List – I	List – II
(i) AIDA Model	(a) Consumer behaviour
(ii) Hierarchy of effects model	(b) Marketing communication
(iii) Howard and Sheth model	(c) Consumer buying-decision process
(iv) Information search	(d) Advertising effectiveness

Codes :

	(i)	(ii)	(iii)	(iv)
(A)	(a)	(b)	(c)	(d)
(B)	(b)	(c)	(d)	(a)
(C)	(b)	(d)	(a)	(c)
(D)	(d)	(a)	(c)	(b)

43. Inability of the firm to meet its obligations results in financial distress which may lead to bankruptcy resulting into the following :

1. Distress sale of assets at lower price.

2. Legal and administrative costs for bankruptcy.

3. Dilution of stakeholders' commitment to the firm.

4. Stretching of payments to suppliers and creditors.

The direct costs of such financial distress may be

(A) 1 and 4   (B) 2 and 3

(C) 1 and 2   (D) 3 and 4

44. Mutually exclusive projects can be more accurately ranked as per

(A) Internal rate of return method

(B) Net Present Value Method

(C) Modified Internal Rate of Returns Method

(D) Accounting or Average Rate of Return Method

45. Which one of the following does not constitute a Standalone Risk Analysis ?
    (A) Simulation Analysis
    (B) Break-even Analysis
    (C) Corporate Risk Analysis
    (D) Scenario Analysis

46. Financial leverage in a firm is positively affected by
    (A) Intensity of tangible assets
    (B) Operating leverage
    (C) Profitability
    (D) Tax Rate

47. Which combination of the following two statements (A) and (R) is correct ?
    Assertion (A) : The IRR of a project is the discount rate which reduces its NPV to zero.
    Reason (R) : A project is worth accepting if the IRR exceeds the cost of capital.
    Codes :
    (A) (A) is right, but (R) is wrong.
    (B) Both (A) and (R) are correct.
    (C) (A) is wrong, but (R) is correct.
    (D) Both (A) and (R) are wrong.

48. **Assertion (A) :** A company should pay minimum dividend to its shareholders.
    Reason (R) : Dividends are heavily taxed than capital gains.
    Codes :
    (A) Both (A) and (R) are correct.
    (B) Both (A) and (R) are incorrect.
    (C) (A) is not correct, but (R) is correct.
    (D) (A) is correct, but (R) is wrong.

49. Dividend irrelevance hypothesis is implied in the
    (A) Traditional Model
    (B) Walter Model
    (C) Gordon Model
    (D) M.M. Model

50. Which one of the following does not serve the main objective of performance appraisal ?
    (A) Developmental uses
    (B) Administrative uses
    (C) Ethical and moral values
    (D) Organisational objectives

51. **Statement (I) :** Job evaluation is a technique of assessing the worth of each job in comparison with others throughout an organization.
    Statement (II): Job evaluation and job rating are one and the same for employees' appraisal purposes.
    Codes :
    (A) Statement (I) is correct, but Statement (II) is incorrect.
    (B) Statement (II) is correct, but Statement (I) is incorrect.
    (C) Both the Statements (I) and (II) are correct.
    (D) Both the Statements (I) and (II) are incorrect.

52. Match the items of List – I with the items of List – II and select the correct answer :

List – I	List – II
(i) Job Rotation	(a) Involves conscious efforts, to organise tasks, duties and responsibilities into a unit of work to achieve certain objectives.
(ii) Job Design	(b) Involves movement of employees from job to job
(iii) Job Evaluation	(c) Seeks to improve both task efficiency and human satisfaction and more opportunity for individual growth
(iv) Job Enrichment	(d) The formal process by which the relative worth of various jobs in the organisation is determined for pay purpose.

Codes :

	(i)	(ii)	(iii)	(iv)
(A)	(a)	(b)	(c)	(d)
(B)	(d)	(c)	(b)	(a)
(C)	(c)	(d)	(b)	(a)
(D)	(b)	(a)	(d)	(c)

53. **Assertion (A)** : Merit rating of an employee is the process of evaluating the employees performance on the job in terms of the requirements of the job.

Reason (R) : Employees' merit rating is a technique for fair and systematic evaluation of an employee's capacities and abilities and performance on the specific job.

Codes :
(A) Both (A) and (R) are correct, and (R) is the right explanation of (A).
(B) Both (A) and (R) are correct, but (R) is not the right explanation of (A).
(C) Both (A) and (R) are incorrect.
(D) (R) is correct, but (A) is incorrect.

54. The major provisions for employees' health and safety are contained in
(A) The Industrial Disputes Act, 1947
(B) The Factories Act, 1948
(C) The Industrial Employment (Standing Orders) Act, 1946
(D) The Employees' Compensation Act, 1923

55. Indicate your choice through the codes given below :
1. A club is an industry under the Industrial Disputes Act, 1947
2. Factory as defined under the Factories Act, 1948 includes a mine.
3. For purpose of the payment of bonus to employees, the gross profits earned by a bank is to be calculated in the manner specified in Schedule – I of the Payment of the Bonus Act, 1965.
4. Various labour laws do not apply to public sector undertakings.

Codes :
(A) While 1 and 2 are correct, others are not.
(B) All the statements are correct.
(C) Only 1 is correct, others are incorrect.
(D) Only 1 is incorrect, all others are correct.

56. Match the items of List – I with the items of List – II and select the correct answer :

	List – I		List – II
(i)	Abraham Maslow	(a)	Achievement Motivation Theory
(ii)	Herzberg	(b)	ERG Theory
(iii)	Alderfer	(c)	Two Factor Theory
(iv)	McClelland	(d)	Need Hierarchy Theory

Codes :

	(i)	(ii)	(iii)	(iv)
(A)	(a)	(b)	(c)	(d)
(B)	(d)	(c)	(b)	(a)
(C)	(c)	(b)	(a)	(d)
(D)	(d)	(c)	(a)	(b)

57. **Assertion (A)** : The Central Bank of the country is responsible to maintain stability of the monetary standard which involves currency circulation

Reason (R) : The Central Bank is the only authorized entity to do so.

Codes :
(A) (A) and (R) both are correct.
(B) (A) and (R) both are incorrect.
(C) (A) is correct, but (R) is incorrect.
(D) (R) is correct, but (A) is incorrect.

58. Identify the quantitative credit control methods among the following :
(i) Bank Rate
(ii) Credit Rationing
(iii) Open Market Operations
(iv) Variable Reserve Ratio
(v) Selective Credit Control
(vi) Liquidity Ratio

Codes :
(A) (i), (ii), (iii) and (iv)
(B) (ii), (iii), (iv) and (v)
(C) (i), (ii), (v) and (vi)
(D) (i), (iii), (iv) and (vi)

59. The following activities are mainly related to which organization ?

(i) Micro Finance

(ii) Rural Finance

(iii) Self Help Groups

(iv) Cooperative Banks Finance

(A) Industrial Finance Corporation of India

(B) Ministry of Finance

(C) Reserve Bank of India

(D) National Bank for Agriculture and Rural Development

60. PIN in banking transaction is known as

(A) Postal Index Number

(B) Permanent Identification Number

(C) Personal Identification Number

(D) Public Interlocking Numeric

61. Reserve Bank of India was nationalized on

(A) January 26, 1948

(B) January 01, 1949

(C) January 26, 1950

(D) January 01, 1956

62. When a banking company is placed under moratorium under Section 45 of the Banking (Regulation) Act, 1949, the RBI must prepare a scheme of

(A) VRS for staff

(B) Capital Buy-Back

(C) Reconstruction of the company or amalgamation with any other bank

(D) IPO of the bank

63. Match the following items of List – I with List – II :

List – I	List – II
(i) SWIFT	(a) 1996
(ii) NEFT	(b) 1988
(iii) BASEL I Accord	(c) 1973
(iv) BASEL II Accord	(d) 2004

Codes :

	(i)	(ii)	(iii)	(iv)
(A)	(a)	(b)	(c)	(d)
(B)	(b)	(c)	(a)	(d)
(C)	(d)	(c)	(b)	(a)
(D)	(c)	(a)	(d)	(b)

64. The main features of TRIMS are :

(i) All restrictions on foreign capital are imposed.

(ii) No restriction is imposed on any area of investment.

(iii) Restrictions on repatriation of dividend is eliminated.

(iv) Imports of raw material is allowed freely.

(v) No limit on the extent of foreign investment.

Indicate the correct combination

(A) (i), (ii), (iii) and (v)

(B) (ii), (iii), (iv) and (v)

(C) (iii), (iv) and (v)

(D) (iv) and (v)

65. **Assertion (A)** : TRIPS requires an understanding about the scope of the new patent regime.

    Reason (R) : Patent protection will be extended to micro organisms, non-biological and micro-biological processes and plant varieties.

    Codes :
    (A) (A) and (R) are not related with each other.
    (B) (R) is related with (A).
    (C) (A) is independent of (R).
    (D) While (R) is related with TRIMS, (A) is related with TRIPS.

66. Possible impact of WTO on various aspects of the Indian economy :
    (i) Quantitative restriction will be allowed.
    (ii) Second hand cars will be imported.
    (iii) There will be dumping of Chinese goods.
    (iv) Increase in population.
    (v) Child labour exploitation
    (vi) Unemployment will increase
    Which combination is appropriate ?
    (A) (i), (ii), (iii)
    (B) (iii), (iv), (v)
    (C) (ii), (iii) & (vi)
    (D) (iv), (v) & (vi)

67. **Assertion (A)** : Economic integration abolishes cross-national economic discrimination.

    Reason (R) : Geographical proximity is an important reason for economic integration.

    Codes :
    (A) (R) does explain (A).
    (B) Both (A) and (R) are correct.
    (C) Both (A) and (R) are not correct.
    (D) (A) is correct, but (R) is not correct.

68. Match the items of List – I and items of List – II and select the correct answer :

	List – I		List – II
(i)	Free Trade Area	(a)	MERCOSUR
(ii)	Customs Union	(b)	European Union
(iii)	OEEC	(c)	EFTA
(iv)	Common Market	(d)	Marshall Plan

    Codes :

	(i)	(ii)	(iii)	(iv)
(A)	(a)	(b)	(c)	(d)
(B)	(b)	(d)	(a)	(c)
(C)	(c)	(a)	(d)	(b)
(D)	(d)	(c)	(b)	(a)

69. **Assertion (A)** : A futures contract specifies in advance the exchange rate to be used, but it is not as flexible as a forward contract.

    Reason (R) : A futures contract is for specific currency amount and a specific maturity date.

    Codes :
    (A) (R) is a correct explanation of (A).
    (B) (R) is not a correct explanation of (A).
    (C) (A) and (R) are not related with each other.
    (D) (R) is irrelevant for (A).

70. Out of the following, which are the important objectives of IMF ?
    (i)   To promote exchange rate stability
    (ii) To create standby reserves
    (iii) To print International currency notes
    (iv) To establish a multilateral system of payments.
    (v)   To maintain orderly exchange rate stability
    (vi) To create employment
    Codes :
    (A) (ii), (iv), (v), (vi)
    (B) (iii), (v), (vi)
    (C) (i), (ii), (iv), (v)
    (D) (i), (ii), (v), (vi)

71. Given that :
    Fair rent of a let out house property is ₹ 75,000. Its Municipal value is ₹ 60,000, standard rent is ₹ 72,000 and actual rent received is ₹ 63,000. What is the Gross Annual Value of this house property ?
    (A) ₹ 60,000   (B) ₹ 63,000
    (C) ₹ 72,000   (D) ₹ 75,000

72. Match the items of List – I with the items of List – II

	List – I		List – II
(i)	Amount deposited in PPF	(a)	80-IA
(ii)	Profits and gains from undertakings engaged in infrastructure development	(b)	80 G
(iii)	Contribution to National Defence Fund	(c)	80-IAB
(iv)	Profits and gains by an undertaking engaged in the development of Special Economic Zone	(d)	80-C

    Codes :
	(i)	(ii)	(iii)	(iv)
(A)	(d)	(c)	(b)	(a)
(B)	(d)	(a)	(b)	(c)
(C)	(d)	(a)	(c)	(b)
(D)	(b)	(a)	(c)	(d)

73. Which of the following deductions will not come under Sec. 80 of the Income Tax Act ?
    (A) Deduction in the case of a person with disability
    (B) Deduction for interest paid on loan taken for pursuing higher education
    (C) Deduction for interest on loan taken for the construction / purchase of house property
    (D) Deduction for repayment of any instalment of principal amount borrowed for the purchase / construction of house property

74. X purchased a land in the P.Y. 1997-98 for ₹ 50,000. This land was sold by him during the P.Y. 2009-10 for ₹ 8,00,000. The fair market value of this land on 1-4-81 was ₹ 1,20,000. If the Cost Inflation Index for the A.Y. 2010-11 is 632, his capital gain for the A.Y. 2010-11 will be
    (A) ₹ 4,84,000
    (B) ₹ 7,50,000
    (C) ₹ 6,80,000
    (D) ₹ 41,600

75. Any amount of money received in excess of ₹ 50,000 without consideration is fully taxable in the hands of
    (A) Individuals
    (B) Individuals and HUF
    (C) Individuals, HUF and Company
    (D) All assessees

UGC - NET DECEMBER 2013

ANSWER KEYS (PAPER III)

SUBJECT : 08 (Commerce)

Qus. No.	Ans.	Qus. No.	Ans.	Qus. No.	Ans.
1	D	26	A	51	A
2	C	27	B	52	D
3	B	28	D	53	B
4	C	29	B	54	B
5	D	30	B	55	A
6	C	31	D	56	B
7	C	32	B	57	C
8	B	33	D	58	D
9	A	34	B	59	D
10	D	35	A	60	C
11	C	36	D	61	B
12	D	37	D	62	C
13	A	38	D	63	B
14	A	39	C	64	B
15	D	40	D	65	A
16	A	41	D	66	C
17	A	42	C	67	B
18	D	43	C	68	C
19	D	44	B	69	A
20	B	45	C	70	C
21	C	46	A	71	C
22	A	47	B	72	B
23	A	48	A	73	C
24	C	49	D	74	D
25	B	50	C	75	B

Sep-2013
COMMERCE
Paper – II

Note : This paper contains **fifty (50)** objective type questions, each question carrying **two (2)** marks. **All** questions are compulsory.

1. Government regulation of business is basically intended to
   (A) make sure all business units have the opportunity to be successful.
   (B) warn consumers against unfair business practices
   (C) make sure business firms are socially responsible.
   (D) protect the public from the negative consequences of business behaviour.

2. What is <u>not</u> the advantage of SEZ ?
   (A) Improvement of infrastructure in the hinterland.
   (B) Diversion of large tracts of farm land.
   (C) Attracting foreign investment.
   (D) All of the above.

3. Which type of the complaints are not to be entertained by Consumer Forums under the Consumer Protection Act, 1986 ?
   (A) A defective product purchased 1½ years back.
   (B) Misleading advertisement in a newspaper.
   (C) Services provided free of cost.
   (D) Tie in sales.

4. Which of the following is a WTO procedure to promote globalisation ?
   (A) Promotion of free trade.
   (B) Reduction of budgetary subsidies.
   (C) Reduction in shipping costs.
   (D) Promotion of foreign portfolio investment.

5. Match the following regarding disinvestment in India :

List – I	List – II
(a) Disinvestment Policy by the Chandrashekhar Government	I. 1999
(b) Rangarajan Committee on disivestment in public sector enterprises	II. 1996
(c) Strategic and nonstrategic classification of public enterprises for disinvestment	III. 1991-92
(d) Formation of Disinvestment Commission	IV. 1993

   Codes :

	I	II	III	IV
(A)	(c)	(d)	(a)	(b)
(B)	(a)	(b)	(c)	(d)
(C)	(c)	(b)	(a)	(d)
(D)	(a)	(d)	(c)	(b)

6. When a partnership is dissolved and the following claims need to be met out piece-meal of the cash released, which is the correct sequence in which these claims have to be met ?
   (a) Any partner's loan
   (b) Capital and Current account balances
   (c) Expenses of dissolution
   (d) Outsider's claim (both payable and accrued)
   Codes :
   (A) (c), (d), (a), (b)
   (B) (b), (c), (a), (d)
   (C) (a), (b), (d), (c)
   (D) (a), (b), (c), (d)

7. In practice, accountants consider revenue from sales if a transaction meets the following condition(s) :
   (A) The seller has passed the legal or economic ownership of the goods to the buyer.
   (B) The seller and the buyer have agreed on the price of the goods.
   (C) The buyer has paid the price of the goods or it is certain that he will pay the price.
   (D) All of the above.

8. The main difference between marginal costing and absorption costing lies in the treatment of
   (A) Direct cost
   (B) Fixed overhead
   (C) Variable overhead
   (D) Semi-variable overhead

9. Which of the following items is not an appropriation of profit for a limited company ?
   (A) Corporate tax payable
   (B) Ordinary dividend payable
   (C) Debenture interest payable
   (D) Preference dividend payable

10. Which of the following is not applicable to responsibility accounting ?
    (A) Accounting Centre
    (B) Cost Centre
    (C) Investment Centre
    (D) Profit Centre

11. Which one of the following is not the basic assumption of Cardinal Utility analysis ?
    (A) Rationality of Consumer.
    (B) Utility cardinally measurable.
    (C) Diminishing marginal utility of money.
    (D) Hypothesis of independent utilities.

12. Which one of the following is not a property of indifference curve ?
    (A) Negatively sloping.
    (B) Convex to the point of origin.
    (C) Indifference curves necessarily have to be parallel.
    (D) Two indifference curves do not intersect each other.

13. Find the correct matching between items of List-I and the items of List-II.

List – I		List – II
(a) Increase in demand	(i)	Leftward movement along the demand curve.
(b) Contraction of demand	(ii)	Rightward shift of the demand curve.
(c) Cross demand	(iii)	Demand of more than one commodity to satisfy one specific want.
(d) Joint demand	(iv)	Demand of one commodity with changes in the prices of another related commodity

Codes :

	(i)	(ii)	(iii)	(iv)
(A)	(b)	(a)	(d)	(c)
(B)	(a)	(b)	(c)	(d)
(C)	(b)	(a)	(c)	(d)
(D)	(a)	(b)	(d)	(c)

14. According to the Law of Variable Proportions, the second stage of production ends when

(A) Marginal productivity of the variable input becomes maximum.

(B) Both marginal productivity and average productivity of the variable input are equal.

(C) Marginal productivity of the variable input becomes zero and average productivity is positive.

(D) Marginal productivity of the variable input is negative but average productivity is positive.

15. Total Revenue (TR) function and the Total Cost (TC) function of a perfectly competitive market firm are as follows :

$$TR = 480\,Q - 8\,Q^2$$
$$TC = 400 + 8\,Q^2$$

The profit maximizing output would be :

(A) 60
(B) 15
(C) 50
(D) None of the above

16. From a population with mean of 220 and standard deviation of 30, a sample of 36 was drawn at random. Calculate the standard error of the sampling distribution and choose the correct answer from the following options.

(A) 7.3   (B) 6.2
(C) 6.0   (D) 5.0

17. A committee of six people is to be formed from a group of seven men and four women. What is the probability that the committee will have exactly two women ?

(A) 0.456
(B) 0.803
(C) 0.962
(D) None of the above

18. From the following Anova table, calculate the 'F' value and select the correct answer from the options given below :

ANOVA Table

Sources of Variation	Sum of Squares	Degrees of Freedom
Between columns	100	3
Between rows	24	16
Total	124	19

(A) 22.2   (B) 31.5
(C) 33.3   (D) 36.2

19. For a hypothesis test, alpha (α) is 0.05 and beta (β) is 0.10. The power of this test is

(A) 0.95
(B) 0.90
(C) 0.80
(D) 0.15

20. Which one(s) of the following statements is (are) correct with respect to Decision Support System (DSS) ?

(i) It (DSS) is used by middle level management.

(ii) DSS applies to mostly structured problems.

(iii) DSS relies on mathematical models for analysis.

(iv) DSS is largely heuristics based.

Codes :

(A) (i) and (ii) are correct.

(B) (i) and (iii) are correct.

(C) (i), (ii) and (iii) are correct.

(D) All the four are correct.

21. Given below are two statements, one labelled as Assertion (A), and the other labelled as Reason (R). Select the correct answer using the code given below :

    Assertion (A) : Strategies necessarily need to be changed over time to suit environmental changes.

    Reason (R) : To remain competitive, organisations develop those strategies that create value for customers.

    Codes :
    (A) (A) is correct, but (R) is incorrect.
    (B) Both (A) and (R) are correct.
    (C) (A) is incorrect, but (R) is correct.
    (D) Both (A) and (R) are incorrect.

22. Which of the following is not true about proactive planning ?
    (A) Way of thinking about managing the future risks.
    (B) Anticipating future contingencies.
    (C) Reacting to external events.
    (D) Getting ready with alternative routes for unforseen situations.

23. Which of the following is not a characteristic of non-programmed decisions ?
    (A) Problems are unique and novel.
    (B) There are no pre-established policies or procedures to rely on.
    (C) The conditions for non-programmed decisions are highly certain.
    (D) These are the responsibility of top-management.

24. Which of the following is an ethical behaviour of a manager ?
    (A) Trading stocks on the basis of inside information.
    (B) Padding expense accounts.
    (C) Not divulging trade secrets to competitors.
    (D) Being severely critical of competitors.

25. Which of the following is suggested by Blake and Mouton as the best leadership behaviour ?
    (A) Low concern for people but high concern for production.
    (B) Low concern for both people and production.
    (C) High concern for both people and production.
    (D) High concern for people and low concern for production.

26. Which segmentation approach is the most compatible with the spirit of the marketing concept ?
    (A) Benefit sought
    (B) Income
    (C) Social class
    (D) Family size

27. Which of the stages of new product development process can be skipped ?
    (A) Business analysis
    (B) Idea screening
    (C) Product testing
    (D) Test marketing

28. The price-setting method which most closely corresponds to the concept of product positioning is
    (A) cost-plus pricing
    (B) going-rate pricing
    (C) perceived value pricing
    (D) psychological pricing

29. The most important retail marketing decision a retailer has to make is to
    (A) select the product assortment.
    (B) identify its target market.
    (C) choose the desired service level.
    (D) develop an effective store atmosphere.

30. Which element of the promotion mix do wholesalers primarily use ?

(A) Advertising

(B) Personal selling

(C) Public relations

(D) Trade show

31. Out of the following alternative methods of project evaluation and selection used in capital budgeting, which one of the combinations in the code corresponds to discounted cash flow methods ?

(i) Internal Rate of Return

(ii) Pay Back Period

(iii) Profitability Index

(iv) Net Present Value

Codes :

(A) (i), (ii), (iii)

(B) (i), (iii), (iv)

(C) (ii), (iii), (iv)

(D) (i), (ii), (iii), (iv)

32. When the expected level of EBIT exceeds the indifferent point for two alternative financial plans, (Equity-financing and Debt-financing), then

(A) The use of debt financing would be advantageous to increase EPS.

(B) the use of equity financing would be advantageous to maximize EPS.

(C) the use of debt-financing would reduce EPS.

(D) the use of equity financing would keep the EPS constant.

33. Which one of the following is not the assumption of the Modigliani-Miller Irrelevance Theory of Dividend Policy ?

(A) No personal or corporate income taxes.

(B) Dividend policy has its effect on firm's cost of equity.

(C) Capital investment policy is independent of its dividend policy.

(D) Stock floatation or transaction cost does not exist.

34. Match the items of List-I with the items of List-II.

List – I	List – II
(i) Financial Break-even-point	(a) Rate of discount at which NPV is zero.
(ii) Cost-Volume-Profit Analysis	(b) Cost of capital remains the same for different degrees of financial leverage.
(iii) Internal Rate of Return	(c) Analysis to study relationship among fixed costs, variable costs, sales volume and profits.
(iv) Net Operating Income Approach	(d) The minimum level of EBIT needed to satisfy all fixed financial charges.

Codes :

	(a)	(b)	(c)	(d)
(A)	(iii)	(iv)	(ii)	(i)
(B)	(i)	(ii)	(iii)	(iv)
(C)	(iv)	(iii)	(i)	(ii)
(D)	(i)	(ii)	(iv)	(iii)

35. **Assertion (A)** : The focus of working capital management revolves around managing the operating cycle of the working capital.

Reason (R) : It is because the concept is useful to ascertain the requirements of cash to meet the operating expenses of a going concern.

Codes :
(A) Both (A) and (R) are true, but (R) is not the explanation of working capital management.
(B) Both (A) and (R) are false.
(C) (A) is true, but (R) is false.
(D) (A) is false, but (R) is true.

36. Which of the following terms, includes the task, duties and responsibilities of a particular job ?
(A) Job Evaluation
(B) Job Enrichment
(C) Job Analysis
(D) Job Enlargement

37. Match the following lists and indicate the correct pairing :

List – I	List – II
1. Simple Ranking	a Evaluation by Superiors, Peers and Subordinates.
2. Paired Comparison	b Order of rating from best to worst.
3. 360-Degree Appraisal	c Standardised quantitative rating.
4. Graphic Rating	d Comparing ratings to one another.

The correct pairing is

	1	2	3	4
(A)	b	d	a	c
(B)	a	b	c	d
(C)	c	d	a	b
(D)	d	a	b	c

38. In which method of performance appraisal, the evaluator keeps a written record of significant events and how difficult employees behaved during such events ?
(A) Field Review Method
(B) BARS Method
(C) Critical Incidents Method
(D) Assessment Centre Method

39. In connection with HRD, what is incorrect ?
(A) It is a reactive function.
(B) It develops total organisation.
(C) It focuses on autonomous work groups.
(D) It is an integrated system.

40. In which method of training, job conditions are duplicated with equipments and machines which are identical with those used at the work place ?
(A) On the job training
(B) Apprenticeship training
(C) Vestibule training
(D) Internship training

41. Which one of the following techniques is used by the Commercial Banks in India to measure the risk arising from trading activity ?
(A) Network Analysis
(B) Sensitivity Analysis
(C) Value at risk methodology
(D) E.V.A.

42. Which of the following schemes introduced by NABARD is intended to provide credit to farmers ?
(A) Rural Infrastructure Development Fund
(B) Kisan Credit Card
(C) Micro-Finance
(D) Co-Operative Development Fund

43. Which one of the following is a recent E-Banking initiative in Commercial Banks in India ?
(A) RTGS
(B) NEFT
(C) NECS
(D) NET Banking

44. Which of the following fee-based services are provided by IDBI ?
(i) Credit syndication
(ii) Corporate trustee services
(iii) Custodial services
(iv) Foreign services
Identify the correct code :
Codes :
(A) (i), (ii) and (iv)
(B) (i) and (ii)
(C) (ii), (iii) and (iv)
(D) (iii) and (iv)

45. SIDBI provides financial assistance in the following forms :
(i) Bills financing
(ii) Project financing
(iii) Re-finance assistance
(iv) Resource support to institutions
Which of the following sequence is correct ?
(A) (i), (iii), (iv) and (ii)
(B) (ii), (iv), (i) and (iii)
(C) (iii), (i), (iv) and (ii)
(D) (iv), (i), (iii) and (ii)

46. BOP problems in India cannot be attributed only to
(A) Large trade deficit
(B) Increase in invisible surplus
(C) Sensitive behaviour of foreign creditors, including NRI foreign-currency depositors.
(D) The declining role of concessional external finance.

47. Arrange the stages in anti-dumping investigation process in right sequence.
(i) Initiation
(ii) Preliminary screening
(iii) Rejection of unsubstantiated information
(iv) Provisional findings
(v) Final findings and measures
(vi) Permitting the exporting country to modify the practices
Codes :
(A) (i), (ii), (iii), (iv), (vi), (v)
(B) (i), (ii), (iv), (iii), (vi), (v)
(C) (ii), (iv), (iii), (i), (vi), (v)
(D) (ii), (iii), (i), (vi), (iv), (v)

48. A situation where any advantage given by one member of the WTO to another member is extended to all WTO members is referred to as
(A) Trade Diversion
(B) Inter Regional Principle
(C) Most Favoured Nation
(D) Least Traded Nation

49. The collapse of which of the following systems is related to the Triffin Paradox ?
(A) Gold Standard
(B) Exchange rate mechanism (in 1992)
(C) Bretton Woods
(D) None of the above

50. Which of the following is/are the assumptions of the Law of One Price ?
(i) Restriction on the movement of goods between countries.
(ii) No transportation costs.
(iii) No tariffs
(A) Both (i) and (ii)
(B) Only (i)
(C) Both (ii) and (iii)
(D) (i), (ii) and (iii)

UGC - NET SEPTEMBER 2013

ANSWER KEYS (PAPER II)

SUBJECT : 08 (Commerce)

Qus. No.	Ans.	Qus. No.	Ans.
1	D	26	A
2	B	27	D
3	C	28	C
4	A	29	B
5	A	30	B
6	A	31	B
7	D	32	A
8	C	33	B
9	C	34	A
10	A	35	A
11	C	36	C
12	C	37	A
13	A	38	C
14	C	39	D
15	B	40	C
16	D	41	C
17	D	42	B
18	A	43	C
19	B	44	A
20	C	45	C
21	B	46	B
22	C	47	D
23	C	48	C
24	C	49	C
25	C	50	C

Sep-2013

COMMERCE
Paper – III

Note : This paper contains **seventy five (75)** objective type questions of **two (2)** marks each. **All** questions are compulsory.

1. The first macro-environmental force that a business firm generally monitors is
   (A) Economic environment
   (B) Demographic environment
   (C) Technological environment
   (D) International, Political environment

2. Which of the following statements is true ?
   (A) The highest growth rate in India is in the Manufacturing Sector.
   (B) Agricultural Sector has the highest share in the GDP in India.
   (C) The biggest source of Central Government's revenue is Central Excise.
   (D) None of the above.

3. Which of the following statements is true ?
   (A) The Competition Commission of India is headed by a person having Judicial background.
   (B) The definition of the term 'goods' as given in the Competition Act, 2002, is the same as given in the Sale of Goods Act, 1930.
   (C) Both (A) and (B) are true.
   (D) None of the above is true.

4. Which one of the following is not included in the Consumer Rights as per the Consumer Protection Act, 1986 ?
   (A) Right to be protected against marketing of hazardous goods and services.
   (B) Right to be heard.
   (C) Right to a physical environment that will protect and enhance quality of life.
   (D) Right to seek redressal of legitimate complaints.

5. A consumer can file a complaint under the Consumer Protection Act, 1986, on any of the following grounds except :
   (A) Sale of defective goods
   (B) Provision of deficient service
   (C) Charging very high price
   (D) Unfair trade practice

6. Financial statements provide a true and fair view if
   (A) It is free from any material error and bias.
   (B) It is prepared using the appropriate accounting policy and applicable accounting standards.
   (C) It is prescribed in the format prescribed by the regulator or, in the absence of a prescribed format, it is prepared in a manner that facilitates analyses of the financial position and the performance of the reporting enterprise.
   (D) It conforms to all of the above (A), (B) and (C).

7. Which of the formula is used to calculate Absolute Liquid Ratio is ?

(A) $\dfrac{\text{Current Assets, Loans \& Advances-Inventories}}{\text{Current Liabilities \& Provisions-Bank Overdraft}}$

(B) $\dfrac{\text{Current Assets, Loans \& Advances}}{\text{Current Liabilities \& Provisions}}$

(C) $\dfrac{\text{Absolute Liquid Assets}}{\text{Current Liabilities}}$

(D) $\dfrac{\text{Absolute Liquid Assets}}{\text{Quick Liabilities}}$

8. A company sells its product at ₹ 15 per unit. In a period if it produces and sells 8,000 units, it incurs a loss of ₹ 5 per unit. If the volume is raised to 20,000 units it earns a profit of ₹ 4. Variable cost per unit will be

(A) ₹ 9 per unit

(B) ₹ 4.5 per unit

(C) ₹ 5 per unit

(D) ₹ 6 per unit

9. Which of the following is a sub-variance of labour efficiency variance ?

(A) Idle time variance

(B) Labour-mix variance

(C) Labour-yield variance

(D) All of the above

10. An investment centre is a responsibility centre where the manager has control over

(A) Costs

(B) Costs and profits

(C) Costs, profits and product quality

(D) Costs, profits and assets

11. According to H.A. Simon, if a firm fails to achieve its target initially, it results in

(A) Search behaviour

(B) Sense of helplessness

(C) Appropriate revision of aspiration level.

(D) Sacking of its managerial team

12. When the demand curve is relatively highly elastic, the marginal revenue is

(A) Zero   (B) Unity

(C) Positive   (D) Negative

13. In which one of the following market situations the practice of price rigidity is found ?

(A) Perfectly competitive market

(B) Monopolistic competitive market

(C) Oligopoly market

(D) Discriminating monopoly market

14. During short-run, the optimum level of output corresponds to that level of output where

(A) MC is the minimum

(B) AVC is the minimum

(C) AC is the minimum

(D) AFC stops declining

15. The opportunity cost is a term which describes

(A) a bargain price for a factor of production.

(B) production cost related at the optimum level of production.

(C) average variable cost.

(D) the loss of the reward in the next best use of that resource.

16. Find chi-square value for the following :

Event	Expected	Observed
X	60	52
Y	40	48

Choose the correct answer from the following options :

(A) 2.67 (B) 2.77
(C) 3.33 (D) 4.33

17. A time series is a set of data collected at

(A) Random intervals
(B) Regular intervals
(C) Convenient intervals
(D) All of the above

18. Given the following data calculate the regression coefficient of X on Y. Pearson's correlation coefficient $= +0.8$.

Regression coefficient of Y on X $= 0.8$

Choose the correct answer from the following :

(A) 0.32 (B) 0.64
(C) 0.80 (D) 0.82

19. Which kind of test from the following options is the right test to use when the hypotheses for testing are stated as :

H_0 : Population mean is equal to the sample mean.

H_1 : Population mean is not equal to the sample mean.

(A) One-tailed test
(B) Two-tailed test
(C) Either one tailed or two tailed test
(D) None of the above

20. The steps in data processing are given below :

Choose the correct sequence of steps in data processing from the following options :

(i)   Data Storage
(ii)   Data Validation
(iii) Data Capture
(iv)   Report Generation
(v)   Data Manipulation

(A) (i), (ii), (iii), (iv), (v)
(B) (ii), (i), (iii), (iv), (v)
(C) (iii), (i), (ii), (iv), (v)
(D) (iii), (ii), (i), (v), (iv)

21. Which of the following steps are essential in the staffing process ?

1. Hiring the right kind of people.
2. Firing the non-performing employees.
3. Developing skills of the employees through training.
4. Collective bargaining.
5. Maintaining the employees by creating favourable conditions of work.

Codes :

(A) 1, 3 and 5   (B) 1, 2 and 3
(C) 3, 4 and 5   (D) 2, 3 and 4

22. F.W Taylor

1. Viewed man as an adjunct of man.
2. Completely neglected the psychological aspects.
3. Emphasized only a limited number of the psychological variables.
4. Under-estimated the meaning of human motivation.

Select the correct answer from the following :

(A) 1, 2 and 3   (B) 3, 2 and 4
(C) 1, 2, 3 and 4 (D) 1 and 4

23. The authoritarian leadership style goes with
    (A) Theory X
    (B) Theory Y
    (C) Theory Z
    (D) None of these

24. Select the four stages of group development from the following :
    1. Forming   2. Storming
    3. Discussing   4. Norming
    5. Warning   6. Performing
    Codes :
    (A) 1, 2, 3 and 5   (B) 2, 3, 4 and 6
    (C) 3, 4, 5 and 6   (D) 1, 2, 4 and 6

25. Match the following :

	List – I	List – II
(a)	To check the quality of work.	1. Speed boss
(b)	To see that work is completed in time.	2. Inspection
(c)	To check absenteeism of workers.	3. Instruction clerk
(d)	To issue instruction regarding method of work	4. Shop discipline

    Codes :

	(a)	(b)	(c)	(d)
(A)	3	2	1	4
(B)	2	1	4	3
(C)	2	1	3	4
(D)	4	3	1	2

26. A company plans to create the largest possible total sales volume. It should use
    (A) Concentrated marketing
    (B) Differentiated marketing
    (C) Homogeneous marketing
    (D) Undifferentiated marketing

27. The third stage in the consumer-buying decision process is
    (A) Evaluation of alternatives
    (B) Information search
    (C) Purchase decision
    (D) None of the above

28. Manufacturers of convenience goods typically seek _____ distribution.
    (A) Exclusive   (B) Intensive
    (C) Restrictive   (D) Selective

29. Which promotional tool is most cost effective when a product is in the decline stage of its product life cycle ?
    (A) Advertising
    (B) Personal selling
    (C) Public relations
    (D) Sales promotion

30. Match the items of List-I with those of List-II.

	List – I		List – II
(a)	Product support service	(i)	Information Technology Act 2000
(b)	Interviewers' bias	(ii)	Information Search
(c)	On-line advertising	(iii)	Marketing Research
(d)	Personal sources	(iv)	User's Manual

    Indicate the correct matching.

	(a)	(b)	(c)	(d)
(A)	(iv)	(iii)	(ii)	(i)
(B)	(iv)	(iii)	(i)	(ii)
(C)	(i)	(ii)	(iii)	(iv)
(D)	(ii)	(iii)	(iv)	(i)

31. Match the items of List-I with the items of List-II.

	List – I		List – II
(a)	A theory of capital structure in which the weighted average cost of capital and the total value of the firm remains constant as financial leverage is changed.	I.	Capital Asset Pricing Model
(b)	The value of the geared company will always be greater than an ungeared company with similar business risk but only by the amount of debt associated tax savings of the geared company.	II.	Traditional Approach
(c)	Capital structure that minimizes the firm's cost of capital and thereby maximizes the value of the firm.	III.	Net Operating Income Approach
(d)	Share price is independent of the degree of financial leverage.	IV.	Modigliani-Miller Theory and Corporate Taxation

Codes :

	I	II	III	IV
(A)	(c)	(d)	(b)	(a)
(B)	(d)	(c)	(a)	(b)
(C)	(a)	(b)	(c)	(d)
(D)	(b)	(a)	(d)	(c)

32. Which one of the following expression represents a correct matching ?

(A) A decrease in the proportional claim on earnings and assets of a share of common stock due to the issuance of additional shares : Dilution.

(B) Anticipated annual dividend divided by the total book value of the firm : Dividend Yield.

(C) When a shareholder receives lesser number of new shares in exchange for a given number of old shares : Stock split.

(D) The costs associated with issuing securities, such as underwriting, legal, listing and printing fees : Transaction Costs.

33. When the internal rate of return of a project is more than the hurdle rate, the Net Present Value would be :

(A) Zero   (B) Positive

(C) Negative   (D) Uncertain

34. **Statement I :** The presence of fixed operating costs in the operating cost structure of a firm regardless of the volume denotes the presence of financial leverage.

Statement II : Super leverage is the result of the multiplicative combination of the degree of operating leverage and financial leverage.

Codes :

(A) Both statements are true.

(B) Both statements are false.

(C) Statement I is true, but Statement II is false.

(D) Statement I is false, but Statement II is true.

35. Which one of the following expressions has incorrect matching ?

(A) A method of financing where each asset would be offset with a financing instrument of the same approximate maturity : <u>Hedging Approach</u>.

(B) A method of financing where all long term funds are used to finance the current assets : <u>Aggressive Approach</u>.

(C) The amount of current assets required to meet a firm's long-term minimum needs : <u>Permanent working capital</u>.

(D) Trade credit and other payables that arise in the firm's day to day operations : <u>Spontaneous Financing</u>.

36. The Equal Remuneration Act, 1976 is primarily applicable to workers working on

(A) Monthly wage basis

(B) Annual wage basis

(C) Daily wage basis

(D) Contractual wage basis

37. In comparing Maslow's and Hertzberg's Theories of Motivation, which motivators of Hertzberg are similar to the need specified by Maslow ?

(A) Affiliation needs

(B) Physiological needs

(C) Security needs

(D) Self-actualisation needs

38. The managerial function of staffing is most closely related to

(A) Controlling (B) Leading

(C) Marketing (D) Organising

39. The 'staffing function' does not include :

(A) Performance appraisal

(B) Placement

(C) Selection

(D) Span of control

40. On-the-job training does <u>not</u> include

(A) job rotation

(B) planned progression

(C) sensitivity training

(D) temporary promotion

41. Generally the following are the important items appearing on the assets side of the Balance Sheet of a Commercial Bank.

(a) Cash in hand

(b) Bills discounted

(c) Money at call and short notice

(d) Loans and advances

(e) Investments

Which of the following sequence is correct in the order of liquidity ?

(A) (a), (b), (d), (c) and (e)

(B) (a), (c), (b), (e) and (d)

(C) (b), (d), (c), (a) and (e)

(D) (c), (d), (b), (e) and (a)

42. Which one of the following is not a correct method of calculating profitability ratio in banking sector ?

(A) Burden ratio = Man power expenses ratio + other establishment expenditure ratio – non interest income ratio.

(B) Profit-ability ratio = Spread ratio – burden ratio

(C) Spread ratio = Interest earned ratio + Interest paid ratio

(D) Interest earned ratio = Interest earned/volume of business

43. Capital adequacy norm is expressed as a percentage of

(A) Standard Assets

(B) Risk adjusted Assets

(C) Sub-standard Assets

(D) Investments

44. The major sources of funds for IFCI Ltd. (during the year 2011-12) are given below :
    (i) Reserves and Surpluses
    (ii) Borrowings in Rupees
    (iii) Share Capital
    (iv) Borrowings in Foreign Currency
    Which of the following sequence is correct ?
    (A) (i), (iii), (iv) and (ii)
    (B) (iii), (i), (ii) and (iv)
    (C) (ii), (i), (iii) and (iv)
    (D) (iv), (ii), (i) and (iii)

45. The Bonds and Debentures issued by State Financial Corporations are guaranteed by
    (A) Reserve Bank of India
    (B) IDBI
    (C) Central Government
    (D) State Government

46. Items given are related to international trade theories. Match the items in List-A with most suitable options in List-B.

List – A	List – B
(a) 'Zero-sum' game	(i) Factor proportion theory
(b) Labour-Capital relationship	(ii) Mercantalism theory
(c) Relative efficiencies of the producing countries	(iii) Theory of 'Absolute advantage'
(d) 'Positive-sum' game	(iv) Theory of Comparative advantage

Codes :

	(a)	(b)	(c)	(d)
(A)	(iii)	(iv)	(i)	(ii)
(B)	(ii)	(iii)	(iv)	(i)
(C)	(ii)	(i)	(iv)	(iii)
(D)	(iv)	(i)	(ii)	(iii)

47. The following are the stages in international business entry process. Arrange them in correct sequence.
    (i) Direct experience
    (ii) In-depth scrutiny
    (iii) Country identification
    (iv) Preliminary screening
    (v) Final selection

    Codes :
    (A) (iv), (iii), (i), (ii), (v)
    (B) (iii), (iv), (i), (ii), (v)
    (C) (iii), (iv), (ii), (v), (i)
    (D) (iii), (iv), (v), (ii), (i)

48. Which of the following intellectual properties were covered under Uruguay Round Agreement on TRIPS ?
    (i) Copy rights
    (ii) Trade marks
    (iii) Industrial designs
    (iv) Undisclosed information, including trade secrets

    Codes :
    (A) (i) and (ii) only
    (B) (i), (ii) and (iii)
    (C) (ii), (iii) and (iv)
    (D) (i), (ii), (iii) and (iv)

49. Which of the following statements is true ?

(A) If the absolute Purchasing Power Parity (PPP) holds good, then the relative PPP also holds good.

(B) If the relative PPP holds good, then the absolute PPP also holds good.

(C) If the absolute PPP does not hold good, then the relative PPP also will not hold good.

(D) If the absolute PPP holds good, then the relative PPP may or may not hold good.

50. A company is planning to enter a foreign market. Which of the following entry strategies will give it the maximum control ?

(A) Direct export

(B) Direct investment

(C) Financing

(D) Licensing

51. The opportunity cost approach in Human Resources Accounting was introduced by

(A) Hckimian and Jones

(B) Rensis Likert

(C) Eric. G. Flamholtz

(D) William C. Pyle

52. The GDRs and ADRs can be listed on

(A) Luxemburg Stock Exchange (LSE)

(B) New York Stock Exchange (NYSE)

(C) Over the Counter Exchange of India (OTCEI)

(D) Any of the Overseas Stock Exchanges

53. Match the following :

List – I	List – II
(Name of the credit rating agency)	**(Ownership)**
(a) CRISIL	1. IFCI
(b) ICRA	2. ICICI
(c) CARE	3. Duff & Phelps Corpn.
(d) Duff and Phelps Credit Rating of India Ltd.	4. IDBI

Codes :

	(a)	(b)	(c)	(d)
(A)	1	2	3	4
(B)	2	1	4	3
(C)	1	2	4	3
(D)	2	4	1	3

54. Which of the following is responsible for investigating cases referred to it and deciding whether a proposed merger is in the 'public interest' ?

(A) Director General of Fair Trading (DGFT).

(B) Secretary of State for Trade and Industry.

(C) Competition Commission of India (CCI).

(D) Prime Minister Office.

55. Match the following :

	List – I		List – II
(a)	A popular windows accounting package providing general ledger, accounts receivables, invoicing, accounts payable, inventory and sales analysis capabilities.	1.	Sage Accounting Software
(b)	A good, entry level accounting package.	2.	M.Y.O.B.
(c)	Simplest, yet most powerful software to handle financial accounting, inventory, sales and purchase orders, invoicing and more.	3.	Best Books
(d)	A complete range of accounting software providing an integrated solution at the heart of one's business.	4.	Tally

Codes :

	(a)	(b)	(c)	(d)
(A)	4	3	2	1
(B)	1	2	4	3
(C)	2	4	1	3
(D)	2	3	4	1

56. In order to be useful, market segments must have each of the following characteristics <u>except</u> :

(A) accessibility

(B) adaptability

(C) measurability

(D) substantiality

57. Mass media has the maximum impact at which stage of consumer adoption process.

(A) Adoption   (B) Awareness

(C) Evaluation   (D) Trial

58. Pricing decisions are most complex at which stage of the product life cycle ?

(A) Decline stage

(B) Introductory stage

(C) Growth stage

(D) Maturity stage

59. Industrial buyers are likely to be most responsive to _____ appeal.

(A) emotional   (B) moral

(C) rational   (D) cognitive

60. Indicate the <u>true</u> statement :

(A) Advertisement's sales effect is easier to measure than its communication effect.

(B) As a tool of promotion, public relations can be more cost-effective than advertising.

(C) A successful salesperson is one who can sell refrigerator to an Eskimo.

(D) All the above are true.

61. Who observed in 54 of the cases studied that high morale related to high productivity in 11 of the cases high morale was associated with low productivity and in 35% of the cases there was no relationship between morale and productivity ?
   (A) Michael J. Jucious
   (B) Richard E Walton
   (C) Frederick Herzberg
   (D) None of the above

62. Who developed the goal-setting theory of motivation ?
   (A) Frederick Herzberg
   (B) Edwin Locke
   (C) Richard Hackman
   (D) None of the above

63. Which of the following concepts, involves setting objectives and comparing performance against those objectives ?
   (A) Performance Appraisal
   (B) Merit Rating
   (C) Management by Objectives
   (D) Formulation of objectives and policies

64. The career development cycle includes :
   (A) Introductory stage → Growth stage → Saturation stage → Decline stage.
   (B) Primary stage → Secondary stage → Stage of self-actualisation.
   (C) Pioneering stage → Growth stage → Maturity stage → Decline stage.
   (D) Exploratory stage → Establishment stage → Maintenance stage → Stage of Decline.

65. It is a mental condition or attitudes of individuals and groups which determine their willingness to cooperate.
   (A) Job satisfaction
   (B) Motivation
   (C) Job Advancement
   (D) Morale

66. Which of the following most appropriately describes the meaning of the term 'option forward' ?
   (A) Forward contract entered into along with buying a call option.
   (B) Forward contract entered into for buying or selling at a future date.
   (C) Forward contract entered into for buying or selling over a period of time.
   (D) Forward contract entered into with writing a put option.

67. 'Dual adaptation strategy', in the context of international product decisions, means :
   (A) Modification of product and packaging it to meet local requirements.
   (B) Changing product and price to meet local requirements.
   (C) Modification of product and the marketing communication to suit the foreign markets.
   (D) None of the above.

68. The main promoter of international trade liberalisation
   (A) GATT - WTO (B) NAFTA
   (C) CEPTA   (D) CISA

69. The most common trade barrier faced by a multinational company is the
    (A) Embargo   (B) Quota
    (C) Sales tax   (D) Tariff

70. Exchange Rate System where the Central Bank intervenes to smoothen out the exchange rate fluctuations is termed as
    (A) Free float
    (B) Clean float
    (C) Managed float
    (D) Fixed rate system

71. Mr. X, after about 20 years' stay in India, returns to America on January 29, 2009. He came to India in June 2011. His residential status for the Assessment year 2012-13 will be
    (A) Ordinarily Resident
    (B) Not Ordinarily Resident
    (C) Non-Resident
    (D) Resident or Non-Resident

72. Mr. X retired from a Pvt. Ltd. Company on 31-3-2011. The company paid ₹ 80,000 in lieu of commutation of 25 percent of pension on 31-01-2012, but does not pay any gratuity to its employees. The amount taxable as commuted pension for the Assessment Year 2012-13 is :
    (A) ₹ 80,000   (B) ₹ 3,20,000
    (C) ₹ 1,60,000   (D) Nil

73. Consider the following :
    The book profit of a firm of Chartered Accountants, which satisfies all the conditions of Section 184 and Section 40(b), for the year ended 31-3-2012, is ₹ 72,190.

    The actual remuneration paid to the partners for the year is ₹ 1,56,000.

    The amount of remuneration permissible under Sec: 40(b) is :
    (A) ₹ 1,56,000   (B) ₹ 72,190
    (C) ₹ 64,971   (D) ₹ 1,50,000

74. 'Winman', software can be used for
    (A) Preparation of Balance Sheet
    (B) Computation of Income Tax
    (C) Filing of e-Returns
    (D) All of the above

75. Which of the following deductions under Chapter VI A of Income Tax Act, 1961, <u>cannot</u> be claimed by a partnership firm ?
    (i) Sec. 80-G   (ii) Sec. 80-C
    (iii) Sec. 80-D   (iv) Sec. 80-IB
    Codes :
    (A) (ii), (iii) and (iv)
    (B) (i) and (iii)
    (C) (i), (ii) and (iii)
    (D) (ii) and (iii)

UGC - NET SEPTEMBER 2013

ANSWER KEYS (PAPER III)

SUBJECT : 08 (Commerce)

Qus. No.	Ans.	Qus. No.	Ans.	Qus. No.	Ans.
1	B	26	B	51	A
2	C	27	A	52	D
3	D	28	B	53	D
4	C	29	D	54	C
5	C	30	B	55	D
6	D	31	B	56	A
7	C	32	A	57	B
8	C	33	B	58	D
9	D	34	D	59	C
10	C	35	B	60	B
11	A	36	B	61	C
12	C	37	D	62	B
13	C	38	D	63	C
14	C	39	D	64	D
15	D	40	C	65	D
16	A	41	B	66	C
17	B	42	C	67	C
18	C	43	B	68	A
19	B	44	C	69	D
20	D	45	D	70	C
21	A	46	C	71	A
22	C	47	C	72	D
23	A	48	D	73	D
24	D	49	A	74	D
25	B	50	B	75	D

June-2013

COMMERCE
Paper – II

Note : This paper contains **fifty (50)** objective type questions, each question carrying **two (2)** marks. **All** questions are compulsory.

1. Direct supervision over depositories and mutual funds is undertaken by
   - (A) NBFCs
   - (B) RBI
   - (C) SEBI
   - (D) All of the above

2. In the call/notice money market, which of the following participants is allowed to trade ?
   - (A) All Banks, Primary Dealers and Mutual Funds
   - (B) All Corporates
   - (C) Only Commercial Banks
   - (D) All of the above

3. Match the items of List-I with the items of List-II and select the correct answer :

	List – I		List – II
(i)	Private ownership and Free Enterprise.	(a)	Secondary Market
(ii)	Government ownership and Central Authority.	(b)	Capitalism
(iii)	The market for the sale and purchase of previously issued securities.	(c)	Primary Market
(iv)	The market for new long term capital.	(d)	Socialism

   Codes :

	(i)	(ii)	(iii)	(iv)
(A)	(b)	(d)	(a)	(c)
(B)	(a)	(b)	(c)	(d)
(C)	(b)	(d)	(c)	(a)
(D)	(a)	(c)	(b)	(d)

4. The apex consumer court in India is referred to as
   - (A) The Consumer Education and Research Centre.
   - (B) The Consumer Unity and Trust Society.
   - (C) National Consumer Disputes Redressal Commission.
   - (D) None of the above

5. Who is Chairman of 13th Finance Commission ?
   - (A) Dr. C. Rangarajan
   - (B) Mr. Vimal Jalan
   - (C) Dr.Vijay C. Kelkar
   - (D) None of the above

6. Insurance expenses paid to bring an equipment from the place of purchase to the place of installation is a type of
   - (A) Revenue expenditure
   - (B) Capital expenditure
   - (C) Deferred revenue expenditure
   - (D) Operating expense

7. ABC Ltd was incorporated with an authorised Share Capital of ₹ 1,00,000 equity shares of ₹ 10 each. The Board of Directors of the company decided to allot 10,000 shares credited as fully paid to the promoters of the company for their services. Which account should be debited in the books of ABC Ltd. ?
   - (A) Promoters' Account
   - (B) Services Account
   - (C) Goodwill Account
   - (D) Share Capital Account

8. In a reconstruction scheme, the reduction of capital may take the form of
(A) Reducing the liability of the shareholders in respect of any unpaid amount on the shares held by them.
(B) Paying-off any paid-up share capital which is in excess of its requirement.
(C) Cancelling any paid-up share capital which is lost or unrepresented by available assets.
(D) All of the above.

9. While determining the normal rate of return for the valuation of shares in Market Value Method, which of the following should be taken into consideration ?
(A) The degree of risk involved.
(B) The current rate of interest on gilt-edged securities.
(C) Weighted average cost of capital.
(D) All of the above.

10. Master budget is a
(A) Functional Budget
(B) Operating Budget
(C) Summary Budget
(D) Financial Budget

11. Assertion (A) : Want-satisfying power of a commodity is called its utility.
Reason (R) : Utility may not have the characteristic of morality.
Codes :
(A) Both (A) and (R) are correct.
(B) (A) is correct, but (R) is not correct.
(C) Both (A) and (R) are not correct.
(D) (R) is correct, but (A) is not correct.

12. Match the items of List-I with those in List-II and select the correct code for the answer :

	List – I		List – II
(a)	Contraction of Demand	(i)	Non-Price change effect
(b)	Decrease in Demand	(ii)	Demand curve remains the same
(c)	Increase in Demand	(iii)	Price change effect
(d)	Expansion of Demand	(iv)	Shifts the Demand curve

Codes :

	(a)	(b)	(c)	(d)
(A)	(iii)	(i)	(iv)	(ii)
(B)	(iv)	(iii)	(ii)	(i)
(C)	(i)	(ii)	(iii)	(iv)
(D)	(ii)	(iv)	(i)	(iii)

13. Assertion (A) : As the proportion of one variable factor in a combination with fixed factor is increased, after a point the marginal product of the factor will diminish.
Reason (R) : Beyond the level of optimum combination of inputs leads to this.
Codes :
(A) (R) is appropriate reason of (A).
(B) (R) is not appropriate reason of (A).
(C) (A) and (R) are not related with each other.
(D) (A) is independent of (R).

14. Match the items of List-I with the items of List-II and select the correct answer.

List – I	List – II
(a) Indifference Curve	(i) Slopes downward to the right
(b) Demand Curve	(ii) P=AR=MR=d
(c) Perfect Competition	(iii) Oligopoly
(d) Price Leadership	(iv) Convex to the origin

Codes :

	(a)	(b)	(c)	(d)
(A)	(ii)	(iii)	(iv)	(i)
(B)	(iii)	(iv)	(i)	(ii)
(C)	(iv)	(i)	(ii)	(iii)
(D)	(i)	(ii)	(iii)	(iv)

15. Price, Marginal Revenue and Elasticity are related to each other. When e = 1, then :

(A) $MR > 0$

(B) $MR < 0$

(C) $MR = 0$

(D) $MR = 1$

16. Consider the following statistical tests :

(i) 'F' test

(ii) 't' test

(iii) 'z' test

(iv) 'Chi-square' test

Which of these are parametric tests ?

(A) (i), (ii) and (iv)

(B) (i), (iii) and (iv)

(C) (i), (ii) and (iii)

(D) (ii), (iii) and (iv)

17. The difference between sample statistic and its corresponding population parameter is

(A) Sampling error

(B) Measurement error

(C) Coverage error

(D) Non-response error

18. Match the items in List-I with items in List-II.

List – I	List – II
(i) Level of significance	(a) Sample mean is equal to population mean
(ii) Standard deviation of sampling distribution	(b) Parameters
(iii) Numerical value that describes the characteristics of the population	(c) Type-I error
(iv) Normally-distributed population	(d) Standard error

Codes :

	(i)	(ii)	(iii)	(iv)
(A)	(d)	(c)	(a)	(b)
(B)	(c)	(d)	(b)	(a)
(C)	(c)	(b)	(d)	(a)
(D)	(d)	(b)	(c)	(a)

19. Kendall's co-efficient of concordance is used to

(A) Test the difference among two or more sets of data.

(B) Test the relationship between variables.

(C) Test the variations in the given data.

(D) Test the randomness of samples.

20. Which of the following softwares are used for data processing ?

(i) EXCEL

(ii) ACCESS

(iii) SPSS

(iv) STAR

(v) PASW

Codes :

(A) (i), (ii), (iii) and (v)

(B) (ii), (iii), (iv) and (v)

(C) (iii) and (iv)

(D) (i), (iii) and (iv)

21. Match the items of List-I with the items of List-II and select the correct answer.

	List – I		List – II
(i)	Grapevine	(a)	Task group
(ii)	Formal group	(b)	Field force theory
(iii)	Informal group	(c)	Gossip
(iv)	Kurt Lewin	(d)	National group

Codes :

	(i)	(ii)	(iii)	(iv)
(A)	(c)	(a)	(d)	(b)
(B)	(d)	(c)	(b)	(a)
(C)	(a)	(b)	(c)	(d)
(D)	(b)	(a)	(d)	(c)

22. Who has suggested that achievement motivation among individuals and nations can be developed through training courses ?

(A) MeClelland

(B) Alderfer

(C) Maslow

(D) Herzberg

23. **Assertion (A) :** When span of control is wide co-ordination and control becomes difficult.

Reason (R) : In a narrow span, levels of authority reduces.

Codes :

(A) Both (A) and (R) are true and (R) is the correct explanation of (A).

(B) Both (A) and (R) are true, but (R) is not a correct explanation of (A).

(C) (A) is true, but (R) is false.

(D) (A) is false, but (R) is true.

24. The general pattern of behaviour, shared belief and values that members have in common is known as

(A) Organisation climate

(B) Organisation culture

(C) Organisation effectiveness

(D) Organisation matrix

25. Which of the following is not a principle of management according to Henri Fayol ?

(A) Subordination of individual interest over the organisational interest

(B) Esprit de crops.

(C) Unity of Managers

(D) Unity of Direction

26. Which of the following concepts is based on development, design and implementation of marketing programmes, processes and activities that recognise their breadth and interdependence ?

(A) Product concept

(B) Sales concept

(C) Societal marketing concept

(D) Holistic marketing concept

27. The concept of marketing-mix, consisting of the 4 P's of marketing, was developed by

(A) E. Jerome McCarthy

(B) Peter F. Drucker

(C) Philip Kotler

(D) William J. Stonton

28. The selling concept is most likely to be used by firms which sell

(A) Convenience goods

(B) Shopping goods

(C) Speciality goods

(D) Unsought goods

29. Match the items of List-I with those of List-II and select the correct answer from the codes given below :

List – I		List – II
(a)	Everitt M. Rogers	(i)	Service Quality Model
(b)	J.D. Power	(ii)	Three types of marketing for services
(c)	Parasuraman, Zeithaml and Berry	(iii)	Quality rating of automobiles
(d)	Gronroos	(iv)	Diffusion of innovation

Codes :

	(a)	(b)	(c)	(d)
(A)	(iii)	(ii)	(i)	(iv)
(B)	(i)	(ii)	(iii)	(iv)
(C)	(ii)	(i)	(iv)	(iii)
(D)	(iv)	(iii)	(i)	(ii)

30. Consumer attitudes and beliefs about diet, health and nutrition are influenced by

(A) Economic environment

(B) Cultural environment

(C) Social environment

(D) Natural environment

31. Positive NPV in project appraised by a firm may not occur an account of

(A) Economics of scale

(B) Market reach

(C) Product differentiation

(D) Intangible benefits

32. In case the projects are divisible under capital rationing an appropriate project appraisal method is

(A) Net Present Value Method

(B) Profitability Index Method

(C) Internal Rate of Return Method

(D) Payback Period Method

33. Permanent working capital is generally financed through

(A) Long term Capital Funds

(B) Government Assistance

(C) Internal Financing

(D) Short term loans from Banks

34. The appropriate ratio for indicating liquidity crisis is

(A) Operating ratio

(B) Sales turnover ratio

(C) Current ratio

(D) Acid test ratio

35. Who proposed a model to apply economic order quantity concept of inventory management to determine the optimum cash holding in a firm ?

(A) Keith V. Smith

(B) Miller and Orr

(C) William J. Baumol

(D) J.M. Keynes

36. Which of the following is not included in the model of the systems approach to Human Resource Management ?

(A) Human Resource Planning

(B) Recruitment and Selection

(C) Performance appraisal

(D) Departmentation

37. It is generally easy to measure the performance of the

(A) Industrial Relations Manger

(B) Research and Development Manager

(C) Sales person

(D) All of the above

38. Which one of the following is not a monetory incentive to sales people ?

(A) Bonus

(B) Staff meeting

(C) Travelling allowance

(D) Both (B) and (C)

39. **Statement (i) :** Sound industrial relations are essential to achieve individual, team goals and organizational goals.

Statement (ii) : Congenial labour management relations create an atmosphere of harmony and low rate of absenteeism.

(A) Statement (i) is true, but (ii) is false.

(B) Statement (ii) is true, but (i) is false.

(C) Both statements are true.

(D) Both statements are false.

40. Out of the following, which are the schemes of Social Security ?

(i) Provident Fund Scheme

(ii) Health Insurance Scheme

(iii) Job Guarantee Scheme

(iv) Maternity Benefit Scheme

(v) Merit Promotion Scheme

(vi) Compulsory and Voluntary Social Insurance Scheme

(vii) Child Insurance Scheme

Codes :

(A) (i), (ii), (iv) and (vi)

(B) (ii), (i), (v) and (vii)

(C) (iii), (v), (iv) and (vi)

(D) (iv), (vii), (iii) and (ii)

41. RBI ensures that banks operate within the set norms by conducting _____ inspections and _____ monitoring.

(A) on site, off site

(B) off site, on site

(C) on site, field

(D) field, on site

42. Under Section 37 of the Banking (Regulation) Act, a moratorium order can be issued by the High Court for a maximum total period of

(A) One month

(B) Six months

(C) One year

(D) One and a half year

43. Bonds or debentures issued by Securitization company should bear interest not less than

(A) Bank Rate

(B) Prime Lending Rate

(C) 1.5% over the Bank Rate

(D) 1.5% over the Saving Rate

44. Section 131 of the Negotiable Instruments Act extends protection to the _____

(A) Collecting Banker

(B) Paying Banker

(C) Advising Banker

(D) Confirming Banker

45. When a customer, by a letter has advised the bank not to honour/pay a particular cheque, such letter is called _____

(A) Cancellation letter

(B) Garnishee letter

(C) Mandate

(D) None of the above

46. Flow of foreign loans and investments affect

(A) Trade balance

(B) Current Account balance

(C) Capital Account balance

(D) None of the above

47. Concessions mainly multinational in character come under the principle of

(A) Non-discrimination

(B) Reciprocity

(C) Market Access

(D) Fair Competition

48. From the following identify the one which is not a commercial counter trade ?

(A) Classical barter

(B) Counter purchase

(C) Pre-compensation

(D) Buy-back agreement

49. If the spot price is higher than the strike price in a call option, it is referred to as

(A) At-the-money

(B) In-the-money

(C) Out-of-the-money

(D) Premium

50. Identity the item which does not include under Current Account transaction.

(A) Services

(B) Non-monetary movement of gold

(C) Unilateral transfer

(D) Investment income

UGC - NET JUNE 2013

ANSWER KEYS (PAPER II)

SUBJECT : 08 (Commerce)

Qus. No.	Ans.	Qus. No.	Ans.
1	C	26	D
2	C	27	A
3	A	28	D
4	C	29	D
5	C	30	B
6	B	31	D
7	C	32	B
8	D	33	A
9	D	34	D
10	C	35	C
11	A	36	D
12	A	37	C
13	A	38	D
14	C	39	C
15	C	40	A
16	C	41	A
17	A	42	B
18	B	43	C
19	B	44	A
20	A	45	D
21	A	46	C
22	*	47	B
23	C	48	D
24	B	49	B
25	C	50	B

COMMERCE
PAPER – III

Note : This paper contains **seventy five (75)** objective type questions of **two (2)** marks each. **All** questions are compulsory.

1. Under the provisions of the Industries (Development and Regulation) Act, 1951, a licence is necessary for
   (A) Changing the location of an existing industrial undertaking.
   (B) producing or manufacturing a 'new article' in an existing industrial undertaking.
   (C) Establishing a new undertaking.
   (D) All of the above.

2. Match the items of List-I with the items of List-II and select the correct answer.

	List – I		List – II
(i)	Political and Legal Environment	(a)	Important for industries directly depending on imports or exports.
(ii)	Demographic Environment	(b)	Close relationship with the economic system and economic policy.
(iii)	Economic Environment	(c)	Related to natural resources.
(iv)	Geographical and Ecological Environment	(d)	Occupational and spatial mobilities of population having implications for business.

   Codes :
	(i)	(ii)	(iii)	(iv)
(A)	(b)	(d)	(c)	(a)
(B)	(b)	(d)	(a)	(c)
(C)	(a)	(b)	(c)	(d)
(D)	(a)	(b)	(d)	(c)

3. Match the items of List-I with the items of List-II and select the correct answer :

	List – I		List – II
(i)	SLR	(a)	Working in the field of consumer protection.
(ii)	SIDBI	(b)	Credit control.
(iii)	CUTS	(c)	Industrial policy.
(iv)	ILPIC	(d)	Facilitating Small Scale Industries.

   Codes :
	(i)	(ii)	(iii)	(iv)
(A)	(a)	(c)	(d)	(b)
(B)	(b)	(d)	(a)	(c)
(C)	(a)	(b)	(c)	(d)
(D)	(a)	(c)	(b)	(d)

4. Match the following :

	List – I		List – II
(i)	National Stock Exchange	(a)	Marks the beginning of the process of dematerialisation of shares of the participating companies.
(ii)	National Securities Depository Limited	(b)	Facilitation of equal access to investors across the country.
(iii)	Securities and Exchange Board of India	(c)	To foster the development of an active secondary market for Government Securities.
(iv)	Securities Trading Corporation of India	(d)	Abolition of Capital issues control and retaining the sale authority for new capital issues.

   Codes :
	(i)	(ii)	(iii)	(iv)
(A)	(b)	(a)	(d)	(c)
(B)	(a)	(b)	(c)	(d)
(C)	(a)	(b)	(d)	(c)
(D)	(d)	(c)	(b)	(a)

5. The United Nations Conference on Trade and Development (UNCTAD) was set up in
   (A) 1944   (B) 1954
   (C) 1960   (D) 1964

6. Indicate the ground on which a complaint under the Consumer Protection Act, 1986, shall be invalid.
   (A) A product having short weight.
   (B) A service provided free of cost.
   (C) A misleading advertisement given in newspaper.
   (D) None of the above.

7. Out of the following, which are the four components of food security ?
   (i) Food availability
   (ii) Food market
   (iii) Food accessibility
   (iv) Food utilization
   (v) Food credit
   Codes :
   (A) (iii), (iv) and (v)
   (B) (i), (iii) and (iv)
   (C) (i), (ii) and (iii)
   (D) (i), (ii) and (iv)

8. Performance evaluation of a responsibility centre can be done by
   (A) ROI
   (B) Return on sales
   (C) EVA
   (D) All of the above

9. Social Balance Sheet shows
   (A) Social costs
   (B) Social revenues
   (C) Value of employees of the organisation
   (D) All of the above

10. Which of the following comes under efficiency ratios ?
    (A) Average collection period
    (B) Inventory turnover ratio
    (C) Fixed assets turnover ratio
    (D) All of the above

11. Match the items of the following two lists :

	List – I		List – II
(i)	Statement of changes in Working Capital	(a)	Cash Flow Statement
(ii)	Deferred Tax	(b)	Fixed Assets
(iii)	Three activities	(c)	Funds Flow Statement
(iv)	Impairment Loss	(d)	Balance Sheet

    Codes :

	(i)	(ii)	(iii)	(iv)
(A)	(a)	(b)	(c)	(d)
(B)	(c)	(d)	(b)	(a)
(C)	(c)	(d)	(a)	(b)
(D)	(d)	(c)	(a)	(b)

12. Match the items of the following two lists and indicate the correct answer :

	List – I		List – II
(i)	Earning ability of firm	(a)	Basis of Accounting
(ii)	Conservatism	(b)	P/V ratio
(iii)	Cash profit	(c)	Cash flow statement
(iv)	Cash and Accrual	(d)	Prudence

    Codes :

	(i)	(ii)	(iii)	(iv)
(A)	(b)	(d)	(c)	(a)
(B)	(b)	(a)	(d)	(c)
(C)	(c)	(d)	(a)	(b)
(D)	(c)	(d)	(b)	(a)

13. Given below are two statements, one labelled as Assertion (A) and the other labelled as Reason (R).

Assertion (A) : Only the relevant costs should be taken into consideration for decision-making.

Reason (R) : All variable costs are relevant costs and all fixed costs are irrelevant costs.

In the above two statements, which one alternative of the following is correct ?

Codes :
(A) Both (A) and (R) are correct.
(B) Only (A) is correct, but (R) is wrong.
(C) Only (R) is correct, but (A) is wrong.
(D) Both (A) and (R) are wrong.

14. Given below are two statements, one labelled as Assertion (A) and the other labelled as Reason (R) :

Assertion (A) : Variance analysis is undertaken for planning and control of costs.

Reason (R) : Future costs are taken into consideration in budgeting and standard costing.

In the above two statements, which one alternative of the following is correct ?

Codes :
(A) Both (A) and (R) are correct and (R) is the Reason for (A).
(B) Both (A) and (R) are correct and (R) is not the Reason for (A).
(C) (A) is correct, but (R) is wrong.
(D) (A) is wrong, but (R) is correct.

15. **Assertion (A)** : Mark-up pricing is a method of determining price.

Reason (R) : P = ATC + (m × ATC) is the expression for that.

Codes :
(A) (A) is correct but (R) is not correct.
(B) Both (A) and (R) are correct.
(C) Both (A) and (R) are not correct.
(D) (R) is correct, but (A) is not correct.

16. Match the items of List-I with the items of List-II and select the correct answer.

	List – I		List – II
(a)	Economic profit	(i)	Total Revenue Explicit cost
(b)	Accounting profit	(ii)	Buyers and Sellers exchanging
(c)	Collusion/ Cartel	(iii)	Total Revenue – Total cost
(d)	Market	(iv)	Oligopoly

Codes :

	(a)	(b)	(c)	(d)
(A)	(iii)	(i)	(iv)	(ii)
(B)	(i)	(ii)	(iii)	(iv)
(C)	(iv)	(iii)	(ii)	(i)
(D)	(ii)	(iv)	(i)	(iii)

17. Which one is not the item of economic cost to the business ?
(A) Owner supplied resources.
(B) Market supplied resources.
(C) Implicit costs.
(D) Non-monetary opportunity costs of using owner supplied resources.

18. Demand must have the elements
(A) Desire
(B) Want
(C) Quantity, Price and Time
(D) All of the above

19. Match the items of List-I and items of List-II and select the correct code for the answer.

	List – I		List – II
(a)	Utilitarian Approach	(i)	Marginal Rate of Substitution
(b)	Ordinal Approach	(ii)	Budget line & Indifference Curve
(c)	Price-Consumption Curve	(iii)	U=f (x, y)
(d)	Consumer Equilibrium	(iv)	$MRS_{xy} = MRS_{yx}$

Codes :

	(a)	(b)	(c)	(d)
(A)	(i)	(iv)	(iii)	(ii)
(B)	(ii)	(iii)	(iv)	(i)
(C)	(iii)	(i)	(ii)	(iv)
(D)	(iv)	(ii)	(i)	(iii)

20. The Learner Index measures
    (A) Market power
    (B) Price
    (C) Price-Marginal cost
    (D) None of the above

21. Match the items of List-I and items of List-II and select the correct answer.

	List – I		List – II
(a)	Perfect competition	(i)	Different prices for the same product
(b)	Monopolistic competition	(ii)	Dominant strategy
(c)	Oligopoly	(iii)	Product differentiation
(d)	Discriminating Monopoly	(iv)	Identical product

    Codes :

	(a)	(b)	(c)	(d)
(A)	(iv)	(iii)	(ii)	(i)
(B)	(i)	(ii)	(iii)	(iv)
(C)	(ii)	(iv)	(i)	(iii)
(D)	(iii)	(i)	(iv)	(ii)

22. If there are 8 possible classes under consideration for a goodness of-fit, the number of degrees of freedom will be
    (A) 8
    (B) 7
    (C) 6
    (D) Cannot be determined from the given information.

23. Identify from the following, the test statistic for which the value of numerator should always be greater than that of denominator.
    (A) 'Chi-square'   (B) 'F' value
    (C) 'Z' value   (D) 't' value

24. Which of the following tests can be applied to ordinal scale data ?
    (i) Chi-square test
    (ii) 'Z' test
    (iii) Kruskal-Wallis test
    (iv) Wilcoxon Mann-Whitney test
    Codes :
    (A) (i), (ii) and (iii)
    (B) (ii), (iv) and (iii)
    (C) (i), (iii) and (iv)
    (D) (i), (ii) and (iv)

25. Which of the following tests can be based on the normal distribution ?
    (A) Difference between independent means
    (B) Difference between dependant means
    (C) Difference between proportions
    (D) All of the above

26. From the following, identify one situation where 'F' test cannot be used ?
    (A) To compare more than two population means.
    (B) To test the hypothesis about a single population variance.
    (C) To test the hypothesis about two-population variance.
    (D) To study about randomized block design.

27. Which statistical test should be applied to test the effectiveness of 'special coaching' on the marks scored by the students ?
    (A) Paired 't' test
    (B) 'Chi-square' test
    (C) 'Z' test
    (D) 'F' test

28. In a linear equation,
    $y = a + bx$, 'a' refers to
    (A) Slope
    (B) Y-intercept
    (C) Dependant variable
    (D) Independent variable

29. Which among the following is the most popular approach for accomplishing the results ?
   (A) Management by exception
   (B) Reward system
   (C) Management by objectives
   (D) Mentor system

30. The managerial function of organizing involves
   (A) Reviewing and adjusting plan in the light of changing conditions.
   (B) Establishing programme for the accomplishment of objectives.
   (C) Creating structure of functions and duties to be performed.
   (D) Getting things done through others.

31. A leader who identifies what subordinates need to do to achieve objectives, clarify organizational roles and tasks, set up an organization structure, reward performance and provide for the social needs of their followers, is
   (A) a transformational leader
   (B) a participative leader
   (C) a transactional leader
   (D) an autocratic leader

32. Which of the following is not an assumption of theory X ?
   (A) An average human being has an inherent dislike of work and will avoid it if he can.
   (B) An average human being prefers to be directed, seeks to avoid responsibility, has relatively little ambition, and want security above all.
   (C) An average human being learns under proper conditions, not only to accept responsibility but also to seek it.
   (D) Most people must be coerced, controlled, directed and threatened with punishment to get them put forth adequate effort.

33. If a network of interpersonal relationship that arise when people associate with each other is an informal organization, then find out which of the following is not an informal organization ?
   (A) The "machine shop" group
   (B) Customers' group
   (C) The "sixth floor" group
   (D) The "Friday evening bowling" gang

34. Which of the following are sources of ethics ?
   (i) Religion
   (ii) Legal system
   (iii) Economic system
   (iv) Culture
   (v) Family system
   Select the correct answer from the codes given below :
   (A) (i), (ii), (iii), (v)
   (B) (i), (ii), (iv)
   (C) (i), (iv), (v)
   (D) (i), (ii), (iii), (iv), (v)

35. Which of the following has refined Maslow's theory of motivation by proposing a hierarchy of three needs ?
   (A) MeClelland   (B) Aldorfer
   (C) Herzburg   (D) Vroom

36. Which segmentation approach is the most compatible with the spirit of the marketing concept ?
   (A) Benefit sought
   (B) Income
   (C) Social class
   (D) Family size

37. The description of a product's quality, features, style, brand name and packaging identifiers the
   (A) Actual product
   (B) Augmented product
   (C) Core product
   (D) Tangible product

38. Consider the following statements and find out the correct alternative from the codes given below :
    (i) A firm's marketing information system is a component of its marketing research system.
    (ii) The most common forms of marketing researches conducted in most of the firms are the measurement of market potential and the analysis of market share.
    (iii) Survey research is seldom used for studying consumer perception and attitudes.
    (iv) The concept of cognitive dissonance is relevant to study consumer's post-purchase behaviour.
    Codes :
    (A) All the statements are true.
    (B) All the statements are false.
    (C) (i) is false and the rest are true.
    (D) (ii) and (iv) are true and the rest are false.

39. In India, which pricing practice is not permissible ?
    (A) Penetrating pricing
    (B) Skimming pricing
    (C) Predatory pricing
    (D) None of the above

40. Consider the following statements and find out the correct alternative from the codes given below :
    (i) A good salesman is one who can sell refrigerator to an Eskimo.
    (ii) Salesmen are born, not made.
    (iii) Physical distribution is an area where high cost-savings is possible.
    Codes :
    (A) (i) and (iii) are correct.
    (B) (i) and (ii) are correct.
    (C) (ii) and (iii) are correct.
    (D) All are correct.

41. Which form of retail outlet has the highest operating costs ?
    (A) Super market
    (B) Consumer co-operative store
    (C) Department store
    (D) Retail chain store

42. Consider the following statements and indicate the correct alternative from the codes given below :
    (i) The product management system often turns out to be costly.
    (ii) When customers belong to different user groups with distinct buying preferences and practices, a market management organization is not suitable.
    (iii) Advertising department has the closest interface with the finance department of the company.
    Codes :
    (A) (i) and (ii) are correct.
    (B) (ii) and (iii) are correct.
    (C) Only (i) is correct.
    (D) All are correct.

43. Match the statements in List-I with dividend models in List-II as follows :

	List – I	List – II
I	Dividend Capitalisation Approach.	1. Traditional Model
II	Dividend Policy has a bearing on the share valuation.	2. Gardon Model
III	Stock Market places more weight on dividends than on retain earnings.	3. Walter Model
IV	Dividend payout is irrelevant to the value of the firm.	4. Modigliani and Miller Model

Codes :

	I	II	III	IV
(A)	2	3	1	4
(B)	1	2	4	3
(C)	4	1	3	2
(D)	3	4	2	1

44. Venture capital financing at starting stage is generally not done through
    (A) Debt instruments
    (B) Deep discount bonds
    (C) Equity shares
    (D) Conditional loans

45. Match the statements in List-I with the types of lease in the List-II as follows :

	List – I	List – II
I	Lessor transfers all risks and rewards of an asset to the lessee.	1. Indirect lease
II	Lessor transfers the assets to the lessee but bears the cost of maintenance	2. Operating lease
III	The owner of the asset sells it to the lessor who in turn leases it back to the owner (now lessee)	3. Finance lease
IV	Lessor owns/ acquires the assets that are leased to a given lessee.	4. Direct lease

    Codes :

	I	II	III	IV
(A)	2	3	4	1
(B)	1	4	2	3
(C)	3	2	1	4
(D)	4	1	3	2

46. Full details for the issue of ADRs by a company must be furnished within 30 days from the date of its closure to
    (A) Securities and Exchange Commission (SEC)
    (B) Reserve Bank of India (RBI)
    (C) Securities and Exchange Board of India (SEBI)
    (D) Company Law Board (CLB)

47. The degree to which the returns of the two securities change together, is reflected by
    (A) Correlation   (B) Leverage
    (C) Covariance   (D) Beta

48. The transfer by a company of one or more of its business divisions to another newly set up company is called
    (A) Demerger
    (B) Merger
    (C) Equity Carve-out
    (D) Disinvestment

49. What combination of the following factors influences the working capital requirement ?
    I   Market Conditions
    II   Production Policy
    III   Firm's goodwill
    IV   Supply conditions
    Codes :
    (A) I, II and III
    (B) II, III and IV
    (C) I, III and IV
    (D) I, II and IV

50. Which of the followings are the modern method of performance appraisal ?
    (i)   360 degree performance appraisal.
    (ii)   Graphic rating scale.
    (iii)   Management By Objectives (MBO).
    (iv)   Forced distribution method.
    (v)   Behaviourally Anchored Rating Scales (BARS).
    Select the correct answer from the codes given below :
    (A) (i), (ii), (iii)   (B) (ii), (iv), (v)
    (C) (i), (iii), (v)   (D) (iv), (ii), (i)

51. Which of the following principle serves as a warning to organisations not to take the selection and promotion process lightly ?
    (A) Promotion Principle
    (B) Drucker Principle
    (C) Validity Principle
    (D) Peter Principle

52. According to D. Katz morale has four dimensions :
    (i) jobs satisfaction
    (ii) satisfaction with wages and promotional opportunities.
    (iii) Identification with company.
    (iv) Pride in the work group.
    (v) Top Management Support.
    Select the correct combination.
    (A) (i), (ii), (iii) and (iv)
    (B) (i), (ii), (iii) and (v)
    (C) (i), (ii), (iv), and (v)
    (D) (i), (iii), (iv) and (v)

53. HRM is viewed as a management process, consisting of four functional activities :
    (i) Acquisition
    (ii) Motivation
    (iii) Development
    (iv) Resolution of industrial disputes
    (v) Maintenance
    Select the correct combination.
    (A) (i), (ii), (iii) and (iv)
    (B) (i), (ii), (iii) and (v)
    (C) (i), (ii), (iv) and (v)
    (D) (i), (iii), (iv) and (v)

54. O C TA PA C stands for
    (A) Order, Co-ordination, Trust, Authority, Personality and Co-operation.
    (B) Openness, Confrontation, Trust, Authenticity, Pro-action and Collaboration.
    (C) Organisation, Conflict, Team, Authority, People and Collaboration.
    (D) Oneness, Compromise, Tress pass, Authority, Protection and Combination.

55. Technique of 'Transaction Analysis' was developed by
    (A) Elton Mayo
    (B) Peter Drucker
    (C) Eric Berne
    (D) Adam Smith

56. Which one of the following methods is not a demand forecasting method of Human Resource Planning ?
    (A) Managerial judgement
    (B) Managerial grid
    (C) Work study techniques
    (D) Statistical techniques

57. Transaction of Internet Banking excludes
    (A) Withdrawal of cash anywhere in India.
    (B) Statement of account for a specific period.
    (C) Transfer of funds from one account to another account.
    (D) Balance enquiry.

58. Which among the following is not a category of Non-Performing Assets ?
    (A) Substandard Assets
    (B) Doubtful Debts
    (C) Loss Assets
    (D) Devaluated Assets

59. When a loan will be NPA ?
    (A) Interest and/or loan instalments overdue for more than 90 days.
    (B) Account is out of order for more than 90 days in case of overdraft/cash credit.
    (C) Bill remains overdue for more than 90 days.
    (D) All of the above.

60. **Assertion (A)** : "The problem of rural credit is not primarily one of rural credit, it may be said to be one of rural minded credit."
    Reason (R) : The Indian economy has yet to come out of rural mentality.
    Codes :
    (A) Both (A) and (R) are correct.
    (B) Both (A) and (R) are incorrect.
    (C) (A) is correct, but (R) is incorrect.
    (D) (R) is correct, but (A) is incorrect.

61. Match the items of List-I with the items of List-II and select the correct answer :

	List – I		List – II
(i)	Debit card	(a)	Several storage
(ii)	Credit card	(b)	Online recovery of amount
(iii)	Electronic purse	(c)	Image processing use
(iv)	Cheque function	(d)	Revolving credit

Codes :

	(i)	(ii)	(iii)	(iv)
(A)	(c)	(a)	(d)	(b)
(B)	(a)	(b)	(d)	(c)
(C)	(d)	(c)	(a)	(b)
(D)	(d)	(c)	(b)	(a)

62. Assertion (A) : The Indian economy could survive in the recent global recession due to its strong banking system.

Reason (R) : The Indian economy contains a large amount of black money.

Codes :

(A) Both (A) and (R) are correct and (R) is the explanation of (A).

(B) Both(A) and (R) are correct, but (R) is not the correct explanation of (A).

(C) (R) is correct, but (A) is not the appropriate assertion of (R).

(D) Both (A) and (R) are incorrect.

63. Assertion (A) : Most of the development bank in India have setup private commercial banks after the introduction of capital adequacy norms.

Reason (R) : Development banks in India have not adhered to their basic objectives.

Codes :

(A) (A) and (R) both are correct, and (R) is correct explanation of (A).

(B) (A) and (R) both are correct, but (R) is not a correct explanation of (A).

(C) (A) is correct, but (R) is incorrect.

(D) (R) is correct, but (A) is incorrect.

64. Match the following items of List-I with List-II :

	List – I		List – II
(a)	Brettonwoods conference	(i)	1947
(b)	General Agreement on Trade and Tariffs	(ii)	1964
(c)	ACCRA conference	(iii)	1944
(d)	United Nations Conference on Trade and Development	(iv)	2008

Codes :

	(i)	(ii)	(iii)	(iv)
(A)	(b)	(d)	(a)	(c)
(B)	(b)	(d)	(c)	(a)
(C)	(b)	(c)	(d)	(a)
(D)	(c)	(a)	(b)	(d)

65. The forces that lend momentum to the process of globalization have been identified by Michael Porter include the following :

(i) Fluid global capital market.

(ii) Technological restructuring.

(iii) Decreasing religious command.

(iv) Ethnic decontrol.

(v) New-global competitors.

(vi) End of the 'cold war' in 1990s.

Codes :

(A) (vi), (v), (iv) and (iii)

(B) (vi), (iii), (ii) and (i)

(C) (vi), (v), (ii) and (i)

(D) (iv), (iii), (ii) and (i)

66. **Statement (I) :** Green Box subsidies include amount spent on Government services such as research, disease control, infrastructure and food security.

Statement (II) : Blue Box subsidies are certain direct payments made to farmers, to limit production, and are certain government assistance programmes to encourage agriculture and rural development.

Codes :

(A) Statement (I) is correct, but (II) is not correct.

(B) Statement (II) is correct, but (I) is not correct.

(C) Both statement (I) and (II) are correct.

(D) Both statement (I) and (II) are incorrect.

67. **Assertion (A) :** The major economic powers have succeeded in creating a new international regime where the profits and the dominance of their transnational corporations will be the decisive consideration.

Reason (R) : This regime will legitimise the process of progressive erosion of the sovereign economic space of the third-world countries.

(A) Both (A) and (R) are correct, and (R) is the right explanation of (A).

(B) Both (A) and (R) are correct, but (R) is not the right explanation of (A).

(C) Both (A) and (R) are incorrect.

(D) (R) is correct, but (A) is not correct.

68. **Assertion (A) :** The 'Balance of Payments' presents a classified record of all receipts on account of goods exported, services rendered and capital received by 'residents' and payments made by them on account of goods imported and services received from capital transferred to 'non-residents' or 'foreigners".

Reason (R) : The 'Balance of Payments' of a country is a systematic record of all economic transactions between the 'residents' of a country and the rest of the world.

(A) Both (A) and (R) are correct and (R) is the right explanation of (A).

(B) Both (A) and (R) are correct, but (R) is not the right explanation of (A).

(C) (R) is correct, but (A) is not correct.

(D) Both (A) and (R) are incorrect.

69. Which among the following is not rightly explained ?

   (i) M_1 = Currency with the public + demand deposits of the public.

   (ii) M_2 = M_1 + Post Office Savings Deposits.

   (iii) M_3 = M_1 + Time Deposits of the public with Banks.

   (iv) M_4 = M_3 + Total Post Office Deposits.

   (v) M_1 = Narrow money

   (vi) M_3 = Broad money

   (A) Only (v) and (vi)

   (B) Only (i) and (iii)

   (C) Only (vi)

   (D) None of the above

70. Which of the followings are not effect of dumping on importing country ?

   (i)   Domestic industry might be affected adversely by a decline in sales and profits.

   (ii) If dumping is continued for a longer period, survival of the domestic industry may be threatened.

   (iii) Dumping may create BOP problems for the country.

   (iv) It finds market for its surplus production.

   Codes :

   (A) (i), (ii), (iii) and (iv)

   (B) (ii), (iii) and (iv)

   (C) (iii) and (iv)

   (D) Only (iv)

71. Donation to National Children's Fund will come in which of the following deduction under Sec. 80G of Income Tax Act, 1961.

   (A) 100 percent deduction without any qualifying limit.

   (B) 50 percent deduction without any qualifying limit.

   (C) 100 percent deduction subject to qualifying limit.

   (D) 50 percent deduction subject to qualifying limit.

72. If the taxable income of a domestic company for the Assessment Year 2011-12 is ₹ 9,00,000, its tax liability will be

   (A) ₹ 2,76,800   (B) ₹ 2,78,100

   (C) ₹ 3,70,800   (D) ₹ 3,70,880

73. Unabsorbed depreciation which could not be setoff in the same assessment year, can be carried forward upto

   (A) 4 years

   (B) 8 years

   (C) 10 years

   (D) Indefinite period

74. If the book profits of a partnership firm is ₹ 1,10,000, the remuneration admissible to working partners under Sec.40(b) of the Income Tax Act, 1961 is

   (A) ₹ 1,10,000

   (B) ₹ 1,50,000

   (C) ₹ 99,000

   (D) None of the above

75. Which of the following expenses is inadmissible while computing income from other sources ?

   (A) Interest paid on amounts borrowed to meet tax liabilities.

   (B) Collection charges paid to the banker or any other person to collect interest/dividend.

   (C) Interest on loan taken to invest in securities.

   (D) Depreciation on let-out machinery and plant.

UGC - NET JUNE 2013

ANSWER KEYS (PAPER III)

SUBJECT : 08 (Commerce)

Qus. No.	Ans.	Qus. No.	Ans.	Qus. No.	Ans.
1	D	26	B	51	D
2	B	27	A	52	A
3	B	28	B	53	B
4	A	29	C	54	B
5	D	30	C	55	C
6	B	31	C	56	B
7	B	32	C	57	A
8	D	33	B	58	D
9	C	34	C	59	D
10	D	35	B	60	C
11	C	36	A	61	B
12	A	37	A	62	B
13	B	38	D	63	C
14	B	39	C	64	A
15	B	40	A	65	C
16	A	41	C	66	C
17	B	42	C	67	B
18	D	43	A	68	A
19	C	44	B	69	D
20	A	45	C	70	D
21	A	46	B	71	B
22	D	47	C	72	B
23	B	48	A	73	D
24	C	49	D	74	B
25	D	50	C	75	A

Note: This paper contains fifty (50) objective type questions of two (2) marks each.
All questions are compulsory.

1. GDP at factor cost is
   (A) P(Q) + P(S)
   (B) GDP - IT- S
   (C) GDP + DT + S
   (D) GDP - DT + S

2. Which one is not the main objective of fiscal policy in India?
   (A) To increase liquidity in the economy.
   (B) To promote price stability.
   (C) To minimize the inequalities of income and wealth.
   (D) To promote unemployment opportunities.

3. Which one is not an element of internal environment?
   (A) Marketing capability.
   (B) Operational capability.
   (C) Money and capital market.
   (D) Personal capability.

4. Out of the following, which four benefits are available to host countries from MNCs?
   i.   Transfer of Technology.
   ii.   Learning of business mannerism.
   iii.   Strategic information sharing.
   iv.   Creation of jobs
   v.   Entertainment
   vi.   Better utilization of resources.
   vii.   Enhancing social contacts.
   viii. Improved competition in local economy.
   (A) i, iii, v, vii
   (B) ii, iv, vi, viii
   (C) i, iv, vi, viii

   (D) iii, vi, vii, viii

5. Environmental degradation does not consist of
   (A) Land degradation and soil erosion.
   (B) Problem of overgrazing and ecological degradation.
   (C) Floods.
   (D) None of the above.

6. Which one of the following concepts is used as fund in the preparation of Fund Flow Statement?
   (A) Current Assets.
   (B) Working Capital.
   (C) Cash.
   (D) All Financial Resources.

7. Window dressing is prohibited due to
   (A) Conservative Convention.
   (B) Convention of Disclosure.
   (C) Convention of Materiality.
   (D) Arrear of Book Accounts.

8. **Assertion (A):** Ratio analysis is one of the tools employed to know the financial health of a concern.
   Reason (R): Ratio analysis is not the only technique to take investment decision.
   (A) Both (A) and (R) are true and (R) is the correct explanation of (A).
   (B) Both (A) and (R) are true and (R) is incorrect explanation of (A).
   (C) (A) is true, but (R) is false.
   (D) (A) is false, but (R) is true.

9. Which of the following relate to measures of non-financial performance of a concern?
   i. Customer satisfaction
   ii. Business process improvement
   iii. Economic value added
   iv. Learning organization
   Choose the right combination
   (A) i, iii, ii, iv
   (B) ii, iv, iii
   (C) iv, i, iii
   (D) i, ii, iv

10. Consider the following parties:
   i. Secured creditors
   ii. Unsecured creditors
   iii. Partners who have granted loans
   iv. Partners who have contributed over and above profit sharing ratio.
   Arrange them in correct sequence in the event of dissolution of a firm.
   (A) ii, i, iii, iv
   (B) i, ii, iii, iv
   (C) i, ii, iv, iii
   (D) ii, i, iv, iii

11. Which kind of economics explains the phenomenon of cause and effect relationship?
   (A) Normative
   (B) Positive
   (C) Micro
   (D) Macro

12. **Assertion (A):** Marginal cost and differential cost do not convey the same meaning in all the circumstances.
   Reason (R): Differential cost increases or decreases due to change in fixed cost.
   (A) (A) is true, but (R) is false.
   (B) (A) is false, but (R) is true.

(C) Both (A) and (R) are true and (R) is the correct explanation of (A).
(B) Both (A) and (R) are true and (R) is incorrect explanation of (A).

13. Consider the following:
   i. Pricing objectives
   ii. Pricing methods
   iii. Pricing strategies
   iv. Pricing decisions
   (A) i, iii, ii, iv
   (B) i, iv, iii, ii
   (C) ii, i, iv, iii
   (D) iv, ii, iii, i

14. A commodity is used for multiple purposes, then the demand for it is known as
   (A) Joint Demand
   (B) Composite Demand
   (C) Direct Demand
   (D) Autonomous Demand

15. Match List - I with List – II and select the correct answer.

	List I		List II
1.	Administered price	a.	Landed cost of imports
2.	Parity pricing	b.	Liberalized economy
3.	Competitive price	c.	Public enterprise
4.	Discriminating Price	d.	Fixed by Govt.

Codes:

	a	b	c	d
(A)	1	2	3	4
(B)	2	3	4	1
(C)	3	4	2	1
(D)	4	2	1	3

16. Sample design involves the following:
    i. Sampling unit
    ii. Size of samples
    iii. Type of universe
    iv. Source list
    v. Sampling procedure
    (A) i, ii, iii, iv, v
    (B) iii, iv, i, ii, v
    (C) iii, i, iv ii, v
    (D) iii, v, i, iv, ii

17. Which one of the following is not a measure of dispersion?
    (A) Quartile
    (B) Range
    (C) Mean Deviation
    (D) Standard Deviation

18. If $b_{xy} = 0.25$ and $b_{yx} = 0.64$, correlation coefficient is
    (A) 0.16
    (B) 0.40
    (C) 0.89
    (D) 0.30

19. Sturge's rule is used to find out directly
    (A) Number of classes in a continuous distribution
    (B) Size of class limits
    (C) Direction of the classification
    (D) None of the above

20. Which of the following software has applications in both Mathematics and Statistics?
    (A) SPSS
    (B) SAS
    (C) R
    (D) None of the above

21. Match the following:
    a. The Practice of   1. Henry Fayol
       Management
    b. Philosophy of   2. F. W. Taylor
       Management
    c. Scientific   3. Oliver Sheldon
       Management
    d. General and   4. Peter F. Drucker
       Industrial
       Administration

    Codes:

	a	b	c	d
(A)	1	2	3	4
(B)	4	3	2	1
(C)	4	3	1	2
(D)	3	4	2	1

22. **Assertion (A):** All decisions taken through mental process are rational.
    Reason (R): Decision making is a mental process.
    (A) (R) is correct, but (A) is not correct.
    (B) (A) is correct, but (R) is not correct.
    (C) Both (A) and (R) are correct.
    (B) Both (A) and (R) are not correct.

23. Who among the following developed the technique of management by Exception?
    (A) Joseph L. Massie
    (B) Lester R. Bittel
    (C) L. F. Urwick
    (D) Peter F. Drucker

24. Which among the following are parts of job description?
    i. Duties performed
    ii. Job summary
    iii. Job identification
    iv. Supervision given
    v. Delegation of authority
    (A) i, ii, iii, iv
    (B) ii, iii, iv, v
    (C) i, iii, iv, v
    (D) i, ii, iii, v

25. Appointment of independent directors is the part of Corporate Governance as per the
(A) SEBI
(B) Indian Companies Act
(C) Government of India
(D) SBI

26. A method for achieving maximum market response from limited marketing resources by reorganizing the differences in the response characteristics of various parts of the market is known as
(A) Market targeting
(B) Market positioning
(C) Market segmentation
(D) Market strategy

27. Who plays their significant role in distribution of goods when they do not sell to ultimate users or consumers?
(A) Retailer
(B) Wholeseller
(C) Mediator
(D) Commission agent

28. In Marketing Mix, which four P's are covered?
(A) Product, Price, Place, Promotion
(B) Product, Price, Power, Promotion
(C) Product, Price, Penetration, Promotion
(D) Product, Price, Positioning, Promotion

29. Which research includes all types of researches into human motives when it refers to qualitative research designed to uncover the consumer's subconsciousness or hidden motivations?
(A) Motivational Research
(B) Marketing Research
(C) Managerial Research
(D) Price Research

30. False and misleading claims and vulgarity in advertisements do not match with
(A) Aggressive Advertising
(B) Ethics in Advertising
(C) Mass level of advertising
(D) Sales Promotion

31. Arrange the following steps involved in capital budgeting in order of their occurrence:
i.   Project selection
ii. Project appraisal
iii. Project generation
iv. Follow up
v.   Project Execution
(A) ii, iii, i, v, iv
(B) iii, ii, i, v, iv
(C) i, iii, ii, v, iv
(D) i, ii, iii, v, iv

32. Which method does not consider the time value of money?
(A) Net Present Value
(B) Internal Rate of Return
(C) Average Rate of Return
(D) Profitability Index

33. Which formula is used to measure the degree of Operating Leverage?
(A) $\dfrac{EBIT}{Sales}$
(B) $\dfrac{C}{EBIT}$
(C) $\dfrac{EBIT}{EBT}$
(D) $\dfrac{EBIT}{C}$

34. Which one is more appropriate for cost of retained earnings?
(A) Weighted Average Cost of Capital
(B) Opportunity cost to the firm

(C) Expected rate of return by the investor

(D) None of the above

35. Match the following with the most suitable option

a.	Modigliani-Miller Approach	1.	Commercial Paper
b.	Net Operating Income Approach	2.	Working Capital
c.	Short Term Money Market Instruments	3.	Capital Structure
d.	Factoring	4.	Arbitrage

Codes:

	a	b	c	d
(A)	4	3	1	2
(B)	3	4	1	2
(C)	3	2	1	4
(D)	4	2	3	1

36. During which plan was the National Apprenticeship Training Scheme introduced?

(A) 1st Five Year Plan

(B) 2nd Five Year Plan

(C) 4th Five Year Plan

(D) Annual Plans

37. Match the following:

a.	An ordinary person does not want to work on his own	1.	Hierarchy Theory
b.	An individual is willing to work on his own	2.	Hygiene Theory
c.	Motivational Factors	3.	X-Theory
d.	Esteem Needs	4.	Y-Theory

Codes:

	a	b	c	d
(A)	1	2	3	4
(B)	3	4	1	2
(C)	1	4	2	3
(D)	3	4	2	1

38. Arrange the following staffing procedures in the correct sequence:

i. Determining sources of personnel supply

ii. Preparing personnel specifications

iii. Selection of personnel

iv. Determining personnel characteristics

(A) ii, i, iv, iii

(B) i, ii, iii, iv

(C) ii, i, iii, iv

(D) ii, iii, i, iv

39. Which among the following is not a voluntary method for prevention and settlement of disputes?

(A) Collective Bargaining

(B) Standing Orders

(C) Joint Consultation

(D) Works Committee

40. **Statement – I:** It is no better to pay employees for little than to pay too much.

Statement – II: Competent employees will remain competent forever.

(A) Statement I is true, but II is false.

(B) Statement II is true, but I is false.

(C) Both statements I and II are true.

(D) Both statements I and II are false.

41. Match the following:

a.	Credit Control	1.	MCA
b.	Corporate Control	2.	SEBI
c.	IPO Control	3.	IRDA
d.	ULIP Control	4.	RBI

Codes:

	a	b	c	d
(A)	4	2	3	1
(B)	4	1	2	3
(C)	2	3	4	1
(D)	4	1	3	2

42. Which one among the following has not started Commercial Banking?
(A) SIDBI
(B) IDBI
(C) ICICI
(D) UTI

43. What is OTP in credit card transactions?
(A) Odd Transaction Password
(B) Owner's Trading Passcode
(C) One Time Password
(D) One Time Pincode

44. The powers of Controller of Capital Issues of India is now shifted to
(A) Ministry of Finance
(B) SEBI
(C) AMFI
(D) Ministry of Corporate Affairs

45. The success of E-banking depends upon:
i. Multi - layer Security System
ii. Risk and Surveillance Management
iii. Updated Flawless Softwares
iv. Stringent Legal Frame-work
(A) i and ii
(B) i, ii and iii
(C) ii,iii and iv
(D) i, ii, iii and iv

46. International liquidity comprises which four of the following?
i. Gold held by Central Banks
ii. Gold held by families

iii. Forex Reserve held by Commercial Banks
iv. Mineral Wealth
v. SDRs
vi. Borrowing facilities
vii. NRIs FDRs
viii. Credit facilities available under SWAP
(A) i, ii, iii, iv
(B) ii, iii, iv, viii
(C) i, iii, v, viii
(D) iii, iv, vii, viii

47. Which among the following are important bodies of WTO?
i. Dispute Settlement Body
ii. NAFTA
iii. Trade Policy Review Body
iv. ASEAN
v. Council for Trade in Goods
vi. IBRD
vii. Council for Trade related aspects of Intellectual Property Rights
viii. GATT
(A) i, ii, iii, iv
(B) ii, iii, iv, v
(C) i, iii, v, vii
(D) iv, v, vi, viii

48. Which one is not the source of External Finance?
(A) WTO Funds
(B) World Bank Group
(C) Export Credit
(D) Foreign Direct Investment

49. Which one is called Bretton-Wood Twins?
(A) IBRD and IDA
(B) IMF and IFC
(C) IMF and IBRD
(D) IDA and IFC

50. UNCTAD stands for

(A) United Nations Committee on Tariff and Development

(B) United Nations Conference on Trade and Deficit

(C) United Nations Conference on Trade and Development

(D) Union of Nations Cause for Trade and Development

UGC - NET DECEMBER 2012

ANSWER KEYS (PAPER II)

SUBJECT : 08 (Commerce)

Qus. No.	Ans.	Qus. No.	Ans.
1	B	26	C
2	A	27	B
3	C	28	A
4	C	29	A
5	D	30	B
6	D	31	B
7	B	32	C
8	A	33	B
9	D	34	B
10	B	35	A
11	B	36	B
12	C	37	D
13	B	38	A
14	B	39	D
15	B	40	A
16	C	41	D
17	A	42	A
18	B	43	C
19	A	44	B
20	D	45	B
21	B	46	C
22	A	47	C
23	B	48	A
24	A	49	C
25	A	50	C

COMMERCE
PAPER – III

Note : This paper contains **seventy five (75)** objective type questions of **two (2)** marks each. **All** questions are compulsory.

1. In accounting, profit prior to incorporation is treated as
   (A) Revenue Reserve
   (B) Secret Reserve
   (C) Capital Reserve
   (D) General Reserve

2. Receipts and Payments Account is prepared by
   (A) Manufacturing concerns
   (B) Non-Trading concerns
   (C) Trading concerns
   (D) Companies registered under Companies Act, 1956

3. Owners equity stands for
   (A) Fixed Assets minus Fixed Liabilities.
   (B) Fixed Assets minus Current Liabilities.
   (C) Current Assets minus Fixed Liabilities.
   (D) Total Assets minus Total outside Liabilities.

4. When the Debt Turnover Ratio is 4, what is the average collection period ?
   (A) 5 months   (B) 4 months
   (C) 3 months   (D) 2 months

5. Which of the following will result into sources of funds ?
   (i) Increase in current assets
   (ii) Decrease in current assets
   (iii) Increase in current liabilities
   (iv) Decrease in current liabilities
   Codes :
   (A) (i) and (iv)   (B) (ii) and (iii)
   (C) (i) and (iii)   (D) (ii) and (iv)

6. In marginal costing, contribution is equal to
   (A) Sales – Fixed cost
   (B) Sales – Variable cost
   (C) Sales – Profit
   (D) Sales – Variable Cost + Fixed cost

7. The funds available with a company after paying all claims including tax and dividend is called
   (A) Net Profit
   (B) Net Operating Profit
   (C) Capital Profit
   (D) Retained Earnings

8. **Assertion (A) :** Accounting information refers to only events which are concerned with business firm.
   Reason (R) : Accounting information is presented in financial statements.
   Codes :
   (A) (A) is correct, but (R) is wrong.
   (B) Both (A) and (R) are correct.
   (C) (A) is wrong, but (R) is correct.
   (D) Both (A) and (R) are wrong.

9. When average cost is declining
   (A) Marginal cost must be declining.
   (B) Marginal cost must be above average cost.
   (C) Marginal cost must be below average cost.
   (D) Marginal cost must be rising.

10. ABC Ltd. has declared 40% dividend. Which one of the following does it mean ?
   (A) The company has declared 40% of net profit as dividend.
   (B) The company has declared 40% of profits after tax as dividend.
   (C) The company will provide dividend 40% on issued capital.
   (D) The company will provide dividend 40% on paid-up capital.

11. The main objective of Accounting Standards is
   (A) To prepare the accounting reports which is easily understood by common man.
   (B) To comply with the legal formalities.
   (C) To harmonise the diversified accounting practices.
   (D) To comply with the requirements of the International Accounting Standards (IAS).

12. Given below are two statements :
   I. Activity ratios show where the company is going.
   II. Balance Sheet ratios show how the company stand.
   Codes :
   (A) I is correct, but II is wrong.
   (B) Both I and II are correct.
   (C) I is wrong, but II is correct.
   (D) Both I and II are wrong.

13. Income and Expenditure Account of non-profit organisation is a
   (A) Real Account
   (B) Nominal Account
   (C) Personal Account
   (D) Representative Personal Account

14. Which of the following statements are correct ?
   I. Inventory includes raw materials, finished goods and work – in – progress.
   II. Inventory is a part of the working capital.
   III. Inventory includes goods likely to be purchased.
   Codes :
   (A) I, II and III
   (B) II and III
   (C) I and III
   (D) I and II

15. If the current ratio is 2 : 1 and working capital is ₹ 60,000, what is the value of the Current Assets ?
   (A) ₹ 60,000
   (B) ₹ 1,00,000
   (C) ₹ 1,20,000
   (D) ₹ 1,80,000

16. Which of the following steps of purchase decision process is in sequence ?
   1. Problem recognition
   2. Search for alternatives
   3. Evaluation of alternatives
   4. Purchase action
   5. Post purchase action
   Codes :
   (A) 1, 3, 2, 4, 5
   (B) 1, 2, 4, 3, 5
   (C) 2, 1, 3, 5, 4
   (D) 1, 2, 3, 4, 5

17. What is customer value ?
   (A) Ratio between the customer's perceived benefits and the resources used to obtain these benefits.
   (B) Excess of satisfaction over expectation.
   (C) Post purchase dissonance
   (D) None of the above

18. Match the items of List – I with items of List – II.

	List – I		List – II
a.	The silent mental repetition of information.	1.	Encoding
b.	The process by which we select a word or visual image to represent a perceived object.	2.	Rehearsal
c.	Where information is kept temporarily before further processing.	3.	Working Memory
d.	The stage of real memory in which information is processed and held for just a brief period.	4.	Store house

Codes :

	a	b	c	d
(A)	2	1	4	3
(B)	1	2	3	4
(C)	3	2	1	4
(D)	4	3	2	1

19. Fill in the blanks :

	Statements		Alternatives
a.	Loyal customers ____ products.	1.	Less attention
b.	Loyal customers are ____ sensitive.	2.	Cheaper
c.	Loyal customers pay ____ to competitor's advertising.	3.	Less price
d.	Serving existing customer is ____	4.	Buy more

Codes :

	a	b	c	d
(A)	3	1	2	4
(B)	4	3	1	2
(C)	2	1	3	4
(D)	4	3	2	1

20. **Assertion (A)** : High customer expectations lead to dissatisfaction as product performance never matches them.

    Reason (R) : Product performance is always customer specific.

    Codes :

    (A) Both (A) and (R) are correct.

    (B) Both (A) and (R) are incorrect.

    (C) (A) is correct, but (R) is incorrect.

    (D) (R) is correct, but (A) is incorrect.

21. Under which concept of marketing do you find greater emphasis on techniques and technology of production ?

    (A) Product

    (B) Selling

    (C) Marketing

    (D) None

22. Which is used for short-term sales achievement ?

    (A) Personal selling

    (B) Advertising

    (C) Sales Promotion

    (D) Public Relations

23. Public distribution system relates to

    (A) Marketing system

    (B) Retailing system

    (C) Industrial system

    (D) Selling system

24. Who do buy more, complain less, spread positive word of mouth, ensure a large customer base and repeat business ?

    (A) Satisfied customers

    (B) Delighted customers

    (C) Industrial customers

    (D) None of the above

25. There are impulses which persuade a customer to buy certain products without evaluating the positive and negative value of the same.

(A) Emotional motives

(B) Blind motives

(C) Egoistic motives

(D) All the above

26. Which subject is relevant to the study of consumer behaviour ?

(A) Economics

(B) Psychology

(C) Sociology

(D) All the above

27. Find an incorrect statement.

(A) Consumer attitude can be summarized as evaluation of an object.

(B) Attitudes are learned.

(C) Attitudes are synonymous with behaviour.

(D) Attitudes have motivational qualities.

28. Who is considered Father of Scientific Management ?

(A) Peter Drucker

(B) F.W. Taylor

(C) Victor Vroom

(D) Henry Fayol

29. Who did give the concept of hierarchy of needs ?

(A) Fredrick Herzberg

(B) Victor Vroom

(C) Douglas Mcgregor

(D) A.H. Maslow

30. **Assertion (A) :** Management is a continuous process.

Reason (R) : Managers first plan, then organise and finally perform the function of controlling.

Codes :

(A) Both (A) and (R) are correct and (R) is correct explanation of (A).

(B) Both(A) and (R) are correct, but (R) is not a correct explanation of (A).

(C) (A) is correct, but (R) is incorrect.

(D) (A) is incorrect, but (R) is correct.

31. Induction of employees relates to

(A) Organisational awareness

(B) Training programme

(C) Introduction

(D) Assignment of duties

32. 'Kinked' demand curve is related with

(A) Monopoly

(B) Discriminating monopoly

(C) Oligopoly

(D) Perfect competition

33. Who is not associated with HRM ?

(A) Michael J Jucius

(B) Dale Yodar

(C) Edvoin B. Flippo

(D) K.K. Devit

34. Merit rating is not known as

(A) Efficiency Rating

(B) Service Rating

(C) Job Rating

(D) Experience Rating

35. Match the items of List – I with the items of List – II.

	List – I		List – II
a.	FEMA	1.	1986
b.	Indian Factories Act	2.	1999
c.	Industrial Dispute Act	3.	1948
d.	Consumer Protection Act	4.	1947

Codes :

	a	b	c	d
(A)	4	2	3	1
(B)	3	1	2	4
(C)	2	3	4	1
(D)	1	4	3	2

36. If price of any commodity decreases by 20% and the demand for that commodity increases by 40%, then elasticity of demand would be

(A) perfectly elastic

(B) perfectly inelastic

(C) unit elastic

(D) highly elastic

37. Which of the following statements is true ?

(A) In case of inferior goods, the income effect is negative, although the substitution effect is positive.

(B) In inferior goods, the income and substitution effects are positive.

(C) In inferior goods, the income and substitution effects are negative.

(D) In case of inferior goods, the income effect is positive although the substitution effect is negative.

38. In perfect competition, the demand curve of a firm is

(A) Vertical

(B) Horizontal

(C) Positively sloped

(D) Negatively sloped

39. Which one is not non-financial incentive ?

(A) Additional bonus on minimum wasteful expenditure.

(B) Permanent job.

(C) Participatory decision making.

(D) Recognition of individuality.

40. HRM does not include

(A) job evaluation

(B) performance appraisal

(C) sales promotion

(D) job enrichment

41. The term (1-B) is called

(A) Level of the test

(B) Power of the test

(C) Size of the test

(D) None of the above

42. The area under normal distribution covered within $\mu \pm 3\sigma$ limits is

(A) 0.6827

(B) 0.9545

(C) 0.9973

(D) 1.0000

43. Sampling distribution of mean is very close to the standard normal distribution when
    (A) Population is normally distributed.
    (B) Population is not normally distributed, but sample size is large.
    (C) Both (A) and (B).
    (D) Neither (A) nor (B).

44. If the value of co-efficient of determination is 0.64, what is the value of coefficient of correlation ?
    (A) 0.40
    (B) 0.80
    (C) 0.08
    (D) 0.04

45. Which one of the following is not a source of conflict in project ranking in capital budgeting decision as per NPV and IRR ?
    (A) Independent Investment Project
    (B) No Capital Budget Constraints
    (C) No time disparity
    (D) None of the above

46. Match the following :

List – I	List – II
a. Trade policy	1. Economic conditions
b. Trade flows	2. Economic policies
c. Price trends	3. Global linkages
d. Internal sectoral linkages	4. Structure and Nature of Economy

    Codes :

	a	b	c	d
(A)	3	1	2	4
(B)	2	3	1	4
(C)	1	2	3	4
(D)	1	2	4	3

47. Which one of the following is not a benefit of privatisation ?
    (A) Encourage entrepreneurship.
    (B) Concentration of economic power.
    (C) Better management of enterprise.
    (D) Freedom from bureaucracy.

48. 'BOLT' system in the Indian Securities market is related to
    (A) National Stock Exchange
    (B) Bombay Stock Exchange
    (C) Over the Counter Exchange of India
    (D) Multi Commodity Stock Exchange

49. Which one of the following is not a money market instrument ?
    (A) Commercial paper
    (B) Participatory certificates
    (C) Warrants
    (D) Treasury Bills

50. Which one is related with micro-financing ?
    (A) SHG
    (B) Anganwadi workers
    (C) Women Entrepreneurs
    (D) None of the above

51. Which one of the following is not an element of internal environment ?
    (A) Mission/Objectives
    (B) Human Resources
    (C) Customers
    (D) Shareholders' values

52. The presence of fixed costs in the total cost structure of a firm results into

(A) Financial leverage

(B) Operating leverage

(C) Super leverage

(D) None of the above

53. "The cost of capital declines when the degree of financial leverage increases." Who advocated it ?

(A) Net operating income approach

(B) Net income approach

(C) Modigliani-Miller approach

(D) Traditional approach

54. A view that the dividend policy of a firm has a bearing on share valuation advocated by James E. Walter is based on which one of the following assumptions ?

(A) Retained earnings is only source of financing.

(B) Cost of capital does not remain constant.

(C) Return on investment fluctuates.

(D) All the above.

55. Match the following :

List – I	List – II
a. Matching approach	1. Dividend Policy
b. Structural ratios	2. Inventory Management
c. Ordering quantity	3. Financing Working Capital
d. Bonus shares	4. Capital Structure

Codes :

	a	b	c	d
(A)	1	2	3	4
(B)	3	4	1	2
(C)	3	4	2	1
(D)	2	1	3	4

56. **Assertion (A) :** Operating style of the international business can be spread to the entire globe.

Reason (R) : The style is limited to the internal economy only.

Codes :

(A) Both (A) and (R) are true.

(B) (A) is true, but (R) is false.

(C) (A) is false, but (R) is true.

(D) Both (A) and (R) are false.

57. The Comparative Cost Advantage Theory was given by

(A) David Ricardo

(B) Adam Smith

(C) Raymond Vernon

(D) Michael E. Porter

58. The companies globalise their operations through different means :

(A) Exporting directly

(B) Licensing/Franchising

(C) Joint ventures

(D) All the above

59. The components of W.T.O. are

(A) Ministerial Conference

(B) Disputes Settlement Body

(C) Director General

(D) All the above

60. India is not associated with

(A) SAARC

(B) NAFTA

(C) BRICS

(D) None of the above

61. Which one of the following is true statement ?

    (A) A balance of trade deals with export and import of invisible items only.

    (B) A balance of payment deals with both visible and invisible items.

    (C) The current account is not a component of balance of payment.

    (D) All the above.

62. SDRs are popularly known as

    (A) Currency Notes

    (B) Paper Gold

    (C) Silver Coin

    (D) Gold Coin

63. Which one is not international institution ?

    (A) IMF

    (B) IDA

    (C) IBRD

    (D) TRAI

64. **Assertion (A) :** Indent may be open or closed. Open indent does not specify the price and other details of the goods. The closed indent specifies the brand, price, number, packing, shipping mode, insurance, etc.

    Reason (R) : This is required as a part of export procedures.

    Codes :

    (A) Both (A) and (R) are correct.

    (B) Both (A) and (R) are not correct.

    (C) (A) is true, but (R) is false.

    (D) (R) is true, but (A) is false.

65. Which one of the statements is not true ?

    (A) Institutional infrastructure facilitates market intelligence.

    (B) STC is the chief canalizing agent for export and import of agricultural products.

    (C) IIPO organizes trade fairs and exhibitions.

    (D) Letter of credit does not indicate that the bank will pay the value of imports to the exporter.

66. Match the items of List – I with items of List – II.

	List – I		List – II
a.	Selective credit control	1.	Consumer Credit Regulation
b.	Encourage credit for desirable use	2.	Cash Reserve Ratio
c.	Quantitative credit control	3.	Variation in Margin
d.	Bank Rate	4.	Re-discounting Rate

    Codes :

	a	b	c	d
(A)	4	2	3	1
(B)	3	1	2	4
(C)	1	3	2	4
(D)	2	1	3	4

67. **Assertion (A) :** Use of paper money is replaced by plastic money. The future will see the electronic money clearance through satellite networking.

    Reason (R) : RBI is encouraging e-banking.

    Codes :

    (A) (A) is false, but (R) is true.

    (B) (A) is true, but (R) is false.

    (C) Both (A) and (R) are false.

    (D) Both (A) and (R) are true.

68. Which one is not Finance Company ?

(A) Hire-Purchase Finance Company

(B) IRDA

(C) Mutual Benefit Finance Companies

(D) Loan Companies

69. The Securities and Exchange Board of India was not entrusted with the function of

(A) Investor Protection.

(B) Ensuring Fair practices by companies.

(C) Promotion of efficient services by brokers.

(D) Improving the earnings of equity holders.

70. Which one is not Non-Marketable securities ?

(A) Corporate Securities

(B) Bank Deposits

(C) Deposits with Companies

(D) Post Office Certificates and Deposits

71. Minimum Alternative Tax (MAT) under Sec.115 JB of the Income Tax Act is applicable on

(A) Partnership firm

(B) Association of persons

(C) Certain companies

(D) All types of companies

72. For the Assessment Year 2011-12, deduction under Sec. 80G is available without any limit but at the rate of 50% on

(A) Prime Minister's National Relief Fund.

(B) National Foundation for communal Harmany.

(C) Jawahar Lal Nehru Memorial Fund.

(D) Chief Minister Relief Fund.

73. Interest on capital paid by a firm to its partners, under the Income Tax Act, 1961, is allowed

(A) 6%

(B) 12%

(C) 15%

(D) 18%

74. Under capital gains head of the Income Tax Act, the income from sale of Household Furniture is

(A) Taxable Income

(B) Capital Gain

(C) Revenue Gain

(D) Exempted Income

75. Under Section 80E of the Income Tax Act, 1961 deduction in respect of payment of interest on loan taken for higher education shall be allowed up to

(A) ₹ 10,000

(B) ₹ 15,000

(C) ₹ 20,000

(D) Without any limit

UGC - NET DECEMBER 2012

ANSWER KEYS (PAPER III)

SUBJECT : 08 (Commerce)

Qus. No.	Ans.	Qus. No.	Ans.	Qus. No.	Ans.
1	C	26	D	51	C
2	B	27	C	52	B
3	D	28	B	53	B
4	C	29	D	54	A
5	B	30	A	55	C
6	B	31	C	56	B
7	D	32	C	57	S
8	B	33	D	58	D
9	C	34	C	59	D
10	D	35	C	60	B
11	C	36	D	61	B
12	B	37	A	62	B
13	B	38	B	63	D
14	D	39	A	64	C
15	C	40	C	65	D
16	D	41	B	66	B
17	A	42	C	67	D
18	A	43	C	68	B
19	B	44	B	69	D
20	B	45	D	70	A
21	D	46	B	71	C
22	C	47	B	72	C
23	B	48	B	73	B
24	B	49	C	74	D
25	D	50	A	75	D

June-2012

COMMERCE
Paper – II

Note : This paper contains **fifty (50)** objective type questions, each question carrying **two (2)** marks. Attempt **all** the questions.

1. Which of the following denote the structural changes in Indian economy ?
   (A) Primary sector contribution has gone down.
   (B) Service sector contribution has gone up.
   (C) Secondary sector has not changed much.
   (D) All of the above

2. Broad Money has to be sensitized through :
   (A) CRR
   (B) SLR
   (C) Repo Rate
   (D) All of the above

3. Which one is not an element of legal environment ?
   (A) Act of Parliamentarians in Lok Sabha
   (B) Indian Contract Act, 1872
   (C) Indian Partnership Act, 1932
   (D) Negotiable instruments Act, 1881

4. Out of the following, which are four dimensions of Human Development Index ?
   (i) Life Expectancy
   (ii) Literacy Level
   (iii) Success Rate of Marriages
   (iv) Standard of Living
   (v) Crime Rate
   (vi) Corruption Level
   (vii) Economic Entitlement
   (viii) Foreign Visits
   Codes :
   (A) (i), (ii), (vi) and (viii)
   (B) (i), (ii), (iv) and (vii)
   (C) (ii), (iii), (vi) and (vii)
   (D) (iii), (v), (vii) and (viii)

5. Public Enterprise is defined as
   (A) An organisation run by joint efforts of Centre and State Governments.
   (B) An organisation which caters to the needs relating to public utilities.
   (C) An organisation in which capital is invested by public.
   (D) An organisation owned and managed by public authorities for definite set of public purposes.

6. Match List-I with List-II and select the correct answer :

	List – I		List – II
(i)	Measurement of income	(a)	Accrues to the equity of owners
(ii)	Recognition of expense	(b)	Recognition of revenue
(iii)	Basis of realization	(c)	Matching revenue with expenses
(iv)	Identification of revenue	(d)	Accounting period

   Codes :

	(i)	(ii)	(iii)	(iv)
(A)	(a)	(b)	(c)	(d)
(B)	(b)	(a)	(c)	(d)
(C)	(c)	(d)	(a)	(b)
(D)	(c)	(d)	(b)	(a)

7. Consider the following items :
   (i) Debentures
   (ii) Prepaid rent
   (iii) Interest accrued
   (iv) Bank overdraft
   Which of them are current liabilities ?
   (A) (i), (ii), (iii) and (iv)
   (B) (iv)
   (C) (ii), (iii) and (iv)
   (D) (i), (ii) and (iii)

8. Conversion cost is the sum of
   (A) Indirect wages and factory overhead
   (B) Direct wages, direct expenses and factory overhead
   (C) Direct material cost and indirect wages
   (D) Prime cost and selling & distribution overhead

9. (A) **Assertion :** Premium received on issue of shares is credited to share premium account but not to Profit and Loss account.

   (R) **Reasoning :** Since share premium is not a trading profit, it is not distributed to shareholders.
   (A) Both (A) and (R) are true but (R) is not correct explanation to (A).
   (B) (A) is false but (R) is correct.
   (C) Both (A) and (R) are true and (R) is correct explanation of (A).
   (D) (A) is correct but (R) is false.

10. Consider the following :
    (i) Basic defensive and interval ratio
    (ii) Current ratio
    (iii) Superquick ratio
    (iv) Quick ratio
    Arrange these ratios in sequence to reflect the liquidity in descending order.
    (A) (ii), (iv), (iii) and (i)
    (B) (i), (ii), (iv) and (iii)
    (C) (iv), (ii), (iii) and (i)
    (D) (iii), (iv), (i) and (ii)

11. Normally Demand curve slopes
    (A) Upward
    (B) Downward
    (C) Horizontal
    (D) Vertical

12. Which of the following refers to Perfect Competition ?
    (i) There are restrictions on buyers and sellers
    (ii) There are no restrictions on movement of goods
    (iii) There are no restrictions on factors of production
    Correct one is
    (A) only (i) and (ii)
    (B) only (ii) and (iii)
    (C) only (i) and (iii)
    (D) only (i)

13. **Assertion (A):** Total utility will be maximum when marginal utility to price of respective products are equal.
    Reason (R) : Deviation from this situation leads to reduction in maximum utility.
    (A) (A) and (R) are not correct.
    (B) (A) is correct but (R) is not correct.
    (C) (A) and (R) are correct.
    (D) (A) is incorrect, (R) is correct.

14. Match List-I with List-II and select the correct answer.

	List – I		List – II
(i)	Survival	(a)	Economic Objective
(ii)	R.O.I	(b)	Natural Urge
(iii)	Growth	(c)	Business Purpose
(iv)	Innovation	(d)	Primary Objective

    Codes :

	(a)	(b)	(c)	(d)
(A)	(ii)	(iii)	(iv)	(i)
(B)	(ii)	(i)	(iii)	(iv)
(C)	(i)	(ii)	(iii)	(iv)
(D)	(iv)	(iii)	(ii)	(i)

15. Consider the oligopoly models :
    (i) Sweezy's kinked demand curve model
    (ii) Newman and Morgenstern Game Theory model
    (iii) Cournal's duopoly model
    (iv) Baumal's sales maximisation model
    Arrange them in correct sequence as per order of evolution.
    (A) (iv), (iii), (ii), (i)
    (B) (ii), (i), (iii), (iv)
    (C) (iii), (i), (ii), (iv)
    (D) (i), (iii), (ii), (iv)

16. Which of the following is not a restricted random sampling technique ?
    (A) Stratified sampling
    (B) Simple random sampling
    (C) Systematic sampling
    (D) Multistage sampling

17. Classification of respondents only on the basis of gender is an application of
    (A) Ordinal scale
    (B) Nominal scale
    (C) Interval scale
    (D) Ratio scale

18. Karl Pearson's co-efficient of correlation between two variables is
    (A) the product of their standard deviations
    (B) the square root of the product of their regression co-efficients
    (C) the co-variance between the variables
    (D) None of the above

19. Statistical software packages for research in social sciences include
    (A) SPSS
    (B) STATA
    (C) MiniTab
    (D) All of the above

20. F-test is used to test the significance of the differences between/among
    (A) Two sample mean
    (B) More than two samples mean
    (C) Variance of two samples
    (D) (B) and (C)

21. Match the following

	List-I		List-II
(i)	The Practice of Management	(a)	Henry Fayol
(ii)	Philosophy of Management	(b)	F.W. Taylor
(iii)	Scientific Management	(c)	Oliver Sheldon
(iv)	General and Industrial Administration	(d)	Peter F Drucker

    Codes :

	(i)	(ii)	(iii)	(iv)
(A)	(a)	(b)	(c)	(d)
(B)	(d)	(c)	(b)	(a)
(C)	(d)	(c)	(a)	(b)
(D)	(c)	(d)	(b)	(a)

22. Identify the correct sequence of steps involved in planning :
    (i) Selecting the best course of action
    (ii) Establishing the sequence of activities
    (iii) Establishment of objectives
    (iv) Evaluating alternative courses
    (v) Determining alternative courses
    (A) (i), (ii), (iii), (iv) and (v)
    (B) (iii), (v), (iv), (ii) and (i)
    (C) (v), (iv), (iii), (ii) and (i)
    (D) (iii), (v), (iv), (i) and (ii)

23. **Assertion (A) :** One can be sure about future course of actions by making good plans.
    Reasoning (R) : Planning brings certainty in future course of actions of an organisation.
    (A) (R) is correct but (A) is not correct.
    (B) (A) is correct but (R) is not correct.
    (C) Both (A) and (R) are correct.
    (D) Both (A) and (R) are not correct.

24. According to Kieth Devis, which one is not a barrier of communication ?

(A) Physical Barriers

(B) Technological Barriers

(C) Personal Barriers

(D) Linguistic Barriers

25. While establishing relation between Maslow's and Herzberg's theories, which Needs of Hierachy Theory will fall under the Hygiene Factors ?

(A) Self actualisation, esteem and social needs

(B) Esteem, social and safety needs

(C) Social, safety and physiological needs

(D) Only social needs

26. Howard-Sueth model of consumer behaviour is popularly known as

(A) Machine Model

(B) Human Model

(C) Marketing Model

(D) Purchase Model

27. To generate and facilitate any exchange intended to satisfy human needs or wants such that the satisfaction of these wants occur with minimal detrimental impact on the natural environment is known as

(A) Aggressive marketing

(B) Operating marketing

(C) Green marketing

(D) All of the above

28. All the activities involved in selling goods or services directly to final consumers for personal non-business uses are done by

(A) Wholesalers

(B) Retailers

(C) Mediators

(D) Commission Agents

29. To manage a business well is to manage its future and to manage the future is to manage information is termed as

(A) Management information system

(B) Marketing information system

(C) Future information system

(D) General information system

30. DAGMAR approach in marketing is used to measure

(A) Public relations

(B) Advertising results

(C) Selling volume

(D) Consumer satisfaction

31. Which one is not an important objective of Financial Management ?

(A) Profit Maximisation

(B) Wealth Maximisation

(C) Value Maximisation

(D) Maximisation of social benefits

32. Which one refers to cash inflow under payback period method ?

(A) Cash flow before depreciation and taxes

(B) Cash flow after depreciation and taxes

(C) Cash flow after depreciation but before taxes

(D) Cash flow before depreciation and after taxes

33. The concept of present value is based on the :

(A) Principle of compounding

(B) Principle of discounting

(C) (A) and (B)

(D) None of the above

34. Cost of capital from all the sources of funds is called

(A) Specific cost

(B) Composite cost

(C) Implicit cost

(D) Simple Average cost

35. Match the following with most suitable option :

(a) Modigiliani-   (i) Commercial
    Miller   papers
    Approach

(b) Net Operating (ii) Working
    Income   Capital
    Approach   Management

(c) Short term   (iii) Capital
    Money
    Market   Structure
    Instrument

(d) Factoring   (iv) Arbitrage

Codes :

	(a)	(b)	(c)	(d)
(A)	(iv)	(iii)	(i)	(ii)
(B)	(iii)	(iv)	(i)	(ii)
(C)	(iii)	(ii)	(i)	(iv)
(D)	(iii)	(ii)	(iv)	(i)

36. Which four are the factors influencing the Human Resource Management of an organisation ?

(i) Size of workforce

(ii) Employee Expectations

(iii) Composition of workforce

(iv) Political influence

(v) Changes in technology

(A) (i), (ii), (iii) and (iv)

(B) (i),(ii), (iii) and (v)

(C) (i), (ii), (iv) and (v)

(D) (i), (iii), (iv) and (v)

37. **Assertion (A) :** One can not be sure about the quality of appraisal on the basis of length of service.

Reasoning (R) : Initial appraisal and promotional appraisal are done separately and differently since the length of service is different.

(A) (R) is correct but (A) is not correct.

(B) (A) is correct but (R) is not correct.

(C) (A) and (R) both are correct.

(D) (A) and (R) both are not correct.

38. Which of the following are covered under the scope of Human Resource Management ?

(i) Forecasting Human Resource Needs

(ii) Replacement Planning

(iii) Human Resource Dynamics

(iv) Human Resource Development Planning

(v) Human Resource Audit

(A) (i), (iii), (v)

(B) (i), (ii), (iii), (iv)

(C) (iii), (v)

(D) (i), (ii), (iii), (iv), (v)

39. On which of the following, at the initial stage, the Indian IT compaies relying more for getting good IT professionals ?

(A) Job Portals

(B) Placement Agencies

(C) Campus Placement

(D) All of the above

40. **Statement (i) :** Labour always get a major share of productivity gains.

Statement (ii) : Partial stoppage of work by workers amounts to strike.

(A) Statement (i) is true but (ii) is false.

(B) Statement (ii) is true but (i) is false.

(C) Both statements are true.

(D) Both statements are false.

41. Imperial Bank was established on January 27, 1921 on the advise of

(A) J. M. Keynes

(B) Lord Illingworth

(C) King George V

(D) Winston Churchill

42. Read the following events :

(i) Allowing convertibility of rupee at the market rate in the current account

(ii) Nationalisation of general insurance business

(iii) Establishment of IDBI

(iv) Nationalisation of life insurance business

(v) Capital adequacy norms for commercial banks

Arrange the events in the ascending order of their occurrence :

(A) (iv), (iii), (ii), (i), (v)

(B) (v), (iv), (iii), (ii), (i)

(C) (i), (ii), (iii), (v), (iv)

(D) (i), (v), (ii), (iv), (iii)

43. In India, the Commercial Banks are given license of operation by

(A) The Government of India

(B) The Ministry of Finance

(C) Reserve Bank of India

(D) Banking Companies Regulation Act, 1949

44. The provisions of General Reserve in Banking Companies are made keeping in view the provisions of

(A) Indian Companies Act, 1956

(B) Banking Companies Act, 1949

(C) SEBI Act, 1992

(D) Statutory Auditor

45. Which among the following is not true with regard to merchant banker ?

(i) It can accept deposits.

(ii) It can advance loans.

(iii) It can do other banking activities.

(iv) It can be manager to a public issue.

(A) (i), (ii) and (iii)

(B) (ii), (iii) and (iv)

(C) (i), (iii) and (iv)

(D) (ii) and (iv)

46. Balance of Payments can be made favourable if

(A) Exports are increased

(B) Imports are increased

(C) Devaluation of money

(D) (A) and (C)

47. Which one is not an objective of IMF ?

(A) To promote international monetary co-operation

(B) To ensure balanced international trade

(C) To finance productive efforts according to peace-time requirement

(D) To ensure exchange rate stability

48. EPCG denotes

(A) Export Potential and Credit Guarantee

(B) Earning Promotion and Credit Guarantee

(C) Export Promotion and Credit Guarantee

(D) Export Potential and Credit Goods

49. Which one of the following matches correspond to the Member and Observer countries of the SAARC ?

(i) India, Pakistan, Bangladesh, Bhutan, Nepal, Sri Lanka, Afghanistan, Maldive

(ii) Iran, China, Japan, USA, South Korea, European Union

(iii) Pakistan, Nepal, India, Bangladesh, Iran

(iv) UK, USA, North Korea, South Africa

(A) (iii) and (iv)

(B) (ii) and (iv)

(C) (i) and (ii)

(D) (ii) and (iii)

50. Which one is not an international organisation ?

(A) SAARC

(B) ASEM

(C) ASEAN

(D) CBDT

UGC - NET JUNE 2012

ANSWER KEYS (PAPER II)

SUBJECT : 08 (Commerce)

Qus. No.	Ans.	Qus. No.	Ans.
1	D	26	A
2	D	27	C
3	A	28	B
4	B	29	A
5	D	30	D
6	D	31	D
7	B	32	D
8	B	33	B
9	C	34	B
10	A	35	A
11	B	36	C
12	B	37	D
13	C	38	D
14	A	39	C
15	C	40	B
16	B	41	A
17	B	42	A
18	B	43	C
19	D	44	B
20	D	45	A
21	B	46	D
22	D	47	C
23	A	48	C
24	B	49	C
25	C	50	D

COMMERCE
PAPER – III

Note : This paper contains **seventy five** (75) objective type questions of **two** (2) marks each. **All** questions are compulsory.

1. If Opening Stock is ₹ 10,000, Net Purchases ₹ 70,000, Wages ₹ 2,500, Carriage inward ₹ 500 and Closing Stock ₹ 15,000, what is the Manufacturing Cost ?

   (A) ₹ 65,000   (B) ₹ 83,000

   (C) ₹ 68,000   (D) ₹ 73,000

2. What does a high payout ratio indicate ?

   (A) A High Earning Per Share (EPS)

   (B) The management is not ploughing back enough profit.

   (C) The management is ploughing back profit.

   (D) The company is earning high profit.

3. Which one of the following statements is true ?

   (A) Capital expenditure does not affect the profitability of a concern but revenue expenditure does.

   (B) Capital expenditure affects the profitability of a concern directly but revenue expenditure does not.

   (C) Capital expenditure affects the profitability of a concern indirectly but revenue expenditure affects directly.

   (D) Both capital expenditure and revenue expenditure affect the profitability of a concern directly.

4. Identify the true statement of the following :

   (i) Balance Sheet is always prepared from the point of view of the business but not from that of the owners.

   (ii) The financial relationship of the business to its owners is shown in the Balance Sheet.

   (iii) Balance Sheet is always related to a period of time.

   Codes :

   (A) (i) and (ii)

   (B) (ii) and (iii)

   (C) (i) and (iii)

   (D) (i), (ii) and (iii)

5. X and Y are partners in a firm sharing profits in the ratios of 2 : 1. Z is admitted with a 1/3 profit sharing. What will be the new profit sharing ratio of X, Y and Z ?

   (A) 3 : 3 : 3   (B) 4 : 3 : 2

   (C) 4 : 2 : 3   (D) 2 : 3 : 4

6. Which one of the following will not affect the working capital ?

   (A) Realisation of cash from debtors.

   (B) Sale of plant and machinery in cash.

   (C) Issue of equity shares.

   (D) Redemption of debentures.

7. Given below are two statements, one labelled as Assertion (A) and the other labelled as Reason (R) :

Assertion (A) : When a company earns profit prior to its incorporation, it is called capital profit.

Reason (R) : Capital profit cannot be used for distribution as dividend to the shareholders.

In the context of the above two statements, which one of the following is correct ?

Codes :

(A) (A) is correct, but (R) is wrong.

(B) Both (A) and (R) are correct.

(C) (A) is wrong, but (R) is correct.

(D) Both (A) and (R) are wrong.

8. Reconstruction of a company takes place when

(i) the company is undercapitalised

(ii) company has incurred heavy losses which must be written off

(iii) the company is overcapitalised

Which one of the following is correct ?

(A) (i) and (ii) only

(B) (i) and (iii) only

(C) (ii) and (iii) only

(D) All the above

9. Match the items of List – I with the items of List – II and select the correct answer using the codes given below the lists :

List – I	List – II
(a) Leverage Ratio	(i) Short-term solvency
(b) Liquidity Ratio	(ii) Earning capacity
(c) Turnover Ratio	(iii) Relationship between debt and equity
(d) Profitability Ratio	(iv) Efficiency of Asset Management

Codes :

	(a)	(b)	(c)	(d)
(A)	(ii)	(i)	(iv)	(iii)
(B)	(iii)	(ii)	(i)	(iv)
(C)	(iv)	(iii)	(i)	(ii)
(D)	(iii)	(i)	(iv)	(ii)

10. Given below are two statements, one labelled as Assertion (A) and the other labelled as Reason (R) :

Assertion (A) : Sinking fund is a charge against Profit and Loss Account.

Reason (R) : Sinking fund is created for repayment of a long term liability.

In the context of the above two statements, which one of the following is correct ?

Codes :

(A) (A) is correct, but (R) is wrong.

(B) Both (A) and (R) are correct.

(C) (A) is wrong, but (R) is correct.

(D) Both (A) and (R) are wrong.

11. Match List – I with List – II and select the correct answer using the codes given below the lists :

List – I	List – II
(a) Goodwill of a company	(i) Current liability
(b) Overdraft	(ii) Fixed Assets
(c) Preliminary Expenses	(iii) Reserves and Surplus
(d) Premium on Issue of Shares	(iv) Fictitious Assets

Codes :

	(a)	(b)	(c)	(d)
(A)	(ii)	(i)	(iv)	(iii)
(B)	(i)	(ii)	(iv)	(iii)
(C)	(i)	(ii)	(iii)	(iv)
(D)	(ii)	(i)	(iii)	(iv)

12. In India, which of the following is prepared on the guidelines of AS-3 (Accounting Standard – 3) ?

(A) Balance Sheet of a Company

(B) Funds Flow Statement

(C) Cash Flow Statement

(D) Consolidated Financial Statement

13. What is the correct sequence of the following actions required for the preparation of financial accounts ?

(i) Trading accounts

(ii) Making adjusting entries

(iii) Balance Sheet

(iv) Profit and Loss Account

Select the correct answer from the codes given below :

Codes :

(A) (iv), (ii), (i), (iii)

(B) (ii), (iv), (iii), (i)

(C) (ii), (i), (iv), (iii)

(D) (iv), (ii), (iii), (i)

14. The main effect of inflation on the financial statement is

(A) Profits are understated

(B) Overstatement of Assets

(C) Adequacy of funds for replacement of assets

(D) Erosion of capital

15. Present value of future earnings is a model of Human Resources Accounting suggested by

(A) Brauch Lev & ABA Schwartz

(B) Jaggi & Lau

(C) S.K. Chakraborty

(D) Eric Flamhaltz

16. Which element of the promotion mix do wholesalers generally apply to obtain their promotional objective ?

(A) Advertising

(B) Personal Selling

(C) Trade Promotion

(D) Direct Marketing

17. Who has given 'fourteen Principles of Management' ?

(A) Barnard

(B) Henry Fayol

(C) F.W. Taylor

(D) Flemming

18. What is M.B.O ?

(A) Management by Objective

(B) Multiple Business Organisation

(C) Management by Organisation

(D) Multiplicity of Business Operations

19. Match items in List – II with items in List – I :

	List – I		List – II
I.	Mega Marketing	1.	Advertising
II.	Penetration Price	2.	Kotler
III.	Promotion Mix	3.	Low price
IV.	Customer Satisfaction	4.	Post Purchase Behaviour

Codes :

	1	2	3	4
(A)	I	II	III	IV
(B)	III	I	II	IV
(C)	IV	III	II	I
(D)	III	IV	I	II

20. **Statement (A) :** Sales promotion has a strong impact on consumer behaviour in rural India.

Reason (R) : Rural people in India give utmost significance to sales promotion schemes.

Codes :

(A) Statement (A) is correct but Reason (R) is incorrect.

(B) Statement (A) is incorrect, but Reason (R) is correct.

(C) Both Statement (A) and Reason (R) are correct.

(D) Both Statement (A) and Reason (R) are incorrect.

21. Market sub-divided on the basis of behavioural characteristics is called

(A) Segmentation

(B) Aggregation

(C) Precision

(D) None of the above

22. What is mass marketing ?

(A) Offering the same products and marketing mix to all consumers.

(B) Offering variety of products to the entire market.

(C) Offering differentiated products to all customers.

(D) Following concentrated marketing strategy.

23. Which concept of marketing is based on the assumption that superior products sell themselves ?

(A) Production   (B) Marketing

(C) Societal   (D) Product

24. In broader sense, marketing communication includes

(A) Product   (B) Price

(C) Place   (D) All

25. Physical distribution provides

(A) Place utility

(B) Time utility

(C) Place and Time utility

(D) Form utility

26. What is relevant to place variable of marketing mix ?

(A) Branding

(B) Price penetration

(C) Sales personnel motivation

(D) None

27. Find incorrect statement :
    (A) Marketers arouse emotional motives
    (B) Marketers satisfy rational motives
    (C) Marketers formulate different sales promotions for different motives
    (D) None of the above

28. Non-store marketing includes
    (A) Home selling
    (B) V.P.P.
    (C) Vending Machines
    (D) All of the above

29. What is customer delight ?
    (A) Performance equal to expectation
    (B) Performance less than expectation
    (C) Performance more than expectation
    (D) Expectation more than performance

30. Which terms are often used inter-changeably in marketing literature ?
    (A) Concept, method, philosophy
    (B) Concept, approach, technique
    (C) Orientation, concept, philosophy
    (D) Philosophy, system, concept

31. Which one of the following is not the operative function of HRM ?
    (A) Development
    (B) Controlling
    (C) Compensation
    (D) Integration

32. Which one of the following is not in sequence of personnel training procedure ?
    1. Instructor Preparation
    2. Present the task
    3. Try out performance
    4. Training preparation
    5. Follow up
    (A) 1, 2, 3, 4, 5
    (B) 2, 1, 4, 3, 5
    (C) 1, 4, 2, 3, 5
    (D) 3, 1, 2, 5, 4

33. Under which method of performance appraisal one person is compared with all others for the purpose of placing them in a simple order of work ?
    (A) Grading
    (B) Person to Person comparison
    (C) Ranking
    (D) None of the above

34. Which one of the following is not the fundamental procedure that should be considered for the collective bargaining ?
    (A) Prenegotiation phase
    (B) Selection of Negotiators
    (C) Tactic and Strategy of Bargaining
    (D) None of the above

35. **Assertion (A) :** Inevitably the firm must go to the external sources for lower entry jobs.

Reason (R) : For positions where required qualification/ experience are not met.

Codes :

(A) Both (A) and (R) are not correct.

(B) (A) is true, but (R) is false.

(C) (R) is true, but (A) is false.

(D) Both (A) and (R) are correct.

36. Match the following items of List – I and List – II :

List – I	List – II
1. Asbestos	I. Lung Cancer
2. Benzene	II. Cancer
3. Ethylene Disbromide	III. Leukemia
4. Kerosene	IV. Acute Nervous System Depression

Codes :

	I	II	III	IV
(A)	4	2	3	1
(B)	4	3	2	1
(C)	1	3	2	4
(D)	3	4	2	1

37. **Assertion (A) :** Business Economics is tool centrics facilitating decision making in business.

Reason (R) : It provides an analytical understanding of economic activities.

Codes :

(A) Both (A) and (R) are not correct.

(B) Both (A) and (R) are correct.

(C) (A) is true, but (R) is false.

(D) (R) is true, but (A) is false.

38. Demand has the following elements :

(A) Quantity

(B) Price

(C) Time

(D) All the above

39. A perfectly competitive firm attains equilibrium when

(A) AC = AR

(B) MR = MC

(C) MC = AC

(D) TC = TR

40. The purpose of job evaluation is

(A) Fixation of Responsibility

(B) Promotion

(C) Wage Determination

(D) Transfer to a better job

41. For testing of hypothesis $H_0 : M_1 = M_2$ and $H_1 : M_1 < M_2$, the critical value of Z at 5% level of significance when size of sample is more than 30 is

(A) 1.96 (B) 2.32

(C) 1.645 (D) 2.5758

42. Which of the following is the non-random method of selecting samples from a population ?

(A) Stratified Sampling

(B) Quota Sampling

(C) Systematic Sampling

(D) Cluster Sampling

43. If the two regression coefficients are 0.8 and 0.2, then the value of coefficient of correlation is

(A) + 0.16 (B) − 0.40

(C) − 0.16 (D) + 0.40

44. Which one of the following is a relative measure of dispersion ?

(A) Standard deviation

(B) Variance

(C) Coefficient of variation

(D) None of the above

45. **Assertion (A) :** Internal factors of business environment are controllable factors.

Reason (R) : The company can alter or modify such factors to suit the environment.

Codes :

(A) Both (A) and (R) are correct.

(B) (A) is correct, but (R) is incorrect.

(C) Both (A) and (R) are incorrect.

(D) (A) is incorrect.

46. The concept of 'Rolling Plan' in India was introduced by the

(A) BJP Government

(B) Janta Government

(C) Congress Government

(D) All of the above

47. Which one of the following is an obstacle to globalisation ?

(A) Wide base

(B) Niche markets

(C) Obsolescence

(D) Competition

48. 'VSAT' technology is first followed for on-line trading by

(A) BSE (B) OTCEI

(C) NSE (D) ISE

49. Match the following :

List – I Years		List – II Act
(a) 1956	(i)	Consumer Protection Act
(b) 1986	(ii)	Indian Companies Act
(c) 1992	(iii)	Securities and Exchange Board of India
(d) 2002	(iv)	Securitisation Act

Codes :

	(a)	(b)	(c)	(d)
(A)	(ii)	(i)	(iii)	(iv)
(B)	(i)	(ii)	(iii)	(iv)
(C)	(ii)	(iii)	(i)	(iv)
(D)	(i)	(iv)	(iii)	(ii)

50. The flagship project of Government of India launched for generating guaranteed employment in rural areas is known as

   (A) PMRY   (B) MNREGA

   (C) JRY   (D) NREP

51. The conflicts in project ranking in capital budgeting as per NPV and IRR may arise because of

   (A) Size disparity

   (B) Time disparity

   (C) Life disparity

   (D) All the above

52. The degree of financial leverage reflects the responsiveness of

   (A) Operating income to changes in total revenue

   (B) EPS to changes in EBIT

   (C) EPS to changes in total revenue

   (D) None of the above

53. The overall capitalisation rate and the cost of debt remain constant for all degrees of financial leverage is advocated by

   (A) Traditional Approach

   (B) Net Income Approach

   (C) Net Operating Income Approach

   (D) M-M-Approach

54. Which of the following is not included in the assumptions on which Myron Gordon proposed a model on stock valuation ?

   (A) Retained earnings, the only source of financing

   (B) Finite life of the firm

   (C) Taxes do not exist

   (D) Constant rate of return on firm's investment

55. Match the following :

List – I	List – II
(i) Factoring services	(a) Cash Management
(ii) Economic Order Quantity	(b) Receivable Management
(iii) Commercial paper	(c) Inventory Management
	(d) Working Capital Financing

   Codes :

	(i)	(ii)	(iii)
(A)	(a)	(c)	(b)
(B)	(c)	(b)	(a)
(C)	(b)	(c)	(d)
(D)	(b)	(a)	(c)

56. **Assertion (A) :** International business focuses on global resources, opportunities to buy/sell worldwide.

   Reason (R) : The efforts of IMF, World Bank and WTO to liberalise their economies led to globalisation.

   Codes :

   (A) Both (A) and (R) are true.

   (B) Both (A) and (R) are false.

   (C) (A) is true, but (R) is false.

   (D) (A) is false, but (R) is true.

57. Match the items of List – I with items of List – II :

	List – I		List – II
(i)	Wider Market	1.	Modes of Entry
(ii)	Turn key Projects	2.	Goal of International Business
(iii)	Expanding the production capacities	3.	Advantages of International Business
(iv)	Geocentric approach	4.	Stage of Globalisation

Codes :

	(i)	(ii)	(iii)	(iv)
(A)	4	2	3	1
(B)	3	1	2	4
(C)	1	2	3	4
(D)	4	3	2	1

58. BRICS includes

(A) Bhutan, Romania, Indonesia, Chile and South Korea

(B) Brazil, Russia, Indonesia, Chile and Sudan

(C) Brazil, Russia, India, China and South Africa

(D) Britain, Russia, India, Czechoslovakia, Sri Lanka

59. Out of the following, one is not related with WTO :

(A) TRIPS

(B) Ministerial Conference

(C) TRIMS

(D) TRAI

60. Balance of Payment includes components

(A) Current Account, Capital Account, Unilateral Payments Accounts, Official Settlement Account

(B) Revenue Account, P & L Account, Capital Account, Official Account

(C) Trade Account, Activity Account, Revenue Account, Currency Account

(D) Forex Account, Trade Account, Funds Account

61. **Assertion (A) :** International Monetary Fund was set up in 1944.

Reason (R) : To promote international monetary cooperation through a permanent institution which provides machinery for consultation and collaboration on international monetary problems.

Codes :

(A) Both (A) and (R) are false.

(B) Both (A) and (R) are true.

(C) (A) is true, but (R) is false.

(D) (R) is true, but (A) is false.

62. The commercial banks do not perform one function out of the following :

(A) Mobilisation of savings

(B) Giving Loans and Advances

(C) Issuing Currency Notes

(D) Financing Priority Sectors

63. There are two lists of items, match the items of List – I with items of List – II :

List – I	List – II
I. Reserve Bank of India	1. NPA
II. EXIM Bank	2. Facilitating Small Scale Industries
III. SIDBI	3. Credit Control
IV. Capital Adequacy	4. Export/Import Financing

Codes :

	I	II	III	IV
(A)	1	2	3	4
(B)	4	3	2	1
(C)	2	3	4	1
(D)	3	4	2	1

64. One of the items is not related with e-banking :

(A) Demand Draft

(B) SPNS

(C) ECS

(D) ATM

65. **Assertion (A) :** The Treasury Manager uses the derivatives in the Bond market as well as in Forex market.

Reason (R) : It helps risk coverage.

Codes :

(A) Both (A) and (R) are false.

(B) Both (A) and (R) are true.

(C) (A) is true, but (R) is false.

(D) (R) is true, but (A) is false.

66. Factoring and forfeiting have not taken off in the Indian economy due to lack of expertise and experience. One is not included in the factoring services rendered.

(A) Purchase of book debts and receivables.

(B) Prepayment of debts partially or fully

(C) Giving advice

(D) Covering the credit risk of the suppliers

67. Which one is not the form of FDI ?

(A) Purchase of existing assets in foreign currency

(B) New Investment in property, plant, equipment

(C) Making investment in the mutual funds

(D) Transfer of many types of assets

68. Match the items of List – I with items of List – II :

List – I	List – II
1. Measures towards globalization	I. Globalisation
2. Off-shoring	II. FEMA
3. FERA	III. Liberalise the inflow of FDI
4. Mr. Aruthur Dunkel	IV. Uruguay Round

Codes :

	1	2	3	4
(A)	III	I	II	IV
(B)	II	I	III	IV
(C)	IV	II	I	III
(D)	I	II	IV	III

69. Which one of the following is not the advantage of MNCs to the host country ?

(A) Increase in social activity

(B) Increase in economic activity

(C) Utilisation of natural resources

(D) R & D efforts enhanced

70. India suffered from deficit balance both in trade balance and net invisibles, hence, took up a number of steps to manage this problem. Which one is not appropriate for this ?

(A) Export control

(B) Current Account Convertibility

(C) Liberalised Export Policy

(D) Unified Exchange Rate

71. Mr. James, a citizen of U.S., arrived in India for the first time on 1st July, 2010 and left for Nepal on 15th December 2010. He arrived to India again on 1st January 2011 and stayed till the end of the financial year 2010-11. His residential status for the assessment year 2011-12 is

(A) Resident (ordinarily resident)

(B) Not ordinarily resident

(C) Non-resident

(D) None of the above

72. The value of free accommodation in Delhi provided by employer in the private sector is

(A) 10% of salary

(B) 15% of salary

(C) 20% of salary

(D) 25% of salary

73. Which of the following is not a capital asset under capital gains head of income ?

(A) Stock in trade

(B) Goodwill of business

(C) Agricultural Land in Delhi

(D) Jewellery

74. Match the items of List – I with List – II :

List – I	List – II
I. Tax Planning	1. Making suitable arrangement of TDS
II. Tax Avoidance	2. Understatement of Income
III. Tax Evasion	3. Availing deduction under Section 10A of IT Act.
IV. Tax Admini-stration	4. Misinterpreting the provisions of the IT Act

Codes :

	I	II	III	IV
(A)	2	1	4	3
(B)	1	4	3	2
(C)	3	4	2	1
(D)	4	1	3	2

75. Under the Income Tax Act, 1961 unabsorbed depreciation can be carried forward for set-off purpose :

(A) For 4 years

(B) For 5 years

(C) For 8 years

(D) For unspecified period

UGC - NET JUNE 2012

ANSWER KEYS (PAPER III)

SUBJECT : 08 (Commerce)

Qus. No.	Ans.	Qus. No.	Ans.	Qus. No.	Ans.
1	C	26	C	51	D
2	B	27	D	52	B
3	C	28	D	53	C
4	A	29	C	54	B
5	C	30	C	55	C
6	A	31	B	56	A
7	B	32	C	57	B
8	C	33	C	58	C
9	D	34	D	59	D
10	C	35	D	60	A
11	A	36	C	61	B
12	C	37	B	62	C
13	C	38	D	63	D
14	D	39	B	64	A
15	A	40	C	65	B
16	C	41	C	66	C
17	B	42	B	67	C
18	A	43	D	68	A
19	B	44	C	69	A
20	A	45	A	70	A
21	A	46	B	71	B
22	A	47	C	72	B
23	D	48	C	73	A
24	D	49	A	74	C
25	C	50	B	75	D

COMMERCE
Paper – II

Note : This paper contains **fifty (50)** objective type questions, each question carrying **two (2)** marks. Attempt **all** the questions.

1. By which Act, the government checks restrictive trade practices ?

   (A) FEMA - 1999

   (B) Consumer Protection Act, 1986

   (C) Industrial Policy Act, 1991

   (D) None of the above

2. In which year the new Industrial Policy was announced ?

   (A) 1997

   (B) 1951

   (C) 1991

   (D) 1998

3. The Narasimham Committee made separate recommendations for the reforms of _____

   (A) Manufacturing sector

   (B) Banking sector

   (C) Agriculture sector

   (D) Insurance Sector

4. **Assertion (A) :** Disinvestment tends to arouse opposition from employees.

   Reason (R) : It may increase the cost of Production.

   (A) Both (A) and (R) are true.

   (B) (A) is true, but (R) is false.

   (C) Both (A) and (R) are false.

   (D) (A) is false, but (R) is true.

5. Match the following :

Books	Authors
a. India and Economic Reforms	i. Bhagwati. J.
b. Development planning : The Indian Experience	ii. Chakravarty. S.
c. India : Economic Development and Social Opportunity	iii. Drenz, J and Amartya Sen
d. Fiscal Policy of Underdeveloped countries.	iv. Chelliah, R.J.

   Codes :

	a	b	c	d
(A)	i	ii	iii	iv
(B)	ii	iii	iv	i
(C)	iii	iv	ii	i
(D)	i	iv	iii	ii

6. Which of the following accounting equations is not correct ?

   (A) Assets   – Liabilities = Equity

   (B) Assets   – Equity   = Liability

   (C) Assets   + Liabilities = Equity

   (D) Liabilities + Equity   = Assets

7. Which one of the following statements is correct ?

(A) Increases in liabilities are credits and decreases are debits.

(B) Increases in assets are credits and decreases are debits.

(C) Increases in capital are debits and decreases are credits.

(D) Increases in expenses are credits and decreases are debits.

8. A and B are partners in a firm sharing profit and loss in the ratio of 3 : 2. They admit C into partnership for ¼ share and the new ratio between A and B is 2 : 1. The sacrificing ratio is

(A) 1 : 1

(B) 2 : 1

(C) 3 : 1

(D) 2 : 3

9. Arrange the following liabilities in the order of company balance sheet.

(i) Bank Overdraft

(ii) Bank Loan

(iii) Share Capital

(iv) Provision for Taxation

(A) i, ii, iii, iv

(B) iv, iii, ii, i

(C) iii, ii, i, iv

(D) iii, ii, iv, i

10. Intrinsic value of a share is given by

(A) $\dfrac{\text{Total net assets}}{\text{No. of shares}}$

(B) $\dfrac{\text{Total assets}}{\text{No. of shares}}$

(C) $\dfrac{\text{Share capital}}{\text{No. of shares}}$

(D) $\dfrac{\text{Market capitalisation}}{\text{No. of shares}}$

11. When demand curve is rectangular Hyperbola, the elasticity of demand will be

(A) Perfectly elastic

(B) Unit elastic

(C) Perfectly inelastic

(D) Highly elastic

12. Opportunity cost is a term which describes :

(A) A bargain price for a factor of production.

(B) Cost related to an optimum level of production.

(C) Average variable cost.

(D) The cost of forgone opportunities.

13. Arrange the following books in order (year) in which they appeared.

a. Economic Theory and Operations Analysis by W.J. Baumol.

b. An introduction to positive Economics by R.G. Lipsey.

c. Economics by P. Samuelson.

d. Managerial Economics by Joel Dean.

(A) a, b, c, d   (B) d, c, a, b

(C) b, d, a, c   (D) c, d, b, a

14. Marginal revenue is _____ at the quantity that generates maximum total revenue and negative beyond that point.

(A) zero   (B) + 2

(C) + 1   (D) – 1

15. **Assertion (A) :** "Utility will be maximised when the marginal unit of expenditure in each direction brings the same increment of utility."

Reason (R) : A consumer will try to maximise his utility.

(A) Both (A) and (R) are true.

(B) Both (A) and (R) are false.

(C) (A) is true, but (R) is false.

(D) (A) is false, but (R) is true.

16. In a predominantly illiterate area consisting of 10,000 population, data has to be collected from 10% of them. The appropriate technique for data collection would be

(A) Questionnaire

(B) Schedule

(C) Interview

(D) All the above

17. In a unimodal and symmetric distribution, the relationship between averages is like this.

(A) mean > median > mode

(B) mean < median < mode

(C) mean = median = mode

(D) mean > median < mode

18. Given the following tests :
(i) 'Z'-test (ii) 't'-test
(iii) 'F'-test (iv) 'χ^2'-test
The concept of degrees of freedom is associated with

(A) (i) and (ii)

(B) (ii) and (iii)

(C) (iii) and (iv)

(D) (ii), (iii) and (iv)

19. Which one of the following is not an accounting software ?
(A) Tally (B) Miracle
(C) Profit (D) SPSS

20. E-marketing is _____

(A) Buying and selling of goods and services through internet.

(B) Buying of goods through internet.

(C) Selling of goods through internet.

(D) All of the above.

21. Match the items in List-I with items in List-II.

List – I	List – II
a. Peter F. Druker	i. M.B.O.
b. F.W.Taylor	ii. Scientific Management
c. Henri J. Fayol	iii. Industrial Psychology
d. Hugo Munsterberg	iv. Functional Theory

Codes :

	a	b	c	d
(A)	i	ii	iii	iv
(B)	i	ii	iv	iii
(C)	iv	iii	ii	i
(D)	iii	i	iv	ii

22. The main advantage of functional organization is

(A) Simplicity

(B) Specialisation

(C) Experience

(D) Authority

23. Which of the following is the most democratic form of organisation ?

(A) Line

(B) Line and Staff

(C) Functional

(D) Committee

24. Plan made in the light of a competitor's plan is known as

(A) Policy

(B) Procedure

(C) Strategy

(D) Under-cover plan

25. A proposed organizational change may create _____.

(A) Emotional Turmoil & Tension

(B) Problem of social displacement

(C) Fear of unknown

(D) All of the above

26. Match the following statements with their authors :

a. "Marketing mix is a pack of four sets of variables, namely; product variables, price variables, promotion variables and place variables".

   i. Wheeler

b. "The marketing mix is the set of marketing tools the firm uses to pursue its marketing objectives in the target market."

   ii. Cundiff, Still & Govoni

c. "Marketing is the managerial process by which products are matched with markets and through which transfers of ownership are affected."

   iii. Mc Carthy

d. "Marketing is concerned with all the resources and activities involved in the flow of goods and services from producer to consumer".

   iv. Philip Kotler

Codes :

	a	b	c	d
(A)	ii	iv	i	iii
(B)	i	ii	iv	iii
(C)	iv	iii	i	ii
(D)	iii	iv	ii	i

27. Which one of the following is not the mode of Direct Distribution system ?
   (A) Multiple shops
   (B) Door to door selling
   (C) Broking agent
   (D) Direct mail order

28. Which one of the following is not matched correctly ?
   (A) Sales Portfolio – Internal Sales Promotion
   (B) Merchandise Allowance – Dealer Promotion
   (C) Count and Recount of Stock – Consumer Promotion
   (D) Advertising – Market Promotion

29. **Assertion (A) :** "Advertising plays a vital role in selling products/services."

   Reason (R) : "Sales promotion is incomplete without a good advertising plan."

   Codes :
   (A) (A) is correct, but (R) is false.
   (B) (A) is false, but (R) is correct.
   (C) Both (A) and (R) are correct.
   (D) Both (A) and (R) are false.

30. Which one of the following contains the three elements of service marketing triangle ?
   (A) Management, Marketing Agency and Consumer.
   (B) Marketing Agency, Government and Consumer.
   (C) Management, Employees and Marketing Agency.
   (D) Management, Employees and Consumer.

31. Read the following statements :
   (i) "The rate of return on investment increases with the shortage of working capital."
   (ii) 'Net working capital is the excess of current assets over current liabilities."
   (iii) "Greater the size of the business unit, larger will be the requirement of working capital."
   (iv) "Working capital is also known as circulating capital."

   Which one of the following consists of the correct statements ?
   (A) (i), (ii) and (iii)
   (B) (ii), (iii) and (iv)
   (C) (iii), (iv) and (i)
   (D) (i), (ii) and (iv)

32. Match the following :
   (a) Capital Budgeting   (i) Time adjusted rate of return
   (b) Profitability Index   (ii) Irreversible
   (c) Internal rate of return (iii) Benefit/cost
   (d) Capital investment decisions (iv) Planning capital Expenditure

   Codes :

	(a)	(b)	(c)	(d)
(A)	(iv)	(iii)	(ii)	(i)
(B)	(i)	(iv)	(ii)	(iii)
(C)	(iv)	(iii)	(i)	(ii)
(D)	(ii)	(i)	(iii)	(iv)

33. Which one of the following is correct ?

    (i) Liquidity ratios measure long term solvency of a concern.

    (ii) Inventory is a part of liquid assets.

    (iii) Rule of thumb for acid test ratio is 2 : 1.

    (iv) The amount of gross assets is equal to net capital employed.

    (A) (i), (ii) and (iv)

    (B) (ii), (iii) and (iv)

    (C) (i), (ii), (iii) and (iv)

    (D) None of the above

34. According to which of the following, the firm's market value is not affected by capital structure ?

    (A) M-M Hypothesis

    (B) Net Income approach

    (C) The Traditional view

    (D) None of the above

35. Modigliani and Miller's dividend policy of a firm is

    (A) Relevant

    (B) Irrelevant

    (C) Unrealistic

    (D) None of the above

36. The concept of Quality circles is a brain child of

    (A) Karou Ishikawa

    (B) Munchu

    (C) Japanese Union for Scientists & Engineers

    (D) None of the above

37. Performance appraisal is

    (A) Morale boosting

    (B) Training and Development Activity

    (C) Job Analysis

    (D) None of the above

38. The mechanism to identify employee's growth potentials is done through

    (A) Job enrichment

    (B) Job evaluation

    (C) Assessment centre

    (D) Position Description

39. Statements :

    (i) High morale always leads to high productivity.

    (ii) High morale need not necessarily lead to high productivity.

    (A) (i) is correct, (ii) is incorrect.

    (B) (i) is incorrect, (ii) is correct.

    (C) Both are correct

    (D) Both are incorrect

40. Arrange the following in order :

    (i) Promotion

    (ii) Performance appraisal

    (iii) Recruitment

    (iv) Training and Development

    (A) (iii), (iv), (ii), (i)

    (B) (iii), (ii), (i), (iv)

    (C) (i), (ii), (iii), (iv)

    (D) (iii), (iv), (ii), (i)

41. Find out the odd one out of the following :

(A) State Bank of India

(B) Reserve Bank of India

(C) Union Bank of India

(D) Central Bank of India

42. SIDBI was set up in _____ as a wholly owned subsidiary of _____

(A) 1985 – EXIM

(B) 1969 – RRBS

(C) 1975 – IFCI

(D) 1990 – IDBI

43. The most important reason for an investor to prefer a Bank deposit is

(A) The credit worthiness of the Bank.

(B) The Bank does not invest in the securities.

(C) The Bank offers a guarantee.

(D) All of the above.

44. Main objectives of CRR and SLR is to ensure :

(i) Liquidity position of Bank

(ii) Financial position of Bank.

(iii) Profit position of Bank

(A) Only (i) is correct.

(B) Only (ii) is correct.

(C) Only (iii) is correct.

(D) All are correct.

45. NABARD has taken over the entire functions of

(A) ARDC

(B) ACD of RBI

(C) RPCD of RBI

(D) All of the above

46. Which of the following is the best example of Agreement between oligopolists ?

(A) GATT   (B) OPEC

(C) WTO   (D) UNIDO

47. Factor Endowment Theory of International Trade was propounded by

(A) David Ricardo

(B) Bertil - Ohlin

(C) J.S. Mill

(D) C.P. Kindleberger

48. **Assertion (A) :** The British established and developed Indian Railways.

Reason (R) : The British are keenly interested in India's economic development.

(A) Both (A) and (R) true.

(B) Both (A) and (R) are false.

(C) (A) is true, but (R) is false.

(D) (A) is false, but (R) is true.

49. Which of the following is also known as World Bank ?

(A) IMF   (B) IBRD

(C) ADB   (D) IFC

50. Special Economic Zones (SEZ) have been created first time in the

(A) EXIM Policy – 2000

(B) EXIM Policy 2005

(C) Industrial Policy – 1956

(D) Industrial Policy – 1991

Note : This paper contains **fifty (50)** objective type questions, each question carrying **two (2)** marks. Attempt all the questions.

1. India abolished the quantitative restrictions on imports of 1429 items in 2000 and 2001 as per the commitment to which of the following ?

   (A) South Asian Free Trade Association (SAFTA)

   (B) General Agreement on Tariffs and Trade (GATT)

   (C) World Trade Organisation (WTO)

   (D) Non-Aligned Movement

2. Globalization is a term used to describe the process of removal of restrictions on which of the following ?

   (A) Foreign Trade

   (B) Investment

   (C) (A) and (B) above

   (D) None of the above

3. When a company takes over another one and clearly becomes a new owner, the action is called

   (A) Merger

   (B) Acquisition

   (C) Strategic Alliance

   (D) None of the above

4. Match the following two lists of statements.

List – I	List – II
I. Rate at which RBI gives loans to Commercial Banks by discounting bills	1. Bank rate
II. Rate at which RBI borrows from Commercial Banks	2. Repo rate
	3. Prime lending rate

   Codes :

	I	II
(A)	3	1
(B)	2	1
(C)	1	2
(D)	3	2

5. The MRTP Act, 1969 was abolished in
   (A) 1991
   (B) 2002
   (C) 2006
   (D) None of the above

6. Read the following statements :
   (i) Financial statements are only interim reports.
   (ii) Financial statements are prepared on the basis of realizable values.
   (iii) The preparation of financial statements is not an ultimate aim.
   (iv) Certain assumptions are necessary to prepare financial statements.

   Which of the following combinations consists of all true statements ?
   (A) (i), (ii) and (iii)
   (B) (ii), (iii) and (iv)
   (C) (i), (iii) and (iv)
   (D) (i), (ii) and (iv)

7. Which of the following is not a subsidiary book ?

(A) Purchase Book

(B) Sales Book

(C) Bills Receivables Book

(D) Assets Book

8. Which of the following are the application of funds ?

(i) Redemption of Preference share capital.

(ii) Payment of Dividend.

(iii) Increase in working capital.

(A) only (i) and (ii)

(B) only (ii) and (iii)

(C) only (i) and (iii)

(D) (i), (ii) and (iii)

9. Accounting concepts are based on

(A) Certain assumptions

(B) Certain facts and figures

(C) Certain accounting records

(D) Government guidelines

10. The main purpose of Cost Accounting is to

(A) assist management in decision making.

(B) maximise profits and minimise losses.

(C) comply norms issued by the Government of India from time to time.

(D) prepare cost accounts in line with the accounting standards.

11. The various degrees of price elasticity of demand can be shown on a single demand curve as per which one of the following ?

(A) Total outlay method

(B) Proportional method

(C) Arc method

(D) Geometrical method

12. Which one of the following is not correct about the price discrimination by a monopolist, who intends to

(A) maximise the sales/profit

(B) share the consumer's surplus

(C) increase the welfare of masses

(D) reduce the welfare of masses

13. Returns to scale involve variations in the quantities of the various factors of production

(1) Simultaneously, and/or

(2) Proportionately

(A) Both (1) and (2) are correct

(B) (1) is correct and (2) is incorrect

(C) (1) is incorrect and (2) is correct

(D) Both (1) and (2) are incorrect.

14. The firm under perfect competition will be in short-run equilibrium when

(A) Rising marginal cost is equal to the minimum average cost

(B) Marginal revenue is equal to rising marginal cost.

(C) Average revenue is equal to average cost

(D) Marginal revenue is equal to

15. Match the following :

	List – I		List – II
(i)	Law of demand is fully applicable	(1)	Giffen goods
(ii)	Law of demand is not applicable at all	(2)	Veblon goods
(iii)	Law of demand is partly applicable	(3)	Normal goods

Codes :

	(i)	(ii)	(iii)
(A)	1	2	3
(B)	2	3	1
(C)	3	1	2
(D)	2	1	3

16. Statement – I : The heading for columns and rows are called caption and stub respectively.

Statement – II : Sturge's Rule is used to decide the nature of manifold classification

Which of the following is correct ?
(A) Both I and II are false.
(B) Both I and II are true.
(C) I is true and II is false.
(D) I is false and II is true.

17. F-test is used to test the significance of the differences between
(A) Co-efficient of correlation between two sample groups.
(B) Co-efficient of correlation among more than two sample groups.
(C) Averages between two sample groups.
(D) Averages of more than two sample groups.

18. Co-variance between two variables is
(A) The average of the product of deviations taken from their averages.
(B) A is further divided by the product of their standard deviations.
(C) A is further divided by the product of their arithmetic averages.
(D) None of the above

19. Statement – A : Standard error of the mean is the standard deviation of the sampling distribution of mean.

Statement – B : Simple random sampling is non-probability sampling method.

Which of the following combination is correct ?
(A) Both A and B are true.
(B) Both A and B are false.
(C) A is true and B is false.
(D) A is false and B is true.

20. Which of the following has RDBMS ?
(i) Access
(ii) Excel
(A) (i) and (ii)
(B) only (i)
(C) only (ii)
(D) None of the above

21. In which type of organization is 'grapewine' communication used ?
(A) Informal organization
(B) Formal organization
(C) Departmental organization
(D) Matrix organization

22. In management science "Grid" refers to

(A) Diverse managerial styles

(B) Co-ordination

(C) Communication

(D) Motivation

23. "SWOT" is used for

(A) Planning   (B) Organising

(C) Motivating   (D) Controlling

24. Which of the following pairs is not matched ?

	List – I		List – II
(A)	Frederick Herzburg	–	Scientific Management
(B)	Henry Fayol	–	Modern Management
(C)	Max Weber	–	Bureaucracy
(D)	Philip Kotlar	–	Marketing

25. Which one of the following is not covered under corporate governance ?

(A) Corporate social responsibility

(B) Business ethics

(C) Role of independent directors

(D) Government monitoring

26. Market gridding means

(A) establishing and running a web marketing facility

(B) a method of survey of expert's opinion.

(C) managing brands and developing brand equity

(D) an analytical technique which facilitates dividing a market into segments.

27. Trade Mark is :

(A) a name, term, symbol or design which is intended to identify the goods and services of a seller.

(B) a brand that has been given legal protection.

(C) giving protection to the product and adding to it's aesthetics and sales appeal.

(D) providing written information about the product.

28. Which of the following is not a part of strategic planning ?

(A) Purposes and mission

(B) Objectives

(C) Choice of businesses

(D) Social responsibility

29. Attitude means

(A) Impulses, desires and considerations of the buyer, which induces him to purchase a product

(B) A sum total of the individuals' faith and feelings towards a product.

(C) The customer turning to his environment/world of information around him.

(D) Creating some relentness in the mind of an individual.

30. Match the following :

	List – I		List – II
(a)	Supply chain management	(i)	putting the product in the mind of the prospective buyer
(b)	Product positioning	(ii)	the process of gathering, filtering and analysing information relating to the marketing environment.
(c)	Marketing environment analysis	(iii)	improving the performance of dealers through sharpening of their sales skills and product knowledge
(d)	Dealer training	(iv)	larger in scope than both physical and marketing logistics

Codes :

	(a)	(b)	(c)	(d)
(A)	(i)	(ii)	(iii)	(iv)
(B)	(iv)	(i)	(ii)	(iii)
(C)	(ii)	(iv)	(iii)	(i)
(D)	(iii)	(iv)	(i)	(ii)

31. Over capitalization may not be as a result of which one of the following ?

(A)　Promotion of a company with inflated assets

(B)　Application of low capitalization rate

(C)　Shortage of capital

(D)　Liberal dividend policy

32. Which one of the following is not matched ?

	List – I		List – II
(a)	Interest is a deductible expense	(i)	Cost of debt capital
(b)	Realised-yield approach	(ii)	Cost of equity capital
(c)	Extended yield approach	(iii)	Retained earnings
(d)	Dividend capitalization approach	(iv)	Cost of preference share capital

Codes :

(A)　(a) and (i)

(B)　(b) and (ii)

(C)　(c) and (iii)

(D)　(d) and (iv)

33. The rate of discount at which NPV of a project becomes zero is also known as

(A)　Average Rate of Return

(B)　Internal Rate of Return

(C)　Alternate Rate of Return

(D)　None of the above

34. The dividend irrelevance theorem to share valuation was propounded by

(A)　James E. Walter

(B)　Myron Gordon

(C)　Modigliani and Miller

(D)　None of the above

35. **Assertion (A)** : Management of working capital refers to the management of current assets and current liabilities.

Reason (R) : But the major thrust of course, is on the management of current assets ; because current liabilities arise in the context of current assets.

Codes :
(A) Both (A) and (R) are incorrect.
(B) (A) is correct and (R) is incorrect.
(C) Both (A) and (R) are correct.
(D) (A) is incorrect, but (R) is correct.

36. Business plans designed to achieve the organizational objectives is called
(A) Human Resource Planning
(B) Human Resource Forecasting
(C) Strategic Plan
(D) Corporate Development Plan

37. "360" degree method relates to
(A) Performance appraisal
(B) Organization climate
(C) Employees morale
(D) Retrenchment

38. Match the following :

List – I	List – II
(a) Adam Smith	(i) Subsistence Theory
(b) Karl Marx	(ii) Wages Fund Theory
(c) John Davidson	(iii) The Surplus Value Theory
(d) David Ricardo	(iv) Bargaining Theory

Codes :

	(a)	(b)	(c)	(d)
(A)	(ii)	(iii)	(iv)	(i)
(B)	(i)	(ii)	(iii)	(iv)
(C)	(iv)	(i)	(ii)	(iii)
(D)	(iii)	(iv)	(i)	(ii)

39. **Assertions :**
(i) High morale leads to high productivity.
(ii) High morale need not necessarily lead to high productivity.
(A) Both (i) and (ii) are correct.
(B) Both (i) and (ii) are incorrect.
(C) (i) is correct and (ii) is incorrect.
(D) (i) is incorrect and (ii) is correct.

40. **Statements :**
(i) Fringe benefits, now-a-days, are a significant component of "compensation".
(ii) Under Piece-rate plan, employees are paid at a stipulated rate per hour of work done by them
(A) Both (i) and (ii) are correct.
(B) Both (i) and (ii) are incorrect.
(C) (i) is incorrect and (ii) is correct.
(D) (i) is correct and (ii) is incorrect.

41. Which one of the following is not an instrument of credit control in the banking system ?
(A) Open market operations
(B) Moral suasion
(C) Cash Reserve Ratio
(D) Tax rates

42. Match the following with their year of establishment :

(a) IDBI	(i) 1982
(b) IFCI	(ii) 1964
(c) NABARD	(iii) 1948
(d) ICICI	(iv) 1955

Codes :

	(a)	(b)	(c)	(d)
(A)	(iii)	(i)	(iv)	(ii)
(B)	(iv)	(ii)	(i)	(iii)
(C)	(ii)	(iii)	(i)	(iv)
(D)	(i)	(iii)	(iv)	(ii)

43. Which of the following is not a function of a Rural Bank ?
    (A) To accept deposits
    (B) To waive loans
    (C) To grant advances
    (D) To supply inputs to farmers

44. From which date have all Banks started sharing their ATM free of cost for transactions ?
    (A) January 1, 2009
    (B) April 1, 2009
    (C) July 1, 2009
    (D) September 1, 2009

45. Which of the following is not the fund based business of commercial banks ?
    (A) D.P. Operations
    (B) Loans
    (C) Deposits
    (D) Discounting of Bills

46. Foreign Exchange and foreign currencies in India are governed by
    (A) SCRA Act
    (B) Banking Regulation Act
    (C) FEMA Act
    (D) SEBI Act

47. The balance of payments of a country on Current Account is equal to
    (A) Balance of trade plus short term capital flows.
    (B) Balance of trade plus net invisible exports.
    (C) Balance of payments minus capital flows.
    (D) Balance of invisible trade plus imports.

48. The following table shows cost per unit of production of two goods, wheat and cloth in two countries X and Y with no transportation cost and free trade :

	X Rs.	Y Rs.
Wheat	50	350
Cloth	100	500

Which one of the following will take place ?
    (A) No trade will take place.
    (B) X will export wheat and import cloth.
    (C) X will export cloth and import wheat.
    (D) There is no enough information to comment.

49. A debit balance of payments occurs due to
    (i) Low imports and high exports
    (ii) High imports and low exports.
    (A) Both (i) and (ii) are correct.
    (B) Both (i) and (ii) are incorrect.
    (C) Only (i) is correct.
    (D) Only (ii) is correct.

50. Match the following economic institutions with the year of their establishment :
    (a) World Bank   (i) 1946
    (b) International   (ii) 1956
        Finance
        Corporation
    (c) International   (iii) 1960
        Development
        Agency
    (d) Asian Development   (iv) 1966
        Bank

Codes :

	(a)	(b)	(c)	(d)
(A)	(i)	(ii)	(iii)	(iv)
(B)	(i)	(iii)	(iv)	(ii)
(C)	(ii)	(i)	(iv)	(iii)
(D)	(iii)	(i)	(ii)	(iv)

June-2010

COMMERCE
Paper – II

Note : This paper contains **fifty (50)** objective type questions, each question carrying **two (2)** marks. Attempt all the questions.

1. The concept of Small Scale Industries (SSIs) was brought to fore by the

(A) Industrial Policy Resolution, 1948

(B) Industrial Policy Resolution, 1956

(C) Industrial Policy Statement, 1977

(D) None of the above

2. Which combination of the following factors has driven globalisation in the recent past ?

I. Growth of multinational corporations.

II. Internationalisation of finance.

III. Increased international trade.

(A) I and II   (B) I and III

(C) II and III   (D) I, II and III

3. **Assertion (A) :** Privatisation process leads to change in management with change in ownership.

Reason (R) : Change in management is not a necessary condition for the process of privatisation.

Which one of the following is correct combination ?

Codes :

(A) Both (A) and (R) are correct.

(B) (A) is correct, but (R) is incorrect.

(C) (A) is incorrect, but (R) is correct.

(D) Both (A) and (R) are incorrect.

4. Match the following two lists of statements.

	List – I	List – II
I.	When one company purchases another one.	1. Conglomeration merger
II.	Merger between two companies having no common business areas.	2. Consolidation merger
III.	Merger between two companies that sell the same products in different markets.	3. Purchase merger
IV.	Two companies are bought and combined under new entity.	4. Market extension merger

Codes :

	I	II	III	IV
(A)	1	2	3	4
(B)	2	3	1	4
(C)	3	1	4	2
(D)	3	4	1	2

5. In which of the industrial policies were the following major changes introduced ?

– Liberalisation of licensed capacity.

– Relaxation of industrial licensing.

– Industrialisation of backward areas.

(A) Industrial Policy Resolution, 1956.

(B) Industrial Policy Statement, 1977.

(C) Industrial Policy of 1980.

(D) Industrial Policy of 1991.

6. Which of the following is not an Accounting concept ?

(A) Matching concept

(B) Dual Aspect concept

(C) True and Fair concept

(D) Going concern concept

7. Deficiency/Surplus Account in liquidation of a company is called

(A) List – C   (B) List – D

(C) List – G   (D) List – H

8. Which of the following statement is not correct ?

(A) P/V ratio can be improved by reducing fixed cost.

(B) Contribution is also known as Gross margin.

(C) P/V ratio can be improved by increasing the selling price.

(D) Margin of safety can be improved by reducing fixed cost.

9. In the context of Standard Costing; Basic Standard is established for

(A) short period

(B) current period

(C) indefinite period

(D) pre-defined period

10. Read the following statements :

(i) Marginal costing and Absorption costing are the same.

(ii) For decision making, absorption costing is more suitable than marginal costing.

(iii) Cost-volume-profit relationships also denote break-even point.

(iv) Marginal costing is based on the distinction between fixed and variable costs.

Which of the following combinations gives true statements with regard to above ?

(A) (i) & (ii)   (B) (ii) & (iii)

(C) (iii) & (iv)   (D) (iv) & (ii)

11. A consumer consuming two goods will be in equilibrium, when the marginal utilities from both goods are

(A) maximum possible positive

(B) minimum possible positive

(C) equal

(D) zero

12. Total production will be maximum when

(A) Marginal production is maximum.

(B) Average production is maximum.

(C) Marginal production is zero.

(D) Average production is equal to the marginal production.

13. Which one of the following is not matched properly ?

	List – I		List – II
I.	High initial price to be lowered later	1.	Product line pricing
II.	Prices to be proportional to cost	2.	Differential pricing
III.	Prices to be increased for providing profit	3.	Pioneer pricing
IV.	Prices to be different in different markets	4.	Incremental pricing

(A) I and 3
(B) II and 1
(C) III and 4
(D) IV and 2

14. As per indifference curve and price line, a consumer will not be in equilibrium when

(A) Ratios of marginal utilities and prices of the respective goods are equal.

(B) Ratio of marginal utilities of the two goods is equal to the ratio of their respective prices.

(C) The marginal rate of substitution is equal to the ratio of prices of the two goods.

(D) The marginal rate of substitution is decreasing.

15. Under kinked demand model, the demand curve for the firm's product is drawn on the assumption that

(A) All rivals charge the same price which is charged by the oligopolist.

(B) All rivals charge a price independent of the price charged by the oligopolist.

(C) All rivals follow the oligopolist upto certain price but beyond that they do not.

(D) All oligopolists charge the price as independent sellers.

16. A graph of a cumulative frequency distribution is called

(A) Ogive
(B) Frequency polygon
(C) Pie diagram
(D) Histogram

17. Which of the following tests is used to test the significance of the co-efficient of association ?

(A) Z-test
(B) t-test
(C) χ^2-test
(D) F-test

18. The total area of a normal distribution between average value ± 1.96 of standard deviation is

(A) 95.45 %
(B) 95 %
(C) 99 %
(D) 68.34 %

19. Which of the following is a relative measure of dispersion ?

(A) Standard deviation
(B) Variance
(C) Co-efficient of variation
(D) None of the above

20. ERP includes (i) SAP, and/or (ii) Resource Planning.
(A) Both (i) and (ii)
(B) Only (i)
(C) Only (ii)
(D) None of the above

21. Which one of the following was <u>not</u> main contribution of F.W. Tailor ?
(A) Scientific management
(B) Time and motion studies
(C) Differential wage plan
(D) Modern management

22. Match the items of List-I with items of List-II.

	List – I		List – II
I.	Hygiene theory	1.	Abraham H. Maslow
II.	Theory of 'X' and 'Y'	2.	Victor Vroom
III.	Expectancy Theory	3.	Fredrick Herzberg
		4.	Doughlas Mcgregor

Codes :

	I	II	III
(A)	3	4	2
(B)	1	4	2
(C)	3	2	4
(D)	1	2	4

23. Which of the following combinations consists of correct statements ?
(i) Control and planning are interlinked.
(ii) Control is not meant for men, but for activities.
(iii) Control is a circular movement.
(A) (i) and (ii)
(B) (i) and (iii)
(C) (ii) and (iii)
(D) (i), (ii) and (iii)

24. Staffing includes
(i) Training   (ii) Appraisal
(iii) Placement   (iv) Directing
Which of the following is correct ?
(A) (i) and (iii)
(B) (i), (ii) and (iii)
(C) (ii) and (iii)
(D) (i), (ii), (iii) and (iv)

25. **Assertion (A)** : Management is a continuous process involving the integration of all functions.

Reason (R) : Managers first plan, then organise and finally perform the function of controlling.

Read the above statements and select the correct answer from the code below :

Codes :
(A) Both (A) and (R) are correct; and (R) is correct explanation of (A).
(B) Both (A) and (R) are correct, but (R) is not a correct explanation of (A).
(C) (A) is correct, but (R) is incorrect.
(D) (A) is incorrect, but (R) is correct.

26. Exchange concept of marketing deals with
(A) Exchange of products between sellers and buyers covering distribution and price aspects.
(B) Mere appendage to production.
(C) Achieving marketing success through product attributes.
(D) Aggressively promote and push the products.

27. Who coined the expression "Marketing Mix"?

(A) Henry Fayol

(B) James Culliton

(C) Peter Drucker

(D) Abraham Maslow

28. Road blocking advertisement refers to

(A) Advertising a product by blocking the road.

(B) Creating big blocks for advertising a product.

(C) Advertising a product on multiple TV channels at the same time.

(D) None of the above.

29. Match the following :

	List – I		List – II
1.	Market segmentation	i.	Pricing high of a new product initially.
2.	Skimming price	ii.	Process of disaggregating a market into a number of sub-markets.
3.	Multilevel marketing	iii.	Translation of the marketing plan into marketing performance.
4.	Sales management	iv.	Modified version of direct marketing.

Codes :

	1	2	3	4
(A)	ii	i	iv	iii
(B)	iii	i	ii	iv
(C)	i	ii	iii	iv
(D)	iv	ii	iii	i

30. Which of the following buying process sequence is correct?

1. Adoption
2. Legitimization
3. Attitude
4. Awareness

(A) 4, 3, 2, 1

(B) 2, 3, 4, 1

(C) 1, 2, 3, 4

(D) 3, 4, 2, 1

31. Discounted cash flow criteria for investment appraisal does not include

(A) Net present value

(B) Benefit-cost ratio

(C) Accounting rate of return

(D) Internal rate of return

32. Working capital represents the portion of current assets financed through long term funds. This indicates (1) net working capital and/or (2) gross working capital.

(A) (1) is correct

(B) (2) is correct

(C) Both (1) and (2) are correct

(D) Neither of the two is correct

33. Dividend policy of a company mainly concerns with

(i) dividend payout and/or

(ii) stability of dividend.

(A) Only (i) is correct.

(B) Only (ii) is correct.

(C) Both (i) and (ii) are correct.

(D) Both (i) and (ii) are incorrect.

34. Match the following :

	List – I		List – II
I.	The presence of fixed cost in the cost structure of a firm.	1.	Super-leverage
II.	The presence of fixed return funds in the capital structure of a firm.	2.	Operating leverage
III.	Impact of changes in sales on the earnings available to shareholders.	3.	Financial leverage

Codes :

	I	II	III
(A)	1	2	3
(B)	2	3	1
(C)	3	2	1
(D)	1	3	2

35. Which one of the following is not used to estimate cost of equity capital ?
(A) External yield criterion
(B) Dividend plus growth rate
(C) Equity capitalisation approach
(D) Capital asset pricing model

36. Which of the following is not a Central Trade Union in India ?
(A) B.M.S.   (B) I.L.O.
(C) INTUC   (D) AITUC

37. Sequence the following in which they are practised :
(i) Promotion
(ii) Performance appraisal
(iii) Recruitment
(iv) Training and Development
(A) (iii), (ii), (iv) (i)
(B) (iii), (ii), (i), (iv)
(C) (iii), (i), (iv), (ii)
(D) (iii), (iv), (ii), (i)

38. Which one of the following purposes is not served by performance evaluation ?
(A) Decisions about promotions, transfers and terminations.
(B) Centralisation and decentralisation of decision making authority.
(C) Identification of training and development needs.
(D) Criterion against which selection and development programmes are validated.

39. Who has introduced the "Seven Point Plan" for taking the best interview method ?
(A) Milton L. Blum
(B) F. E. Burt
(C) Prof. A. Rozar
(D) Filippo

40. The last stage in a grievance redressal procedure is handled by
(A) Union
(B) Voluntary Arbitrator
(C) H.R. Department
(D) Grievance Committee

41. The Commercial Banks in India are governed by
(A) Reserve Bank of India Act, 1934
(B) Indian Companie's Act, 1956
(C) Indian Banking Regulation Act, 1949
(D) Securities and Exchange Board of India Act, 1992

42. Which of the following limits the power of credit creation by Commercial Banks ?
(A) Fiscal Policy
(B) Banking Laws
(C) Business Pessimism
(D) None of the above

43. Match the following with the years of establishment/nationalisation.

	List – I		List – II
(a)	Reserve Bank of India	i.	1975
(b)	Nationalisation of 14 Major Commercial Banks	ii.	1935
(c)	Nationalisation of 6 Commercial Banks	iii.	1969
(d)	Regional Rural Banks	iv.	1980

Codes :

	(a)	(b)	(c)	(d)
(A)	i	iii	ii	iv
(B)	iii	ii	iv	i
(C)	iv	iii	i	ii
(D)	ii	iii	iv	i

44. Capital adequacy norm helps to Banks
   (i) For strengthening capital base of Banks.
   (ii) For sanctioning more loans.
   (A) Both (i) and (ii) are correct.
   (B) Both (i) and (ii) are incorrect.
   (C) (i) is correct, but (ii) is incorrect.
   (D) (i) is incorrect, but (ii) is correct.

45. Which one of the following is the main objective of Unit Trust of India ?
   (A) To mobilize the savings of high income groups.
   (B) To mobilize the savings of low and high income groups.
   (C) To mobilize the savings of corporates.
   (D) To mobilize the savings of low and middle income groups.

46. Which of the following is the basic objective of the World Bank ?
   (A) To provide social services
   (B) To provide financial assistance
   (C) To promote economic growth
   (D) To eradicate poverty

47. Which of the following is not an International Financial Institution ?
   (A) I.C.I.C.I.   (B) I.M.F.
   (C) I.D.A.   (D) World Bank

48. In balance of payment accounts, all goods exported and imported are recorded in _____.
   (A) Capital Account
   (B) Visible Account
   (C) Invisible Account
   (D) Merchandise Account

49. The devaluation of currency of a country is done when _____.
   (i) It has adverse balance of payments.
   (ii) It has favourable balance of payments.
   (A) Both (i) and (ii) are correct.
   (B) Both (i) and (ii) are incorrect.
   (C) Only (i) is correct.
   (D) Only (ii) is correct.

50. Match the following with the year of establishment :

	List – I		List – II
(a)	World Trade Organisation	i.	1993
(b)	Uruguay Round Negotiation	ii.	1995
(c)	W.T.O. – Trade Policy Review Body	iii.	1997
(d)	The Patents (Amendment) Act.	iv.	1999

Codes :

	(a)	(b)	(c)	(d)
(A)	i	iii	iv	ii
(B)	i	iv	iii	ii
(C)	ii	i	iii	iv
(D)	iv	ii	i	iii

Dec-2009

COMMERCE
Paper – II

Note : This paper contains **fifty (50)** objective type questions, each question carrying **two (2)** marks. Attempt **all** the questions.

1. If the amount claimed by a consumer as compensation is Rs. 89 lacs, the case under The Consumer Protection Act shall be filed with

   (A) District Consumer Redressal Forum

   (B) State Consumer Disputes Redressal Commission

   (C) National Consumer Disputes Redressal Commission

   (D) Supreme Court

2. Which of the following does not fall within the jurisdiction of MRTP Commission ?

   (A) Prevention of Monopolistic Trade Practices.

   (B) Prevention of Restrictive Trade Practices.

   (C) Prohibition of Unfair Trade Practices.

   (D) Regulation of Combinations.

3. Which of the following is not a part of the economic environment of business ?

   (A) Competitive Environment   (B) Economic System

   (C) Changes in Patent Laws   (D) None of these

4. Laissez faire policy is adopted in

   (A) Socialistic economic system

   (B) Capitalistic economic system

   (C) Mixed economic system

   (D) Communist economic system

5. Relaxing the restrictions and controls imposed on business and industry means

   (A) Liberalisation   (B) Privatisation

   (C) Globalisation   (D) None of these

6. A variable such as activity that causes cost over a given time is

   (A) Cost Driver   (B) Cost Behaviour

   (C) Cost Centre   (D) None of the above

7. The concept of budget that requires all levels to work from scratch is
   (A) Flexible Budget
   (B) Total Budget
   (C) Master Budget
   (D) Zero Base Budget

8. Accounting Standard on the "Effect of Changes in Foreign Exchange Rates" is
   (A) AS 11
   (B) AS 13
   (C) AS 18
   (D) None of the above

9. Land is not depreciable asset because
   (A) Its value always increases
   (B) There is no maintenance required
   (C) Life of land is unlimited
   (D) None of the above

10. The sales at which a firm would earn profit after tax @ 8% of sales, if fixed cost is Rs. 45,000 ; selling price Rs. 50 per unit, variable cost Rs. 30 per unit and tax rate 20% :
    (A) Rs. 90,000
    (B) Rs. 1,50,000
    (C) Rs. 1,68,000
    (D) None of the above

11. The elasticity of demand for luxury goods is
    (A) Infinite
    (B) More than one
    (C) Less than one
    (D) Equal to one

12. Profits are maximised at a point where
    (A) MR = MC
    (B) MR < MC
    (C) MR > MC
    (D) AC > MC

13. The concept of "consumer surplus" was introduced and developed by
    (A) E.A.G. Robinson
    (B) J.M. Keynes
    (C) Lionel Robbins
    (D) Alfred Marshall

14. In Law of Variable Proportions, initially when MP rises
    (A) TP rises at a decreasing rate.
    (B) TP rises at an increasing rate.
    (C) AP rises less than proportionately.
    (D) AP rises more than proportionately.

15. Which one of the following statements is correct ?

    (A)   Monopolist charges the maximum possible price.

    (B)   Monopolist always makes (economic) profit.

    (C)   Monopolist operates on an inelastic demand curve.

    (D)   None of the above

16. The Central Processing Unit of a computer consists of

    (A)   Input, Output and Processing.

    (B)   Control Unit, Primary Storage and Secondary Storage.

    (C)   Control Unit, Arithmetic-logic Unit and Primary Storage.

    (D)   None of the above.

17. If the sample size increases, the sampling error

    (A)   Decreases   (B)   Increases

    (C)   Remains constant   (D)   None of the above

18. Goodness of fit of a distribution is tested by

    (A)   t-test   (B)   Chi-square test

    (C)   F-test   (D)   None of these

19. Probability of rejecting the null hypothesis when it is true, is called

    (A)   Type-II-error   (B)   Type-I-error

    (C)   Standard error   (D)   None of these

20. Standard error of mean is defined as

    (A)   standard deviation of the sampling distribution of mean.

    (B)   standard deviation of data.

    (C)   inter-quartile range of the data.

    (D)   none of these.

21. Who first propounded the principle of 'unity of command' ?

    (A)   F.W. Taylor   (B)   Elton Mayo

    (C)   Peter F. Drucker   (D)   Henry Fayol

22. Which element is not necessary in each objective under MBO Approach ?

(A) Time element

(B) Cost element

(C) Human Relation element

(D) Measurable element

23. Techniques of managerial control are useful in

(A) selection of plant location.

(B) identifying appropriate technology

(C) profit planning

(D) conducting shareholders' meeting

24. The function of attracting, acquiring, retaining and developing human resources in an organisation is called

(A) recruitment

(B) induction

(C) training and development

(D) staffing

25. In terms of Blake-Mouton's managerial grid approach, a production oriented leader will be one who adopts

(A) 1.1 style

(B) 9.1 style

(C) 9.9 style

(D) 5.5 style

26. The strategy of introducing a product with high introductory price is called

(A) penetration strategy

(B) skimming strategy

(C) pull strategy

(D) push strategy

27. The concept of four P's as elements of marketing mix was given by

(A) Philip Kotler

(B) W.J. Stanton

(C) E.J. McCarthy

(D) Bruce J. Walker

28. Which out of the following is not a type of non-store retailing ?

(A) Limited line stores

(B) Automatic vending

(C) Direct selling

(D) Telemarketing

29. A product line strategy wherein a company adds a higher priced product to a line in order to attract a broader market which helps the sale of its existing lower priced products is called

(A) Trading up   (B) Trading down

(C) Life cycle extension   (D) Product line extension

30. Which of the following is not a tool of sales promotion ?

(A) Sales contests   (B) Free gifts

(C) Point of purchase display   (D) Public Relations

31. Use of fixed interest securities in the capital structure is called

(A) operating leverage   (B) financial leverage

(C) overall leverage   (D) none of the above

32. If NPV is positive, the IRR will be

(A) Positive   (B) $K = R$

(C) $K < R$ (D) None of the above

33. According to Walter, firm should pay 100% dividend if

(A) $r > k$ (B) $r = k$

(C) $r < k$ (D) none of the above

34. Sensitivity analysis is performed to

(A) Ascertain risk

(B) Determine profitability

(C) Build scenario for risk profile

(D) None of the above

35. Right shares enjoy preferential rights with regard to

(A) Payment of dividend   (B) Payment of retained earnings

(C) Repayment of capital   (D) None of the above

36. The Industrial Disputes Act, 1947 provides the following industrial relations machinery for resolution of conflicts except

(A) Conciliation   (B) Arbitration

(C) Negotiations   (D) Adjudication

37. Job evaluation is a technique which aims at
    (A) Establishing fair and equitable pay structure.
    (B) Analysing requirement of updating technology.
    (C) Assessing safety requirement of jobs.
    (D) Improving productivity.

38. Induction is an integral part of
    (A) Training   (B) Selection
    (C) Recruitment   (D) None of the above

39. PIP test seeks to measure
    (A) IQ
    (B) Personality, Interest and Preferences
    (C) Quality of a product
    (D) Preferred Investment Plans

40. The Government of India introduced "The Workers' Participation in Management" Bill in Parliament in
    (A) 1983   (B) 1988
    (C) 1990   (D) 1981

41. The features of the Commercial Paper are
    (A) It is an unsecured money market instrument issued in the form of promissory note.
    (B) The highly rated corporate borrowers can raise short term funds through this instrument.
    (C) It is an additional instrument to the investing community.
    (D) All of the above

42. Banking ombudsman may reject the complaint
    (A) immediately after receipt.   (B) after hearing both parties.
    (C) at any stage.   (D) none of the above

43. Which of the following entities provide "Take out Finance" to banks engaged in financing of infrastructure projects ?
    (A) ICICI   (B) SIDBI
    (C) IDFC   (D) RBI

44. Currency chest balance will be periodically verified by

    (A) Bank's own officials   (B) RBI officials

    (C) Both (A) and (B)   (D) Officials of AG's office

45. SEBI is

    (A) Regulatory Authority   (B) Statutory Authority

    (C) Both (A) and (B)   (D) None of these

46. The International Monetary Fund has estimated India's contribution to World Gross Domestic Product in Purchasing Power Parity (PPP) terms for 2007

    (A) 4.6 percent   (B) 6.4 percent

    (C) 7.1 percent   (D) 8.9 percent

47. The World Bank is known as

    (A) IMF   (B) IDA

    (C) IFC   (D) IBRD

48. "De-coupling" denotes

    (A) Indian market may be cut off from global markets so that it may not be affected by global volatility.

    (B) separating the birds affected by bird-flu.

    (C) that markets are independent.

    (D) None of the above

49. Which of the country's banking have been brought under "Sanctions by U.S.A. recently" ?

    (A) Iraq   (B) North Korea

    (C) Pakistan   (D) Iran

50. How many member countries are there in the "World Customs Organisation" ?

    (A) 160   (B) 162

    (C) 172   (D) 180

June-2009

COMMERCE

PAPER – II

Note : This paper contains **fifty** (50) objective-type questions, each question carrying **two** (2) marks. Attempt **all** of them.

1. Which of the following is *not* an objective of competition Act 2002 ?
   (A) Prohibition of abuse of dominant position
   (B) Prohibition of Restrictive Trade Practices
   (C) Prohibition of Anti Competitive Agreements
   (D) Regulation of combinations

2. Consumers have the right :
   (i) to be protected against goods and services that are hazardous to life and property.
   (ii) to assured , wherever possible, access to a variety of goods and services at notional prices.
   Code :
   (A) Both (i) and (ii) are correct
   (B) Both (i) and (ii) are wrong
   (C) Only (i) is correct
   (D) Only (ii) is correct

3. Which of the following is *not* an element of the micro environment of business ?
   (A) Suppliers   (B) Competitors
   (C) Trade Policy   (D) Publics

4. Match the following legislations with the year of their enactment :
   (a) Industries (Development and Regulation) Act   (i) 1969
   (b) Foreign Exchange Management Act   (ii) 1951
   (c) Securities Exchange Board of India Act   (iii) 1999
   (d) Monopolies and Restrictive Trade Practices Act   (iv) 1992
   Codes :

	(a)	*(b)*	*(c)*	*(d)*
(A)	(i)	(iii)	(iv)	(ii)
(B)	(i)	(iv)	(iii)	(ii)
(C)	(ii)	(iii)	(iv)	(i)
(D)	(ii)	(iii)	(i)	(iv)

5. Which of the following is *not* an instrument of monetary policy ?
   (A) Deficit financing   (B) Statutory Liquidity Ratio
   (C) Cash Reserve Ratio   (D) Open Market Operations

6. A and B are partners sharing profits in the ratio of 2:3. They admit C for $1/4^{th}$ share in the business. The sacrificing ratio of A and B is :
   (A) 3 : 1   (B) 1 : 4   (C) 2 : 3   (D) 1 : 1

7. Premium on redemption of debenture is :
   (A) Personal Account   (B) Real Account
   (C) Nominal Account   (D) None of the above

8. If profit and fixed cost are Rs. 80,000 and Rs 2,80,000 respectively, the total variable cost and break-even sales are :
   (A) Rs. 5,40,000 and Rs. 9,00,000   (B) Rs. 5,40,000 and Rs. 7,00,000
   (C) Rs. 4,20,000 and Rs. 7,00,000   (D) Rs. 4,20,000 and Rs. 9,00,000

9. The extent to which an organization uses fixed cost in its cost structure is called :
   (A) Overall leverage   (B) Fixed leverage
   (C) Financial leverage   (D) Operating leverage

10. Direct costs are :
    (A) Traceable to the cost object   (B) Allocated to cost object
    (C) Total cost of the cost object   (D) None of the above

11. In a typical demand schedule, quantity demanded :
    (A) Varies directly with price   (B) Varies proportionately with price
    (C) Varies inversely with price   (D) Is independent of price

12. Opportunity cost is a term which describes :
    (A) A bargain price for a factor of production
    (B) Cost related to an optimum level of production
    (C) Average variable cost
    (D) None of the above

13. The principle which states that an input must be so allocated between various uses that the value added by the last unit of input is the same in all its uses is called :
    (A) Marginal Principle   (B) Incremental Principle
    (C) Equal-marginal Principle   (D) Discounting Principle

14. An example of derived demand is :
    (A) Money   (B) Car
    (C) Cigarette   (D) Mobile phone

15. "Kinked Demand curve approach " is concerned with :
    (A) Price Discrimination   (B) Price Flexibility
    (C) Price Rigidity   (D) Dual Pricing

16. Karl Pearson's coefficient of correlation between two variables X and Y is equal to :
    (A) the covariance between two variables
    (B) the product of their standard deviations
    (C) the square root of product of two regression coefficients.
    (D) None of the above

17. "Parameter " refers to the characteristic of the :
    (A) Population   (B) Sample
    (C) Both   (D) None of these

18. If the probability of inclusion of every unit of the population in the sample is equal, it is called :
    (A) Simple Random Sampling   (B) Stratified Random Sampling
    (C) Systematic Sampling   (D) None of these

19. For 3×2 contingency table, the degrees of freedom for testing the hypothesis is :
    (A) 6   (B) 2   (C) 3   (D) 4

20. The "word length" of a computer is measured in :
    (A) Bytes   (B) Millimeters (C) Meters   (D) Bits

21. 'Motivation Hygiene Theory ' was propounded by :
    (A) Herzberg   (B) Maslow
    (C) Mc Gregor   (D) Peter F Drucker

22. 'Grapevine' communication is a type of :
    (A) Formal communication   (B) Informal communication
    (C) Written communication   (D) Vertical communication

23. 'Span of control' refers to :
    (A) Controlling technique
    (B) Number of units under a company
    (C) Number of subordinates under a manager
    (D) Supply area of a company

24. A written statement of main duties and responsibilities which a particular job entails is called :

(A) Job evaluation
(B) Job analysis
(C) Job description
(D) None of the above

25. Elton Mayo is main contributor to :

(A) Classical approach
(B) Bureaucracy
(C) Modern Theory of Management
(D) Human relations approach

26. Which one of the following is an example of non-store retailing ?

(A) Limited Line Stores
(B) Discount Stores
(C) Tele Marketing
(D) Super Markets

27. Promotional efforts directed primarily at end users so that they will ask middle men for the product, is called :

(A) Pull strategy
(B) Push strategy
(C) Single segment strategy
(D) Penetration strategy

28. A product line strategy where in a company adds a lower priced products to a line to reach a market that cannot afford higher priced items, is called :

(A) Trading up
(B) Trading down
(C) Product Line Extension
(D) Life cycle extension

29. Which is the step following the 'test marketing' in the process of new product development ?

(A) Idea Screening
(B) Prototype Development
(C) Business Analysis
(D) Commercialisation

30. Which of the following is *not* a demographic basis of market segmentation ?

(A) Income
(B) Life Style
(C) Occupation
(D) Family Life Cycle

31. Taffler's (1995) Z score does *not* include :

(A) Current ratio
(B) Acid test ratio
(C) Stock turnover
(D) None of the above

32. Approximately, *IRR* is inverse of :
   (A) Pay back period
   (B) *NPV*
   (C) Adjusted Accounting Rate of Return
   (D) None of the above

33. Auction pricing is a superior method of price discovery because :
   (A) All can participate
   (B) None can participate
   (C) It Leads to speculation
   (D) None of the above

34. Cost of leasing is lower than :
   (A) Cash credit
   (B) Hire purchase
   (C) Bank Loan
   (D) None of the above

35. Market Efficiency is dependent on :
   (A) Information
   (B) Accounts
   (C) Technology
   (D) Management

36. The process of integrating the employees' needs and aspirations with organisational needs is called :
   (A) Organisational Planning
   (B) Human Resource Planning
   (C) Career Planning
   (D) Succession Planning

37. Productivity means :
   (A) An act of increasing the knowledge and skills of an employee for doing a particular job
   (B) Using the minimum amount of resources needed to produce goods and services
   (C) One's skills, abilities in meeting the needs of the job which one is holding currently
   (D) The ratio of an organisation's output to its inputs

38. Human Resource Department is :
   (A) Line Department
   (B) Functional Department
   (C) Authority Department
   (D) Service Department

39. Business Plans designed to achieve the organisation's objectives is called :
   (A) Human Resource Planning
   (B) Human Resources forecasts
   (C) Strategic Plan
   (D) Corporate Development Plan

40. A performance Appraisal System can be used for the following except :

(A) Human Resource Planning

(B) Tone up performance

(C) Identify individuals with high potential

(D) Discipline employees

41. Banking in India has its origin as early as _____ period.

(A) Vedic   (B) Moughal

(C) British   (D) None of the above

42. The maturity period of Treasury Bill is :

(A) 91 days   (B) 364 days

(C) (A) and (B) both   (D) None of the above

43. " Blue Card" denotes :

(A) A Credit Card

(B) A Debit Card

(C) A Proposition by EU to attract highly qualified professionals from other countries

(D) None of the above

44. "Repo Rate" refers to the rate at which :

(A) *RBI* borrows short term money from the market

(B) Banks keeps the money with *RBI*

(C) Bills are discounted by *RBI*

(D) Forex is purchased by *RBI*

45. 'Retail Banking' means :

(A) Credit facilities extended to retail traders

(B) Providing personal banking services directly to the consumers

(C) Collection of large number of dividend/interest warrants

(D) Providing services to the employees of large organisations

46. *NOSTRO* Account :

    (A)   Refers to a current account denominated in a foreign currency maintained by a bank in the currency of home country

    (B)   Carries no interest

    (C)   Provides for nominal interest on over night investments

    (D)   All of the above

47. Which of the following is not a mode of foreign capital inflow to India ?

    (A)   *FDI*   (B)   *FII*

    (C)   *NRI* Accounts   (D)   None of the above

48. *IMF* has raised the quota and voting share of India which places India at the _____ place among 184 members of the organisation.

    (A)   10th (B)   11th (C)   12th (D)   13th

49. Foreign Trade Policy 2008–09 forecasts the share of India's trade in World Trade at :

    (A)   1.2 %   (B)   1.3 %   (C)   1.4 %   (D)   1.5 %

50. On the basis of the size and composition of external debt, World Bank has classified India as a :

    (A)   heavily indebted country

    (B)   moderately indebted country

    (C)   less indebted country

    (D)   severely indebted country

-oOo-

www.ingramcontent.com/pod-product-compliance
Lightning Source LLC
Chambersburg PA
CBHW081116170526
45165CB00008B/2462